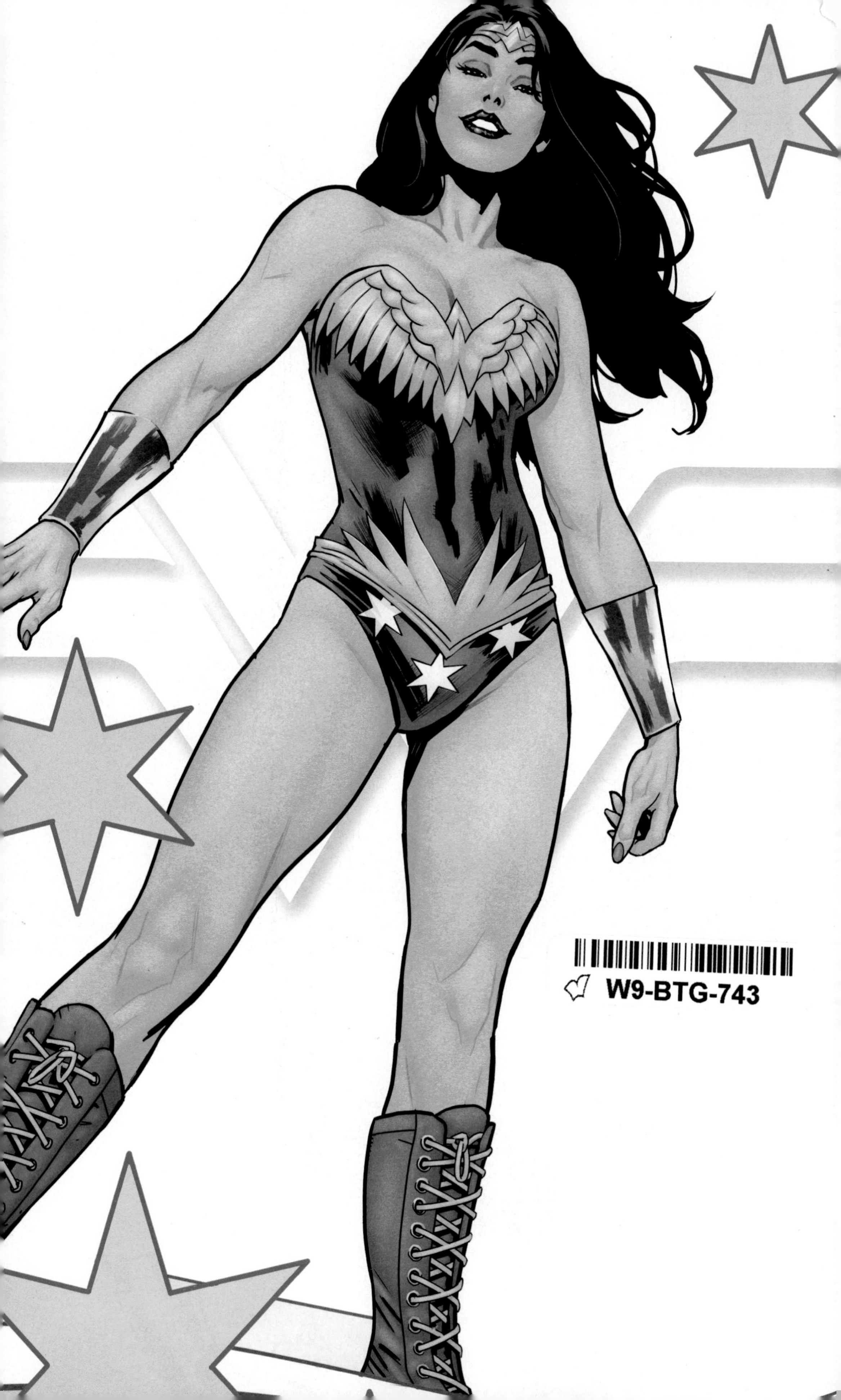

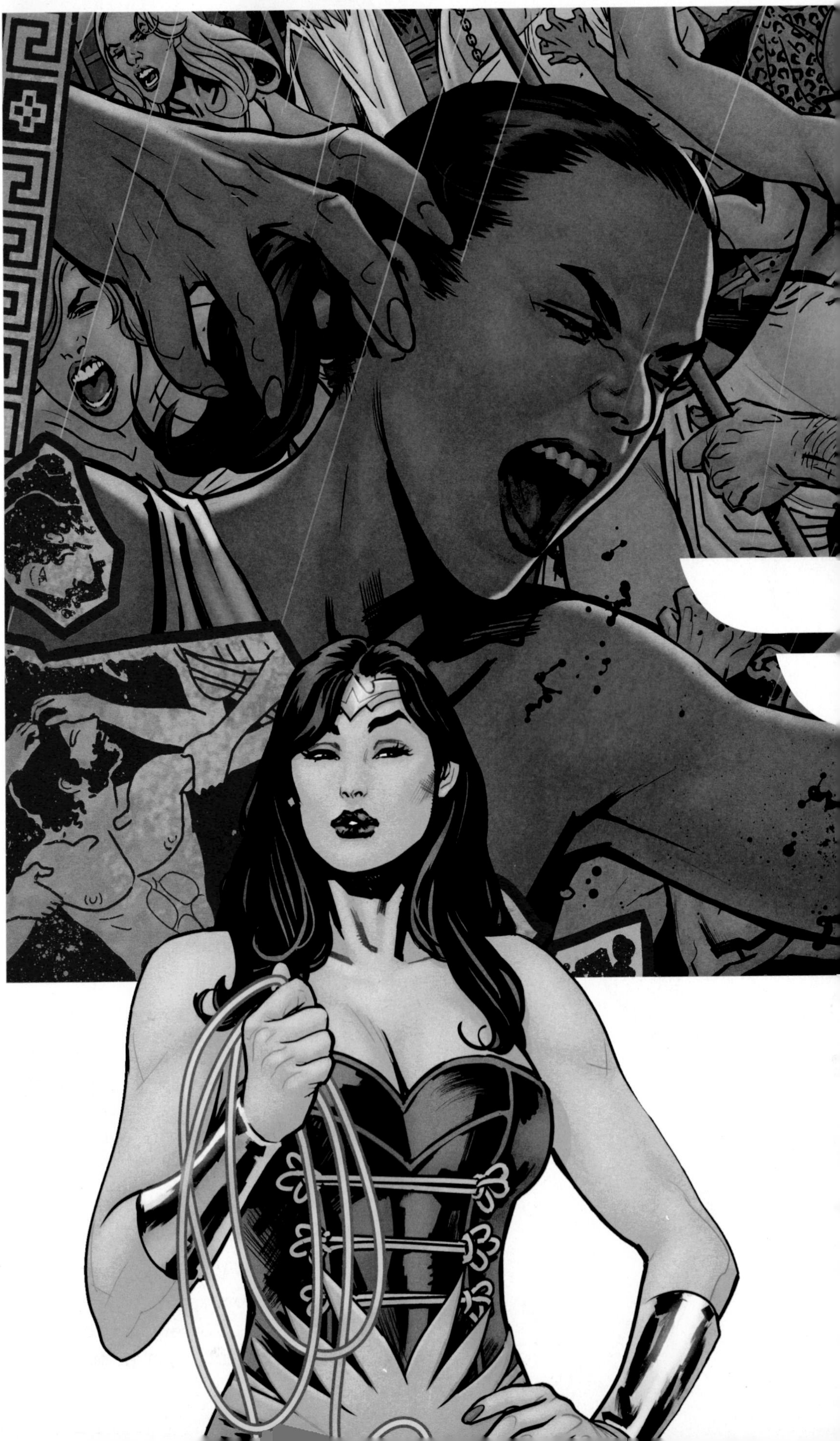

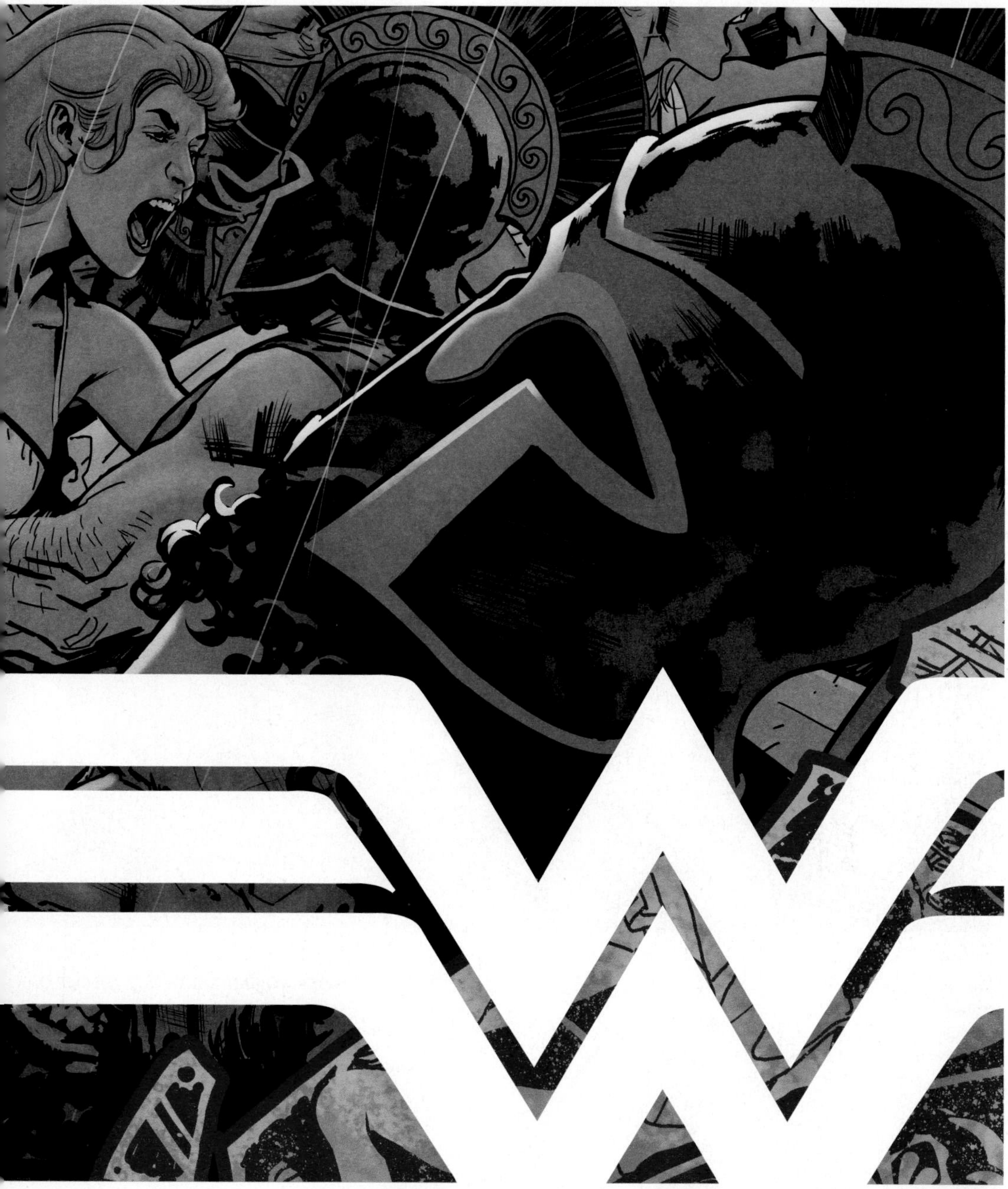

EARTH ONE

Written by Grant Morrison

Art by Yanick Paquette

Colors by Nathan Fairbairn

Letters by Todd Klein

Wonder Woman created by William Moulton Marston.

Eddie Berganza Editor
Andrew Marino Assistant Editor
Steve Cook Design Director – Books
Louis Prandi Publication Design

Bob Harras Senior VP – Editor-in-Chief, DC Comics

Diane Nelson President
Dan DiDio Publisher
Jim Lee Publisher
Geoff Johns President & Chief Creative Officer
Amit Desai Executive VP – Business & Marketing Strategy,
Direct to Consumer & Global Franchise Management
Sam Ades Senior VP – Direct to Consumer
Bobbie Chase VP – Talent Development
Mark Chiarello Senior VP – Art, Design & Collected Editions
John Cunningham Senior VP – Sales & Trade Marketing
Anne DePies Senior VP – Business Strategy, Finance & Administration
Don Falletti VP – Manufacturing Operations
Lawrence Ganem VP – Editorial Administration & Talent Relations
Alison Gill Senior VP – Manufacturing & Operations
Hank Kanalz Senior VP – Editorial Strategy & Administration
Jay Kogan VP – Legal Affairs
Thomas Loftus VP – Business Affairs
Jack Mahan VP – Business Affairs
Nick J. Napolitano VP – Manufacturing Administration
Eddie Scannell VP – Consumer Marketing
Courtney Simmons Senior VP – Publicity & Communications
Jim (Ski) Sokolowski VP – Comic Book Specialty Sales & Trade Marketing
Nancy Spears VP – Mass, Book, Digital Sales & Trade Marketing

 **WONDER WOMAN: EARTH ONE VOLUME ONE**

DC Comics, 2900 W. Alameda Ave., Burbank, CA 91505

ISBN: 978-1-4012-6863-3

Library of Congress Cataloging-in-Publication Data is available

PEFC Certified

Printed on paper from
sustainably managed
forests, controlled
sources

PEFC/29-31-337   www.pefc.org

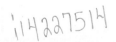

DEDICATIONS

"To all the Wonder Women — "
Grant Morrison

"This one is for Diane, my mother, who shares
with Wonder Woman more than just the name.
Being raised in a feminist household offered
me a modern view of the world, allowing me
to define my relation to women in a fulfilling,
egalitarian way and to find my own path to
manhood Merci, Diane."
Yanick Paquette

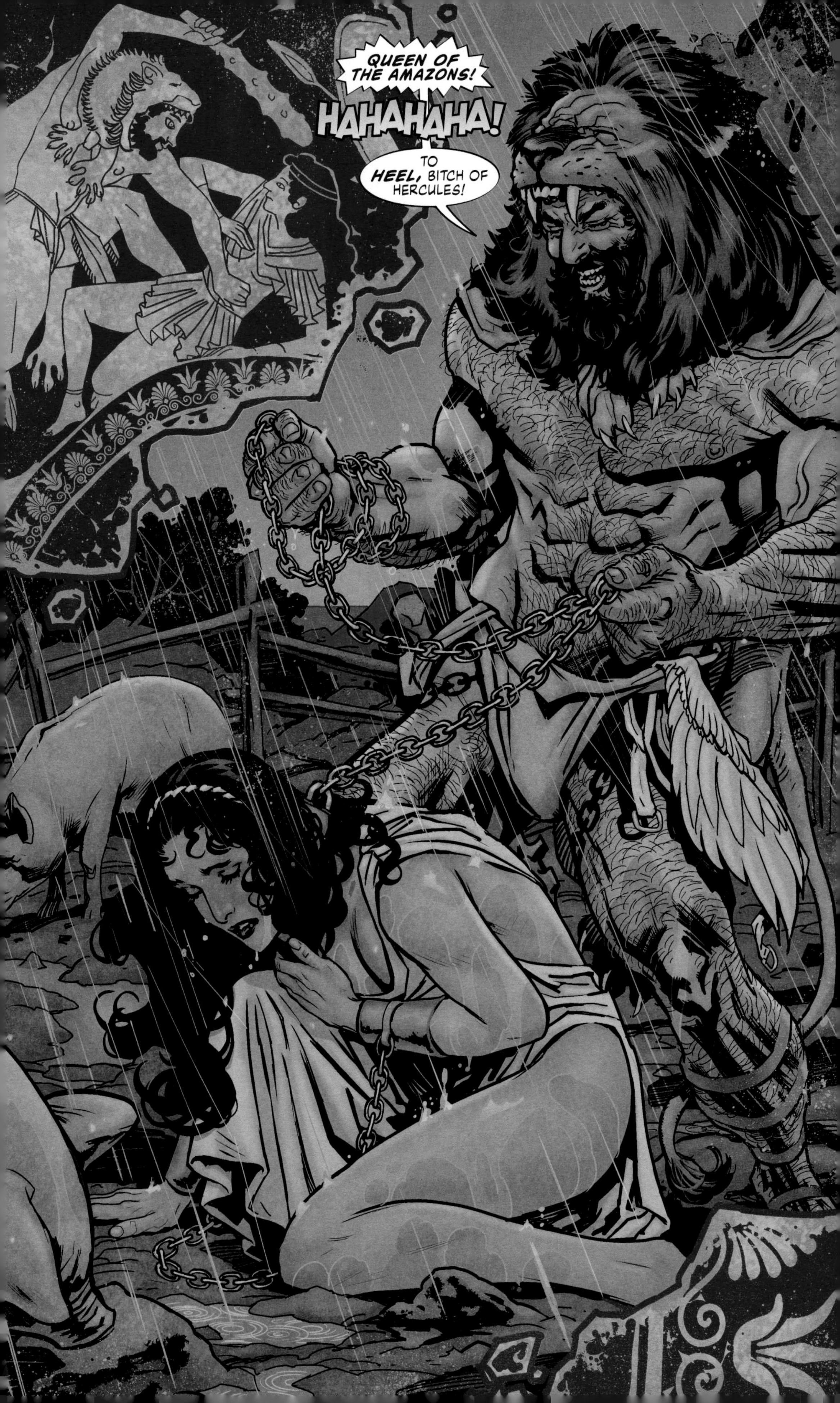
QUEEN OF THE AMAZONS!
HAHAHAHA!
TO HEEL, BITCH OF HERCULES!

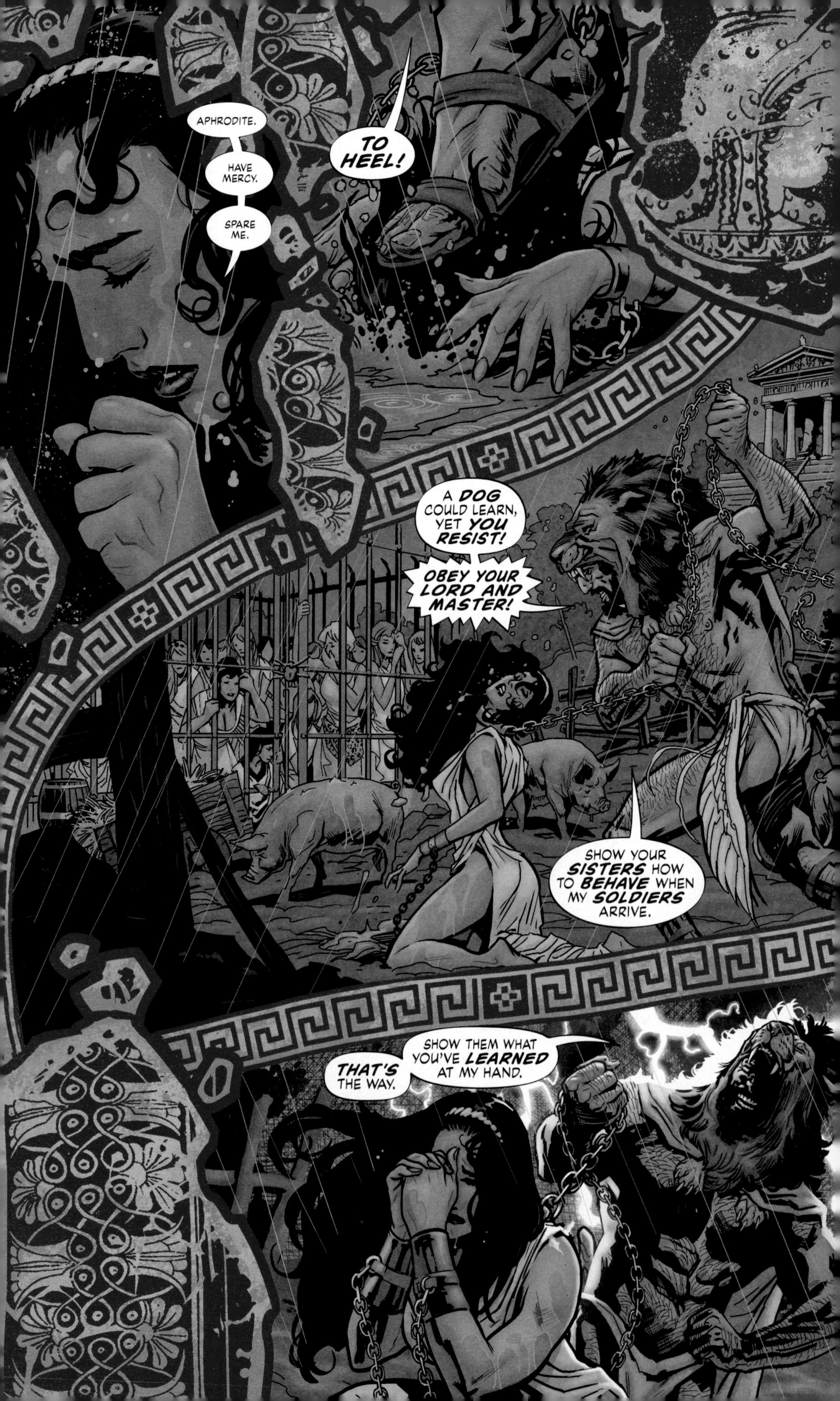
APHRODITE.
HAVE MERCY.
SPARE ME.
TO HEEL!
A DOG COULD LEARN, YET YOU RESIST!
OBEY YOUR LORD AND MASTER!
SHOW YOUR SISTERS HOW TO BEHAVE WHEN MY SOLDIERS ARRIVE.
THAT'S THE WAY.
SHOW THEM WHAT YOU'VE LEARNED AT MY HAND.

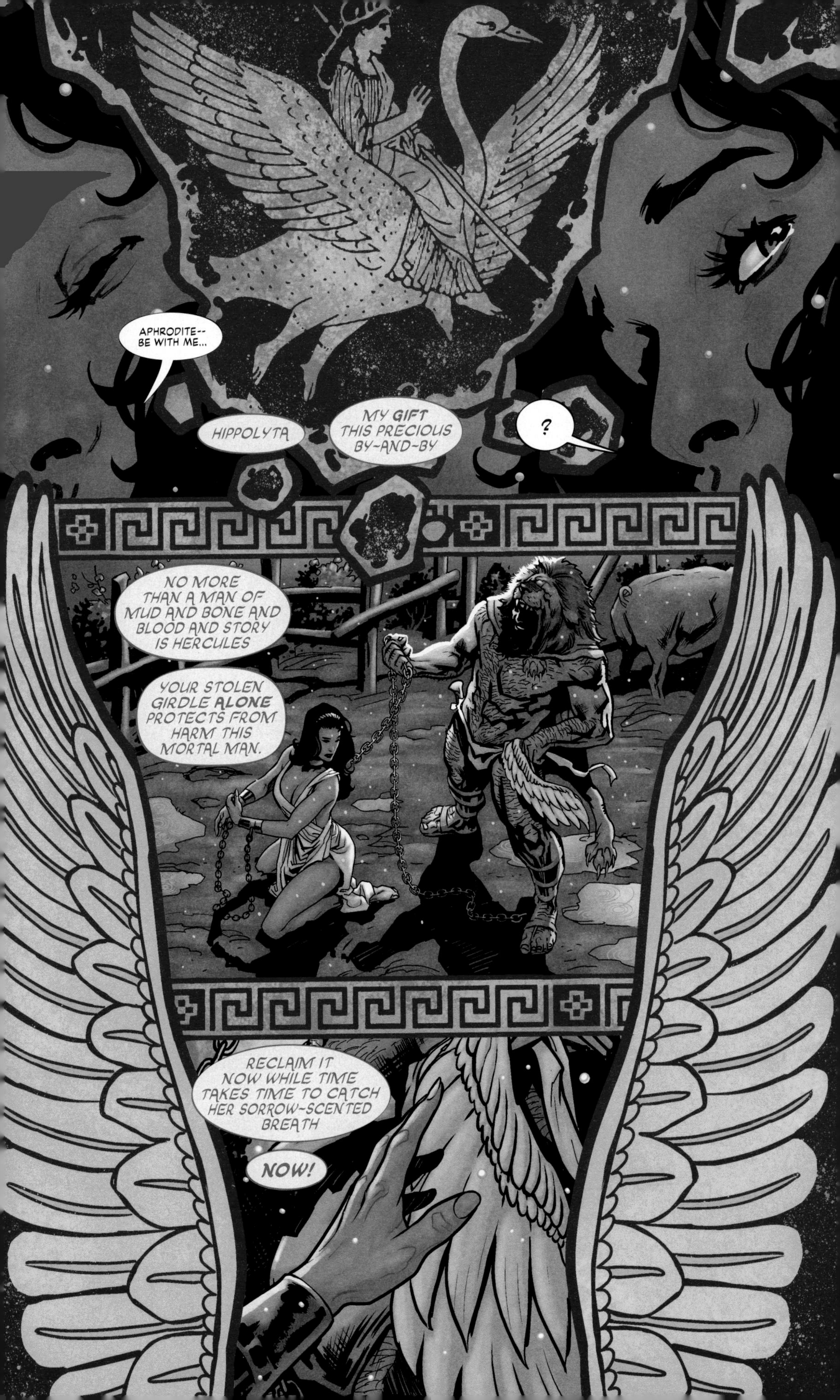

APHRODITE-- BE WITH ME...
HIPPOLYTA
MY GIFT THIS PRECIOUS BY-AND-BY
?
NO MORE THAN A MAN OF MUD AND BONE AND BLOOD AND STORY IS HERCULES
YOUR STOLEN GIRDLE ALONE PROTECTS FROM HARM THIS MORTAL MAN.
RECLAIM IT NOW WHILE TIME TAKES TIME TO CATCH HER SORROW-SCENTED BREATH
NOW!

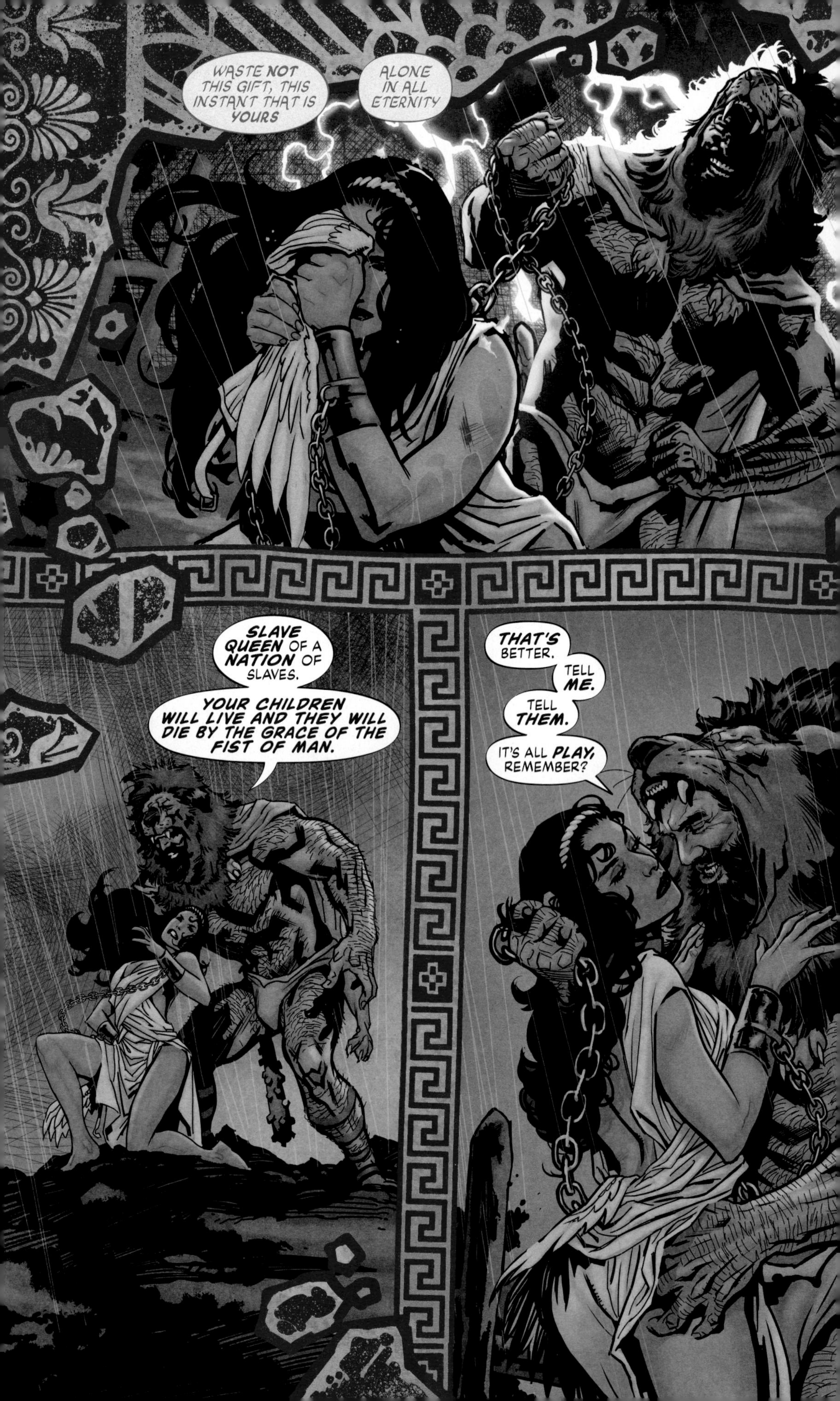
WASTE NOT THIS GIFT, THIS INSTANT THAT IS YOURS
ALONE IN ALL ETERNITY
SLAVE QUEEN OF A NATION OF SLAVES.
YOUR CHILDREN WILL LIVE AND THEY WILL DIE BY THE GRACE OF THE FIST OF MAN.
THAT'S BETTER.
TELL ME.
TELL THEM.
IT'S ALL PLAY, REMEMBER?

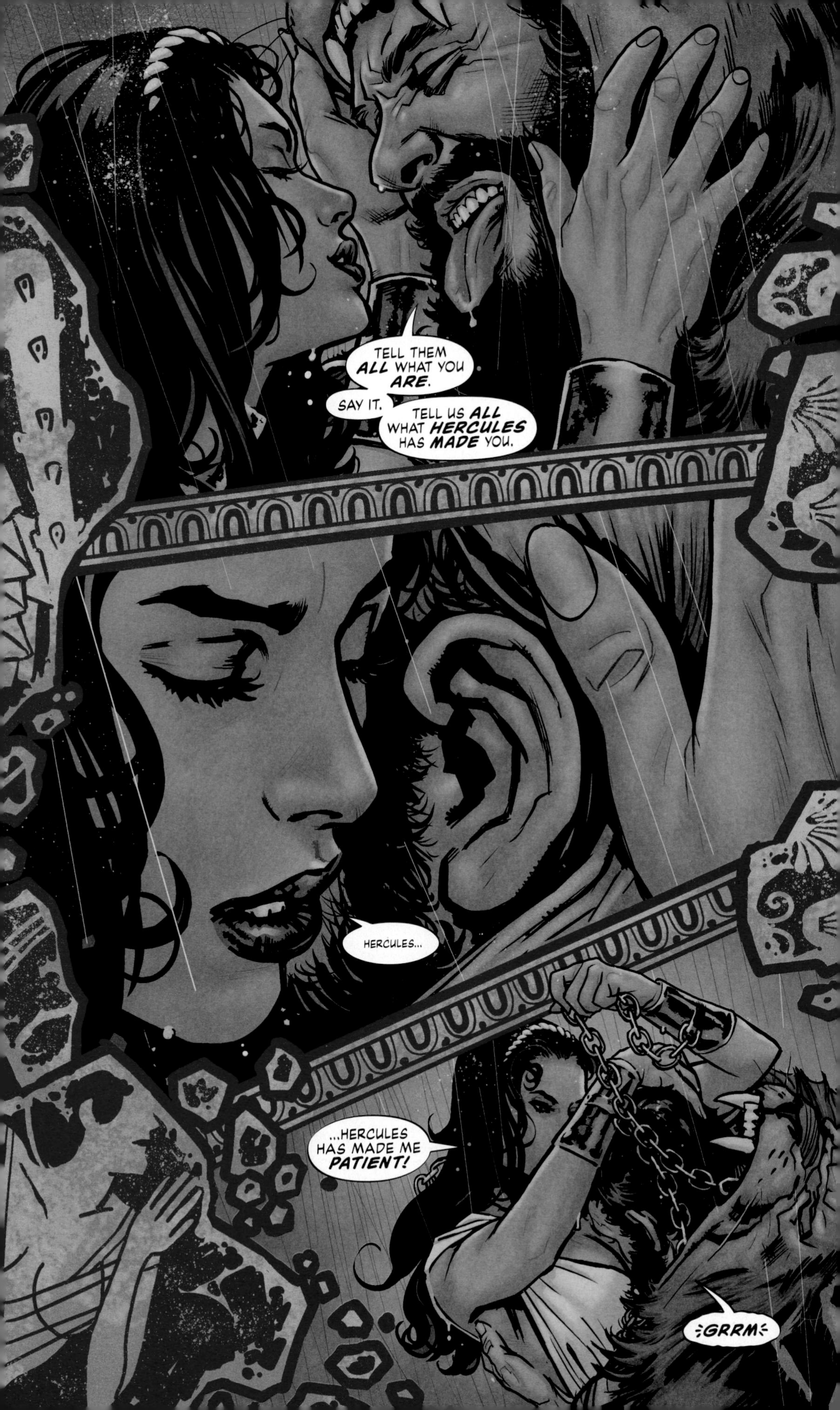
TELL THEM ALL WHAT YOU ARE.
SAY IT.
TELL US ALL WHAT HERCULES HAS MADE YOU.
HERCULES...
...HERCULES HAS MADE ME PATIENT!
GRRM

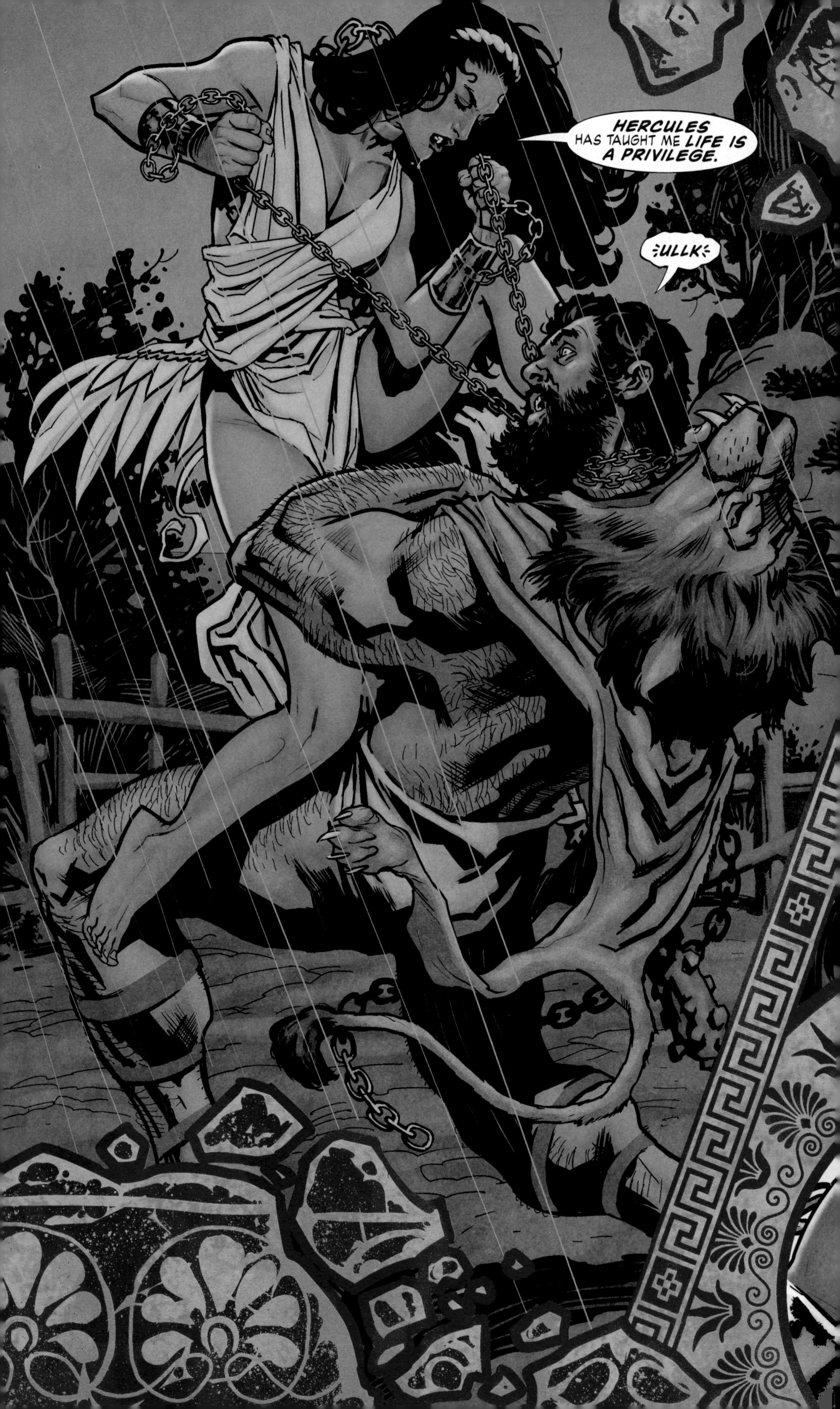
HERCULES HAS TAUGHT ME LIFE IS A PRIVILEGE.
:ULLK:

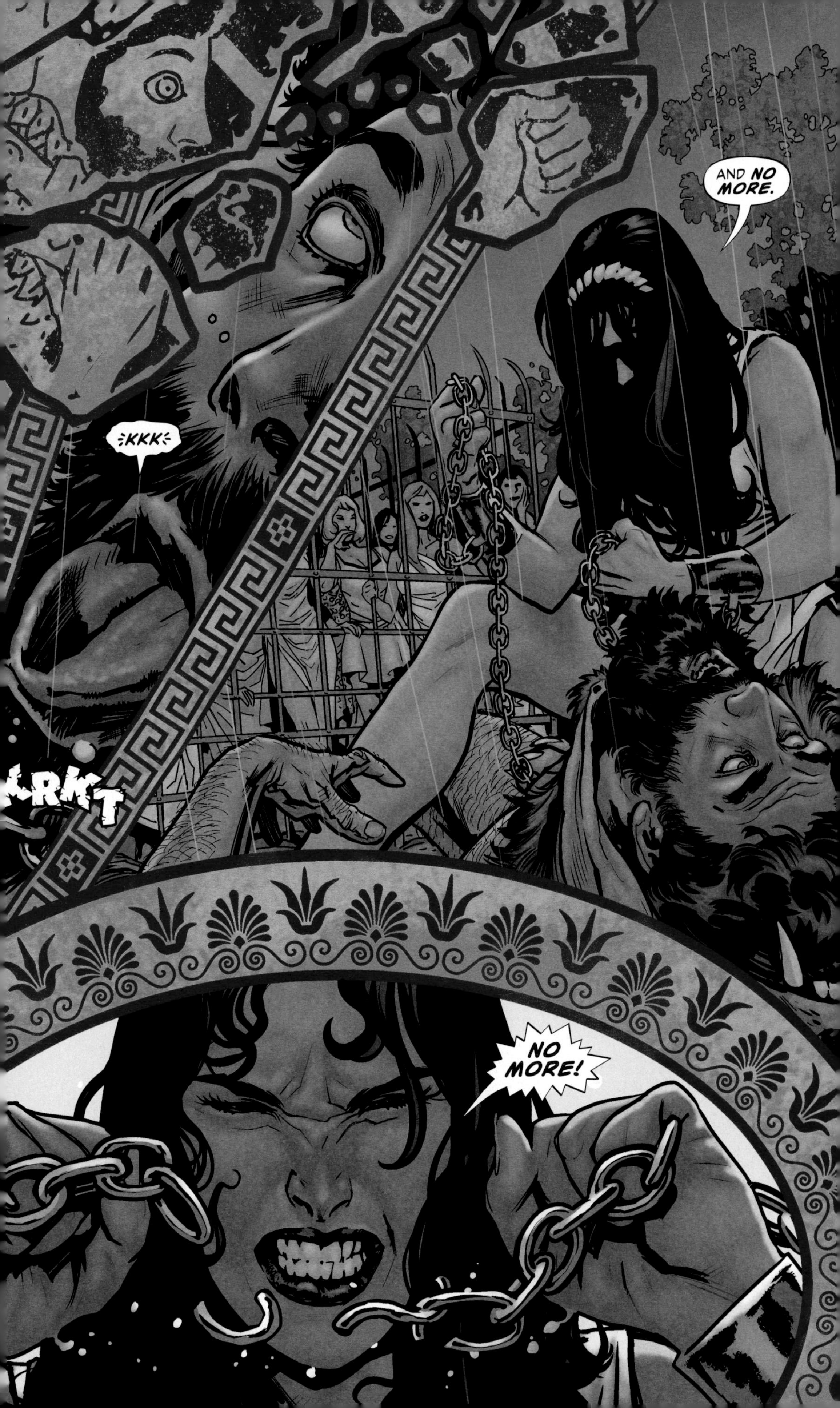
AND NO MORE.
KKK
RKT
NO MORE!

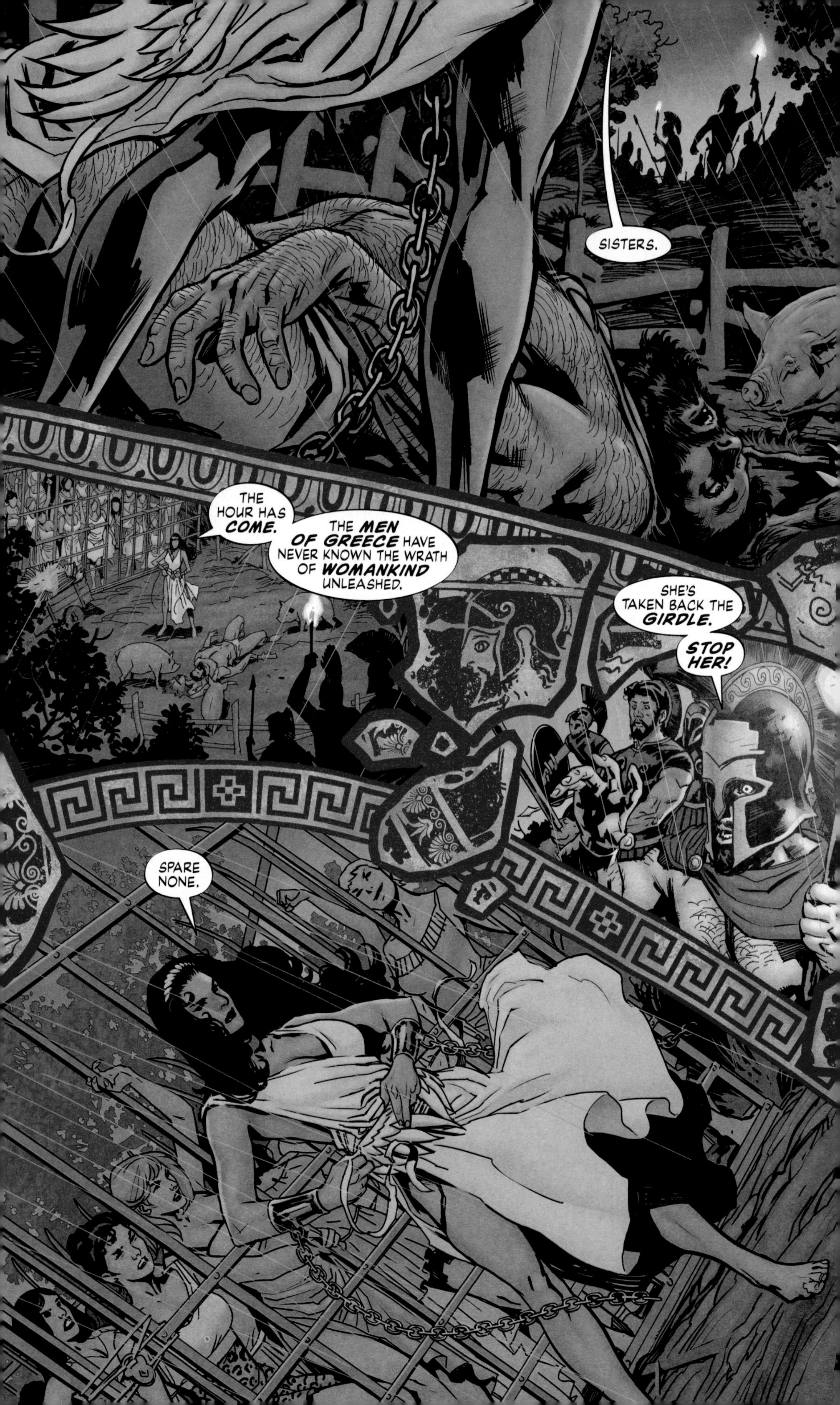

SISTERS.
THE HOUR HAS COME.
THE MEN OF GREECE HAVE NEVER KNOWN THE WRATH OF WOMANKIND UNLEASHED.
SHE'S TAKEN BACK THE GIRDLE.
STOP HER!
SPARE NONE.

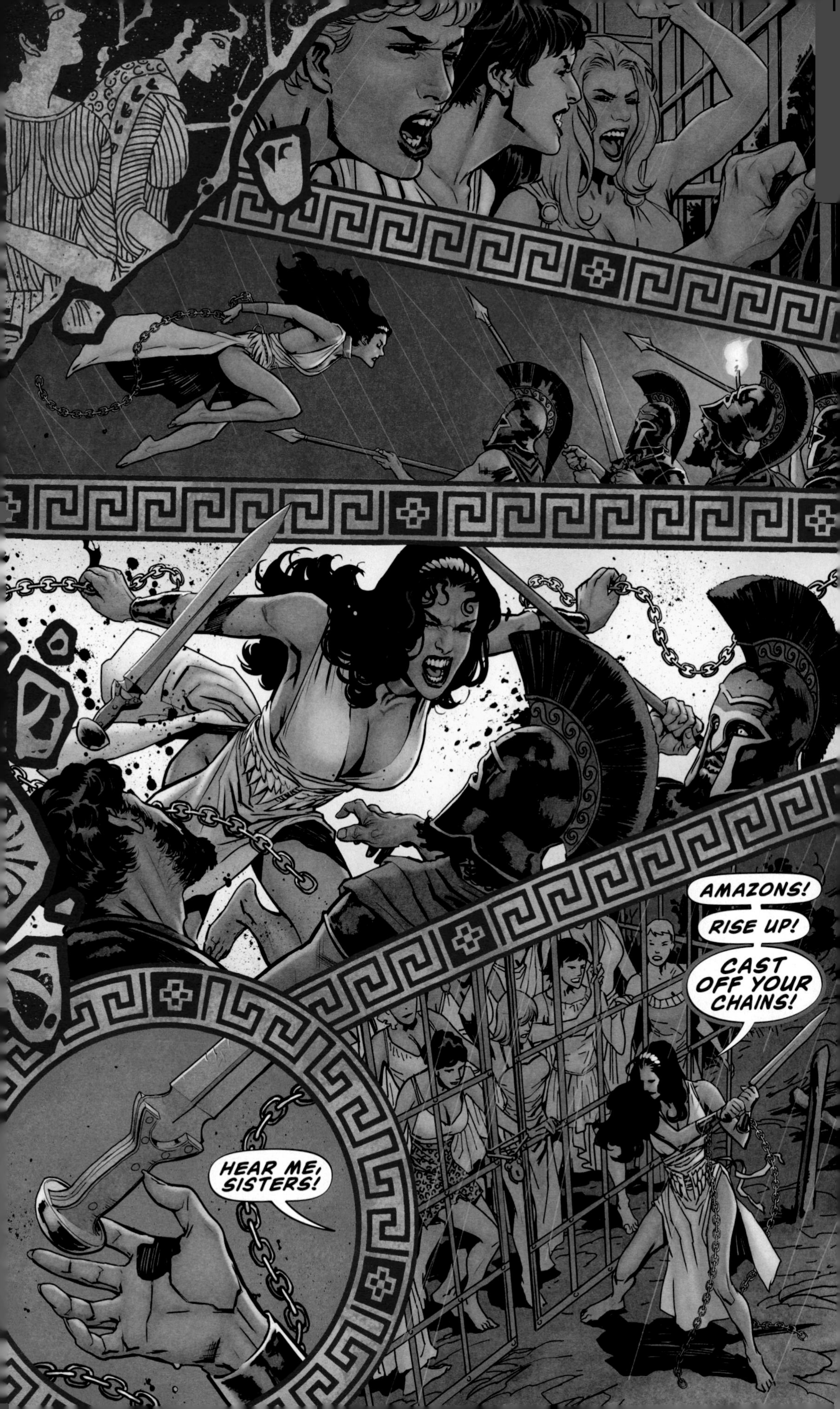
AMAZONS!
RISE UP!
CAST OFF YOUR CHAINS!
HEAR ME, SISTERS!

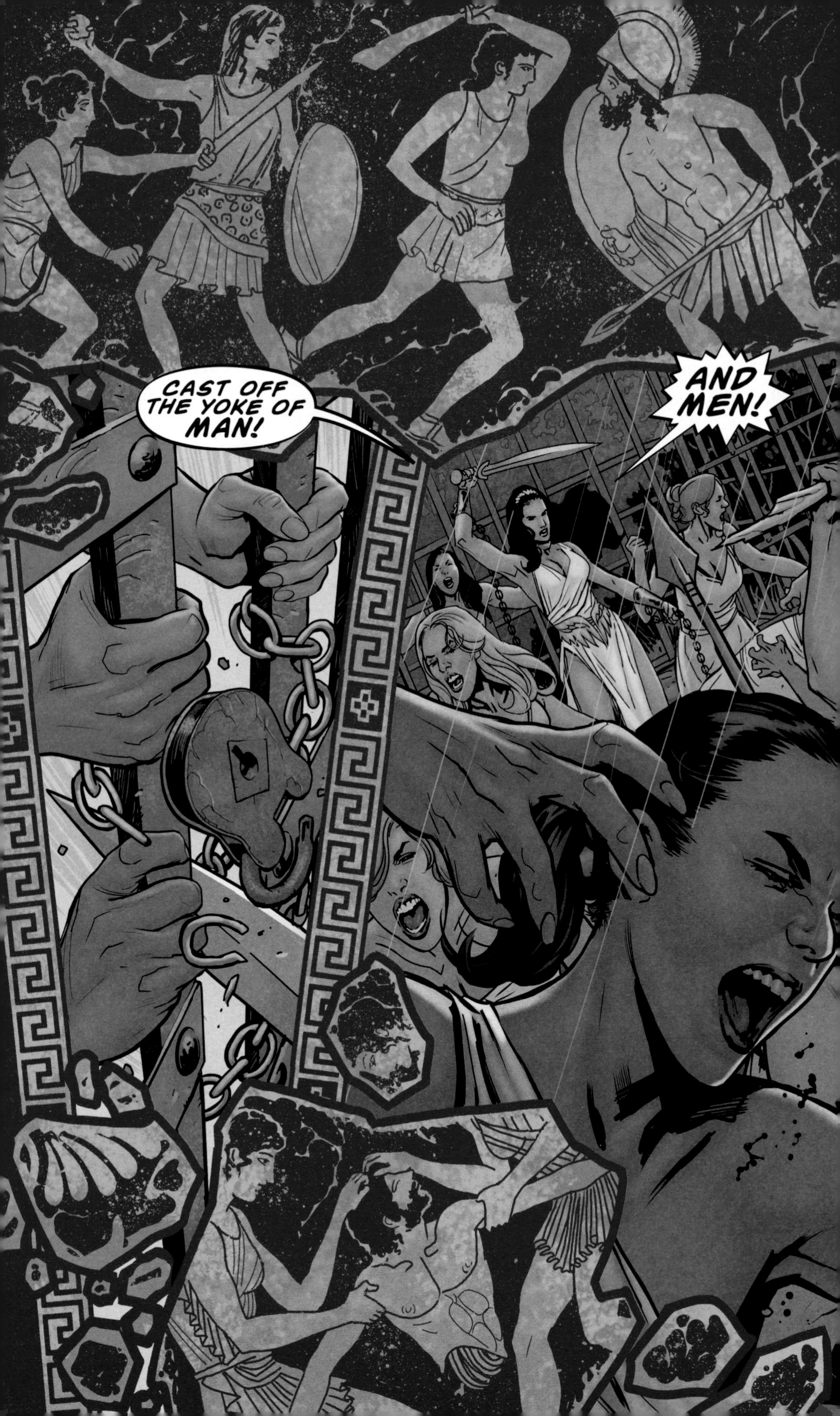
CAST OFF THE YOKE OF MAN!
AND MEN!

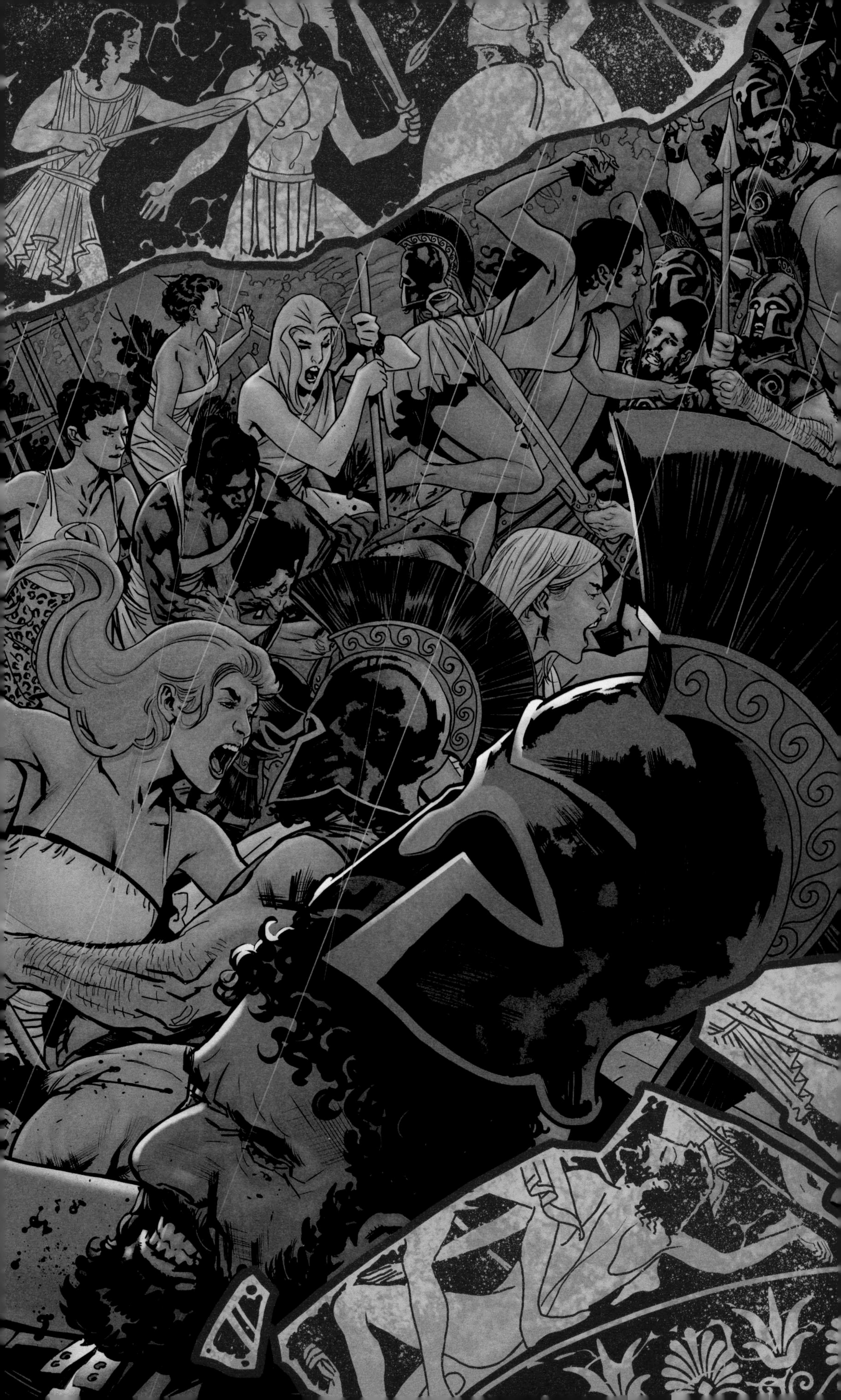

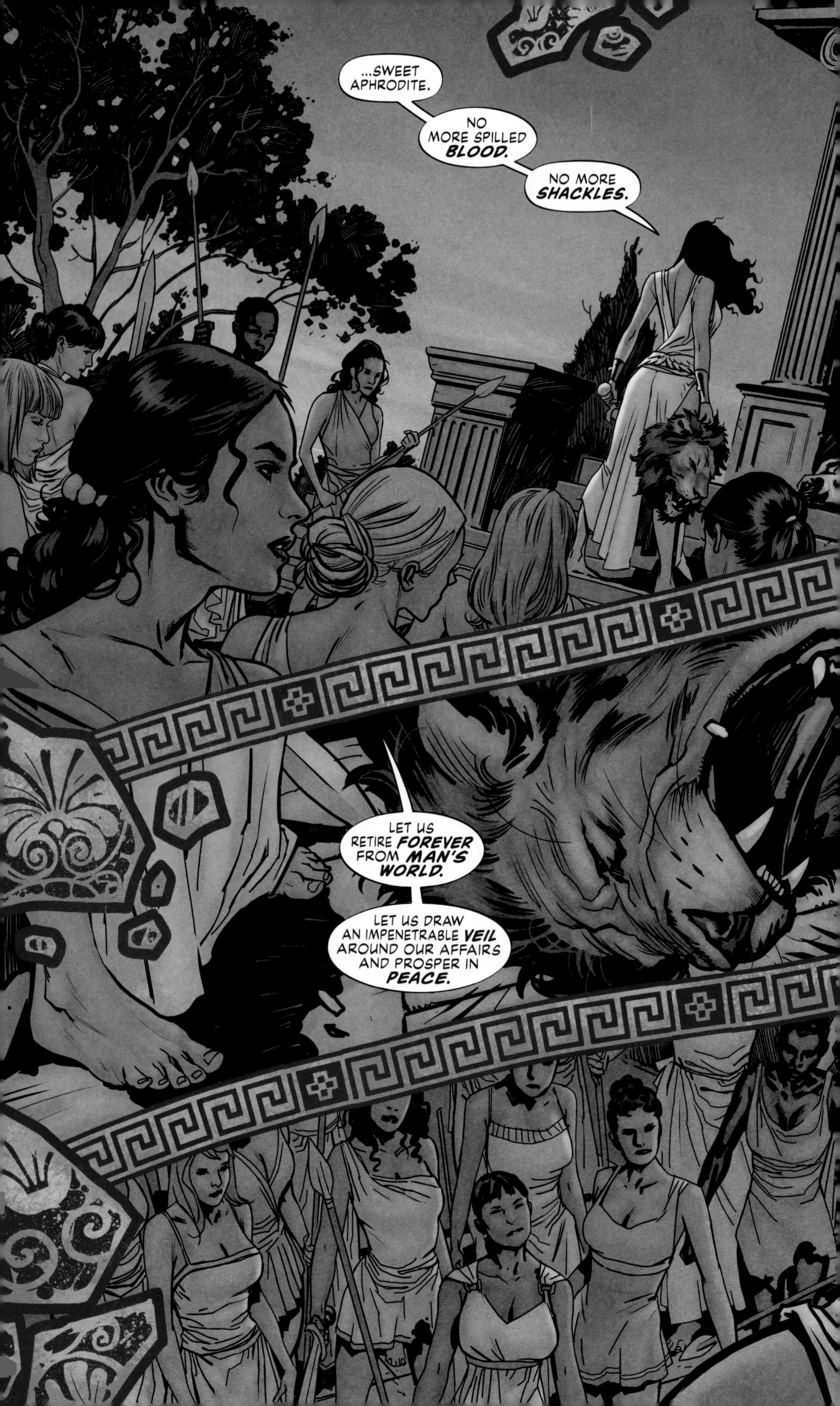

...SWEET APHRODITE.
NO MORE SPILLED BLOOD.
NO MORE SHACKLES.
LET US RETIRE FOREVER FROM MAN'S WORLD.
LET US DRAW AN IMPENETRABLE VEIL AROUND OUR AFFAIRS AND PROSPER IN PEACE.

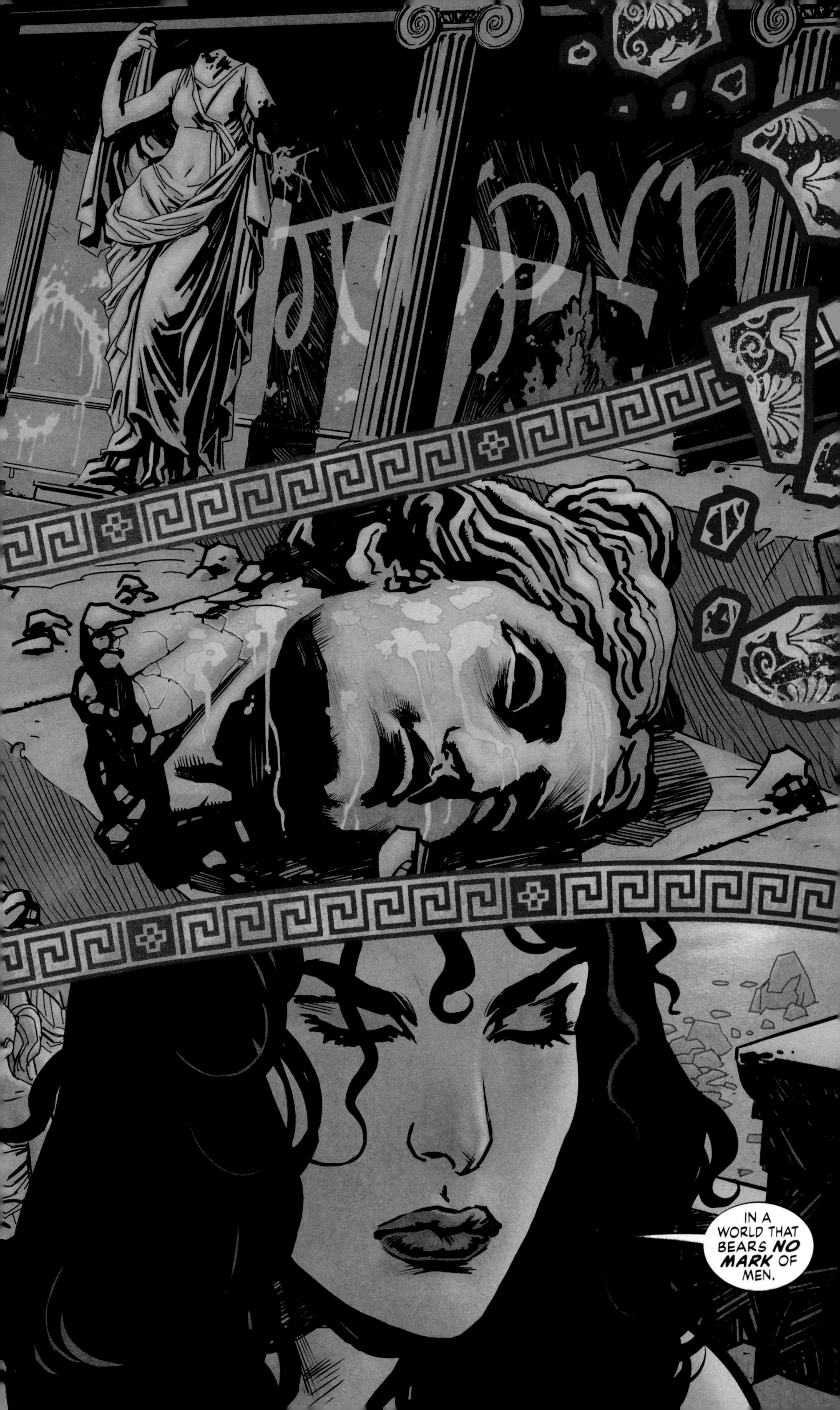
IN A WORLD THAT BEARS NO MARK OF MEN.

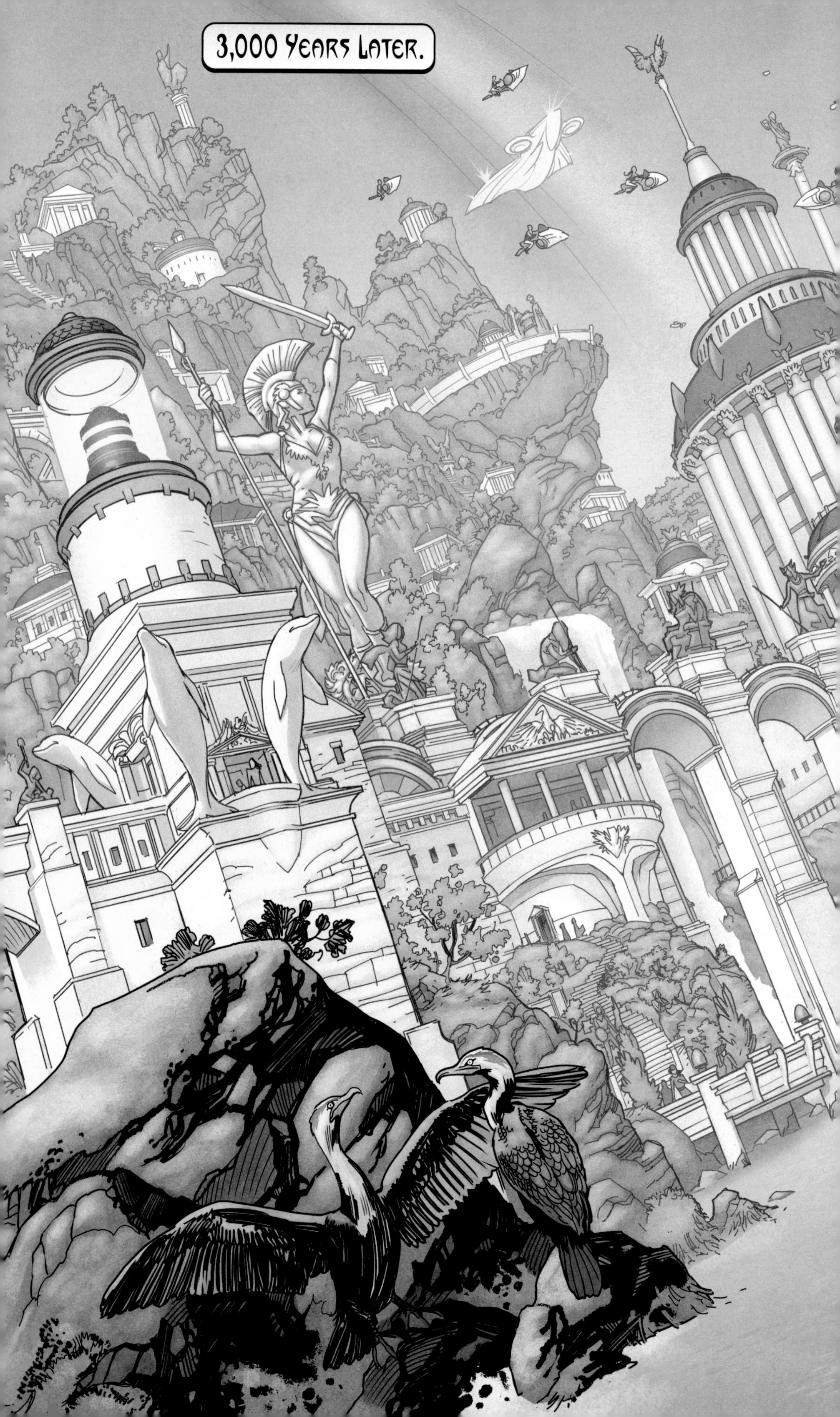
3,000 Years Later.

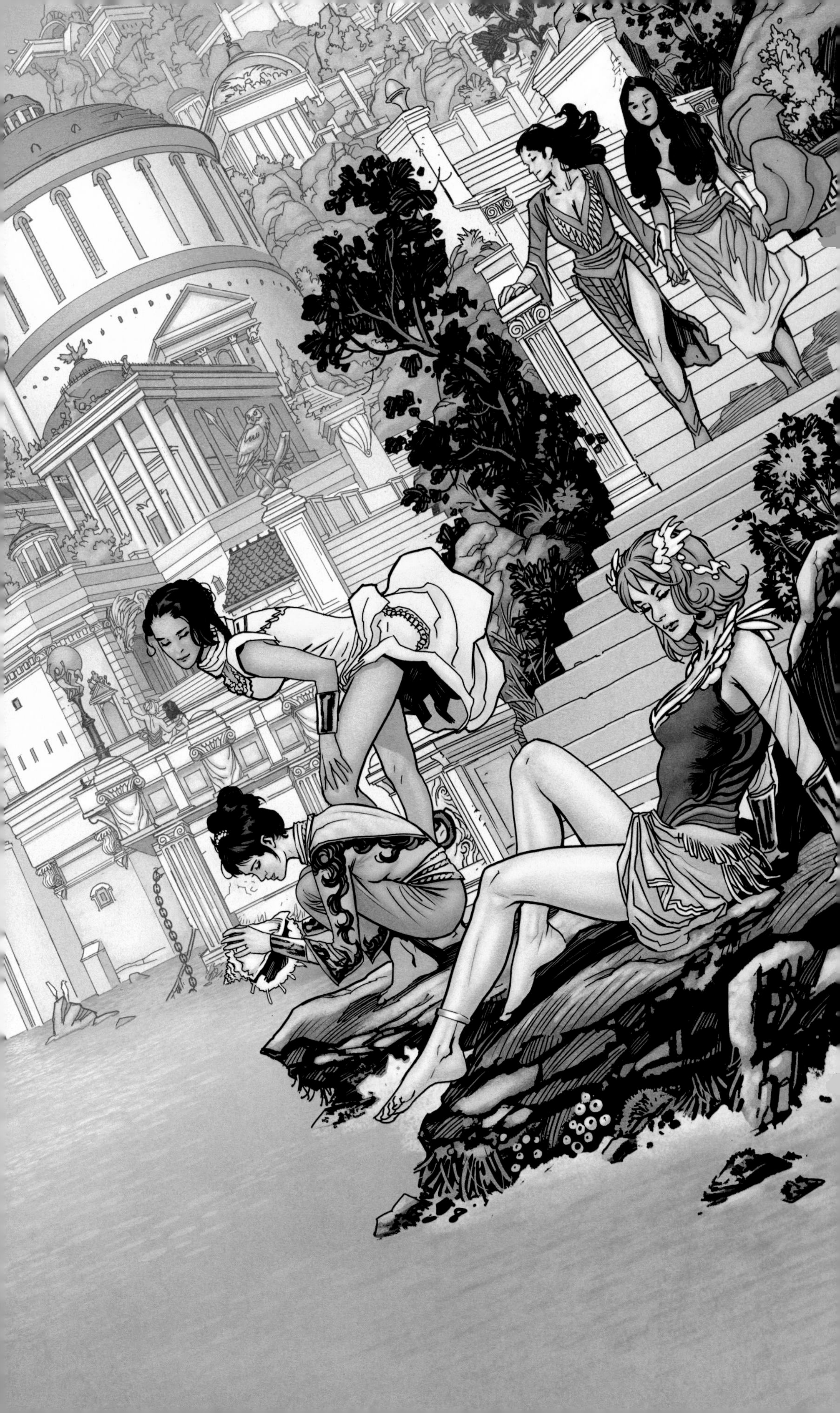

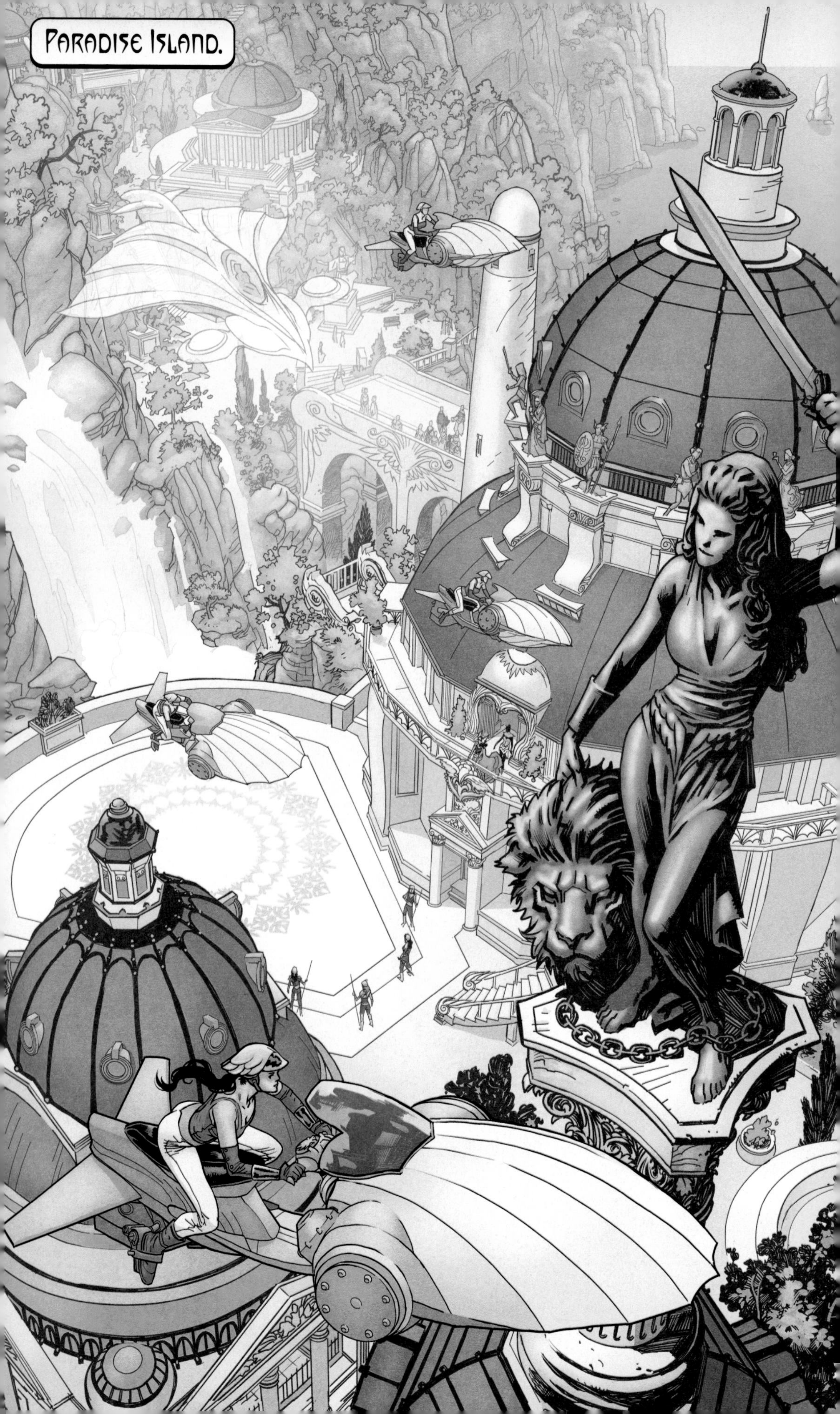
PARADISE ISLAND.

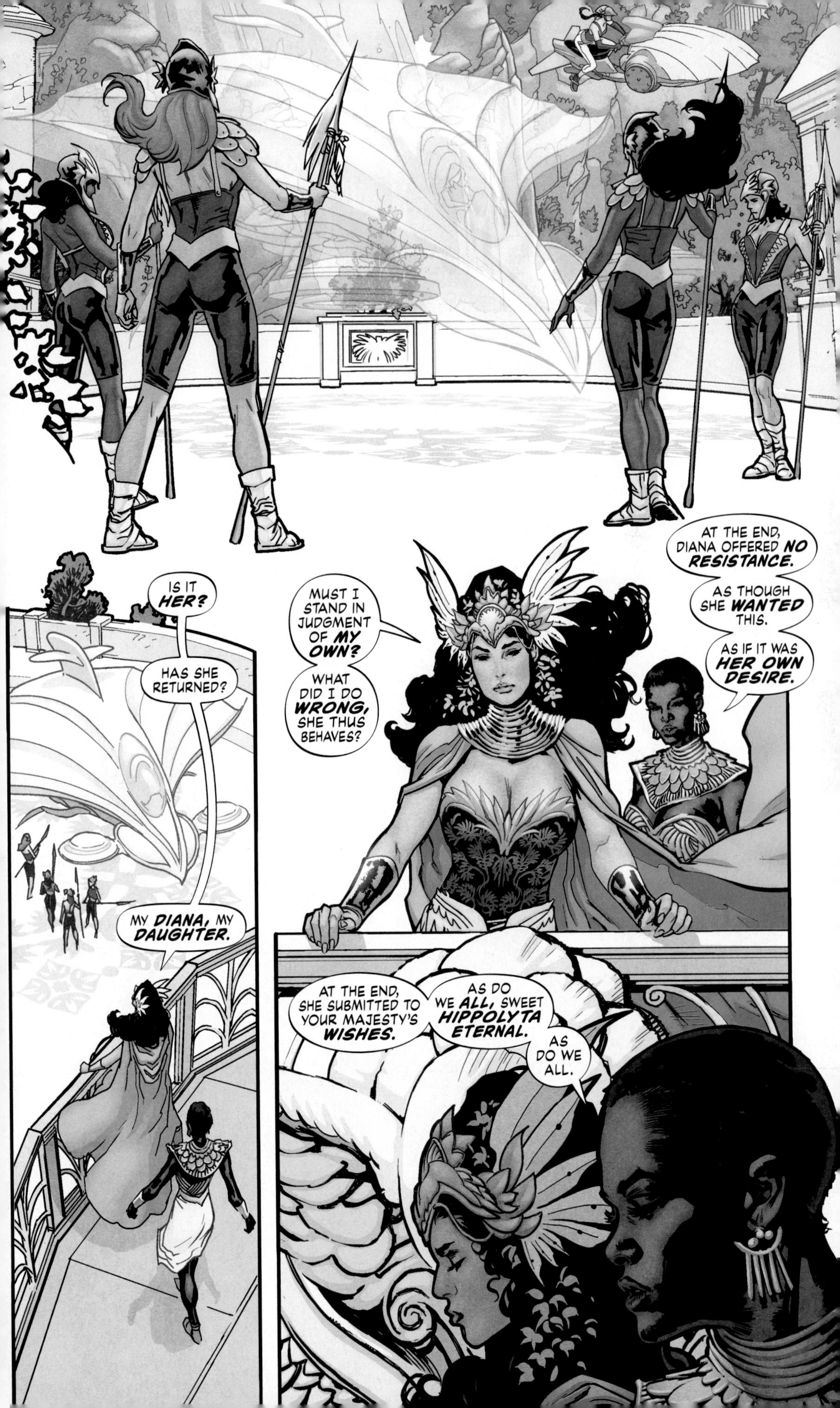

IS IT HER?
HAS SHE RETURNED?
MY DIANA, MY DAUGHTER.
MUST I STAND IN JUDGMENT OF MY OWN?
WHAT DID I DO WRONG, SHE THUS BEHAVES?
AT THE END, DIANA OFFERED NO RESISTANCE.
AS THOUGH SHE WANTED THIS.
AS IF IT WAS HER OWN DESIRE.
AT THE END, SHE SUBMITTED TO YOUR MAJESTY'S WISHES.
AS DO WE ALL, SWEET HIPPOLYTA ETERNAL.
AS DO WE ALL.

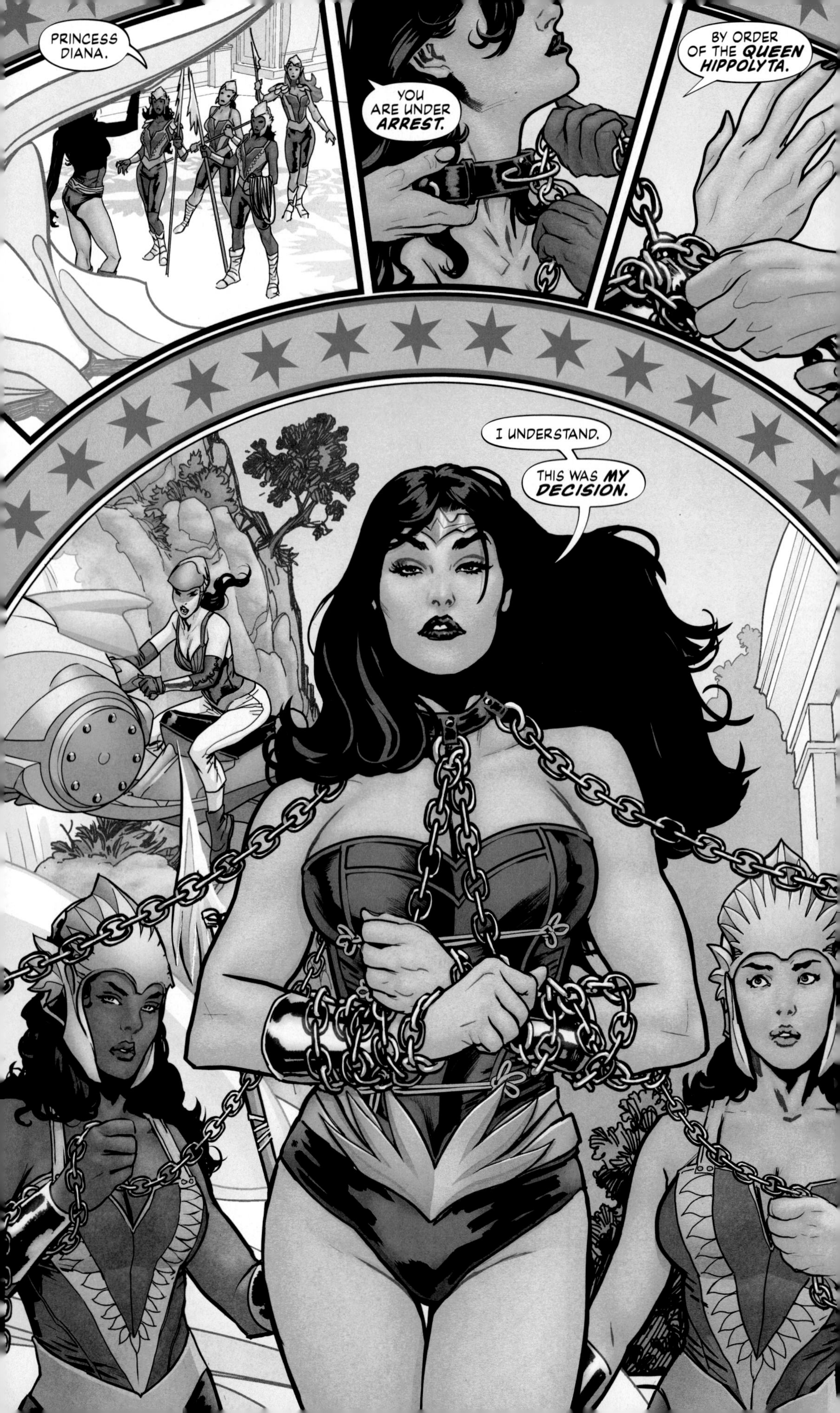
PRINCESS DIANA.
YOU ARE UNDER ARREST.
BY ORDER OF THE QUEEN HIPPOLYTA.
I UNDERSTAND.
THIS WAS MY DECISION.

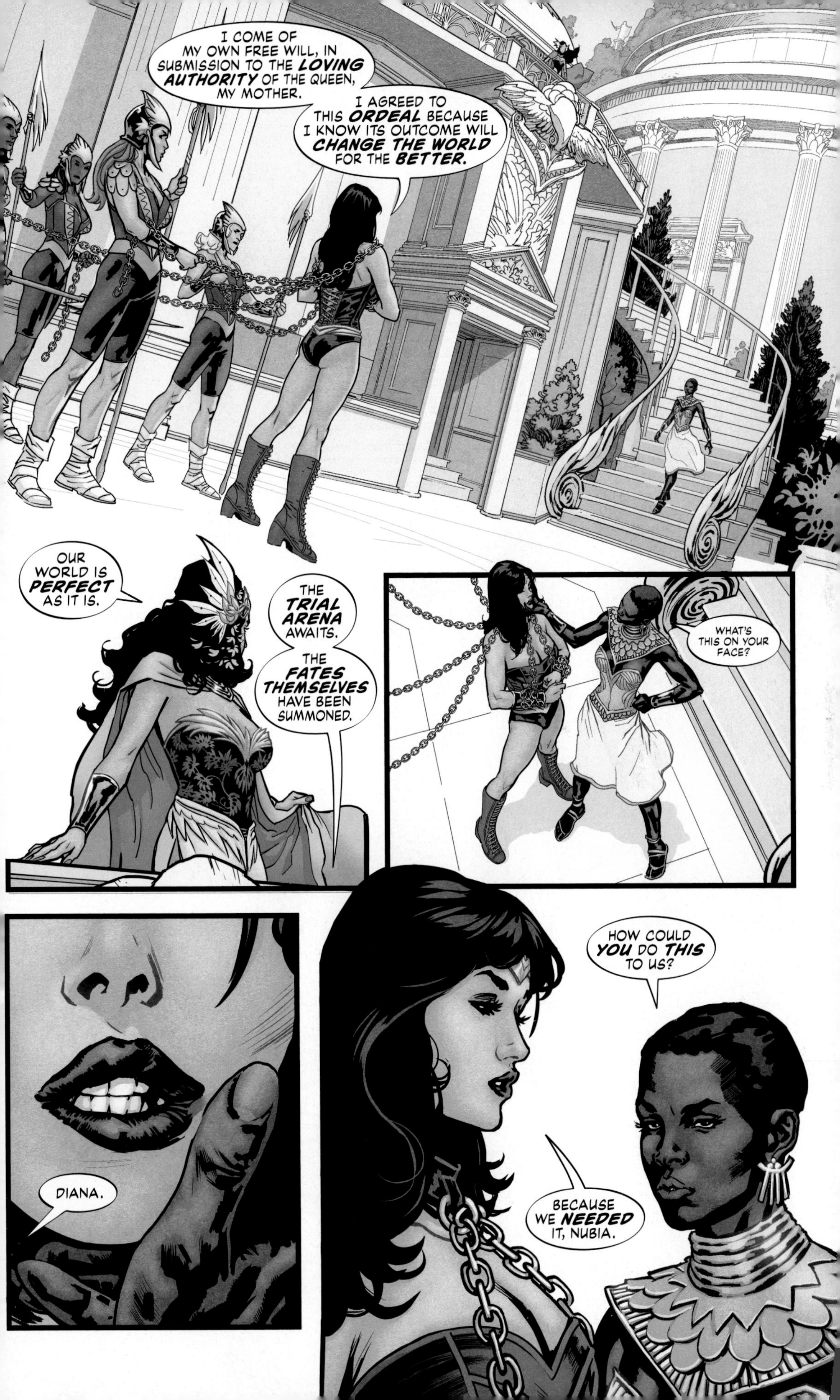

I COME OF MY OWN FREE WILL, IN SUBMISSION TO THE LOVING AUTHORITY OF THE QUEEN, MY MOTHER.
I AGREED TO THIS ORDEAL BECAUSE I KNOW ITS OUTCOME WILL CHANGE THE WORLD FOR THE BETTER.
OUR WORLD IS PERFECT AS IT IS.
THE TRIAL ARENA AWAITS.
THE FATES THEMSELVES HAVE BEEN SUMMONED.
WHAT'S THIS ON YOUR FACE?
DIANA.
HOW COULD YOU DO THIS TO US?
BECAUSE WE NEEDED IT, NUBIA.

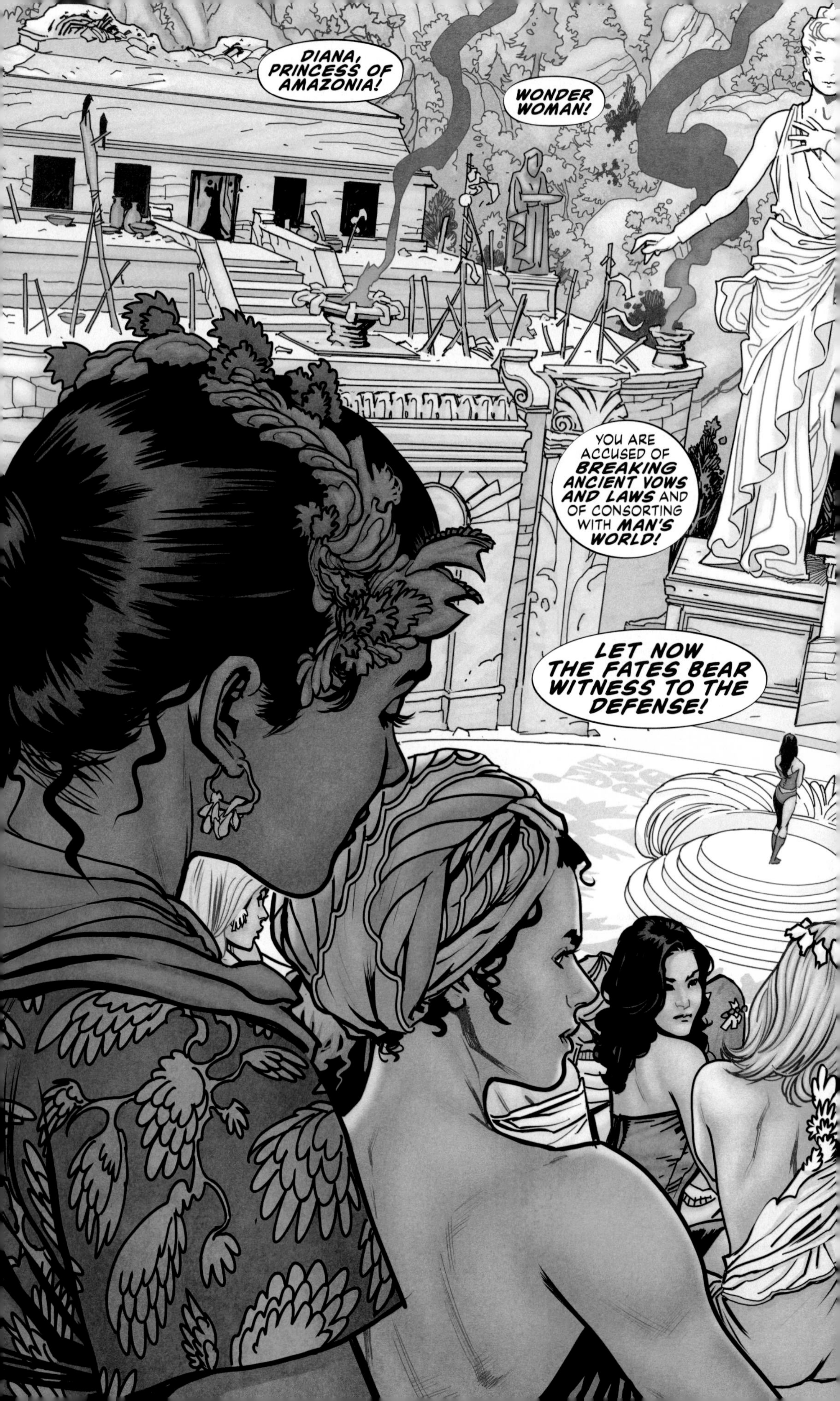
DIANA, PRINCESS OF AMAZONIA!
WONDER WOMAN!
YOU ARE ACCUSED OF BREAKING ANCIENT VOWS AND LAWS AND OF CONSORTING WITH MAN'S WORLD!
LET NOW THE FATES BEAR WITNESS TO THE DEFENSE!

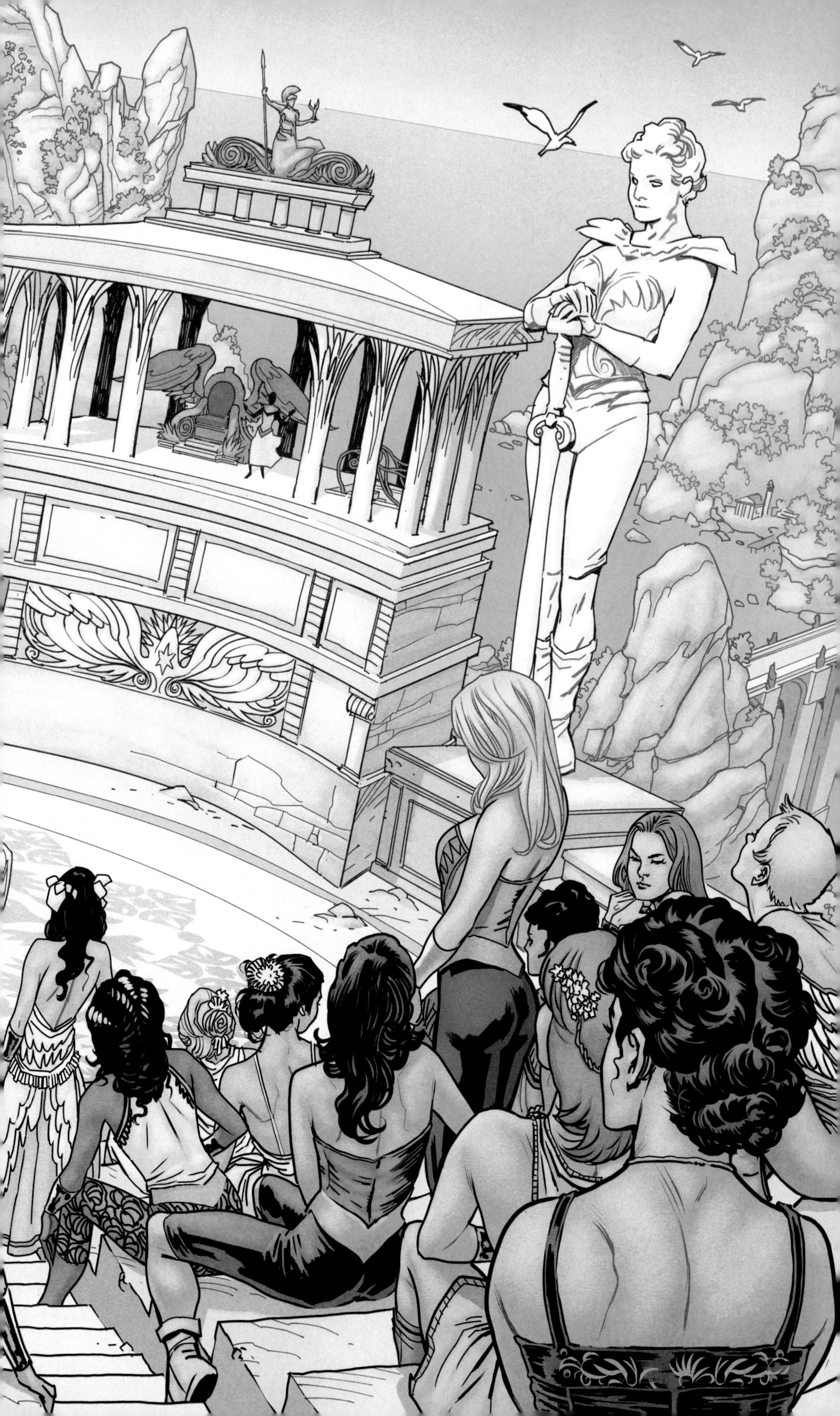

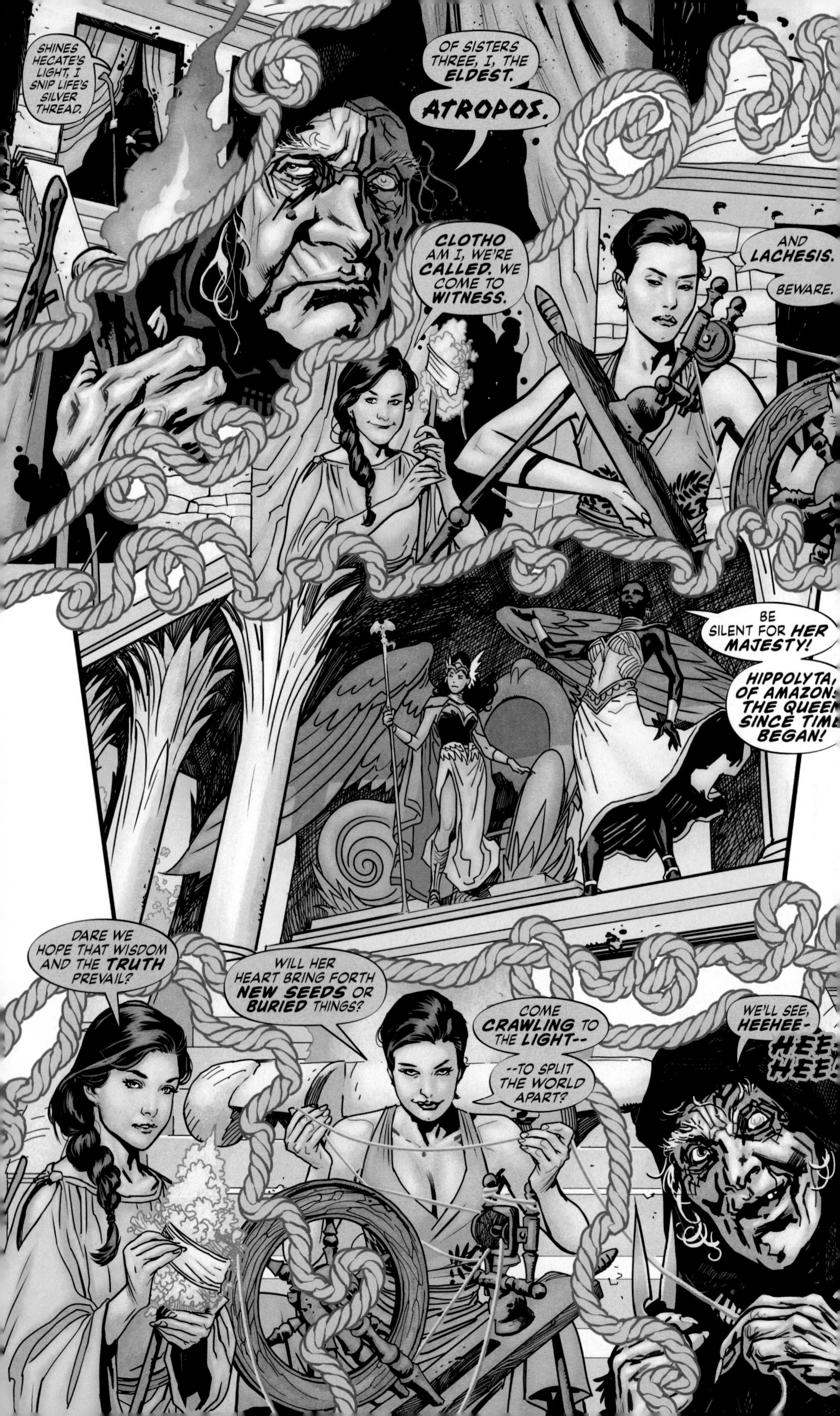

SHINES HECATE'S LIGHT, I SNIP LIFE'S SILVER THREAD.
OF SISTERS THREE, I, THE ELDEST.
ATROPOS.
CLOTHO AM I, WE'RE CALLED. WE COME TO WITNESS.
AND LACHESIS.
BEWARE.
BE SILENT FOR HER MAJESTY!
HIPPOLYTA, OF AMAZON THE QUEE SINCE TIM BEGAN!
DARE WE HOPE THAT WISDOM AND THE TRUTH PREVAIL?
WILL HER HEART BRING FORTH NEW SEEDS OR BURIED THINGS?
COME CRAWLING TO THE LIGHT--
--TO SPLIT THE WORLD APART?
WE'LL SEE, HEEHEE-
HEE HEE

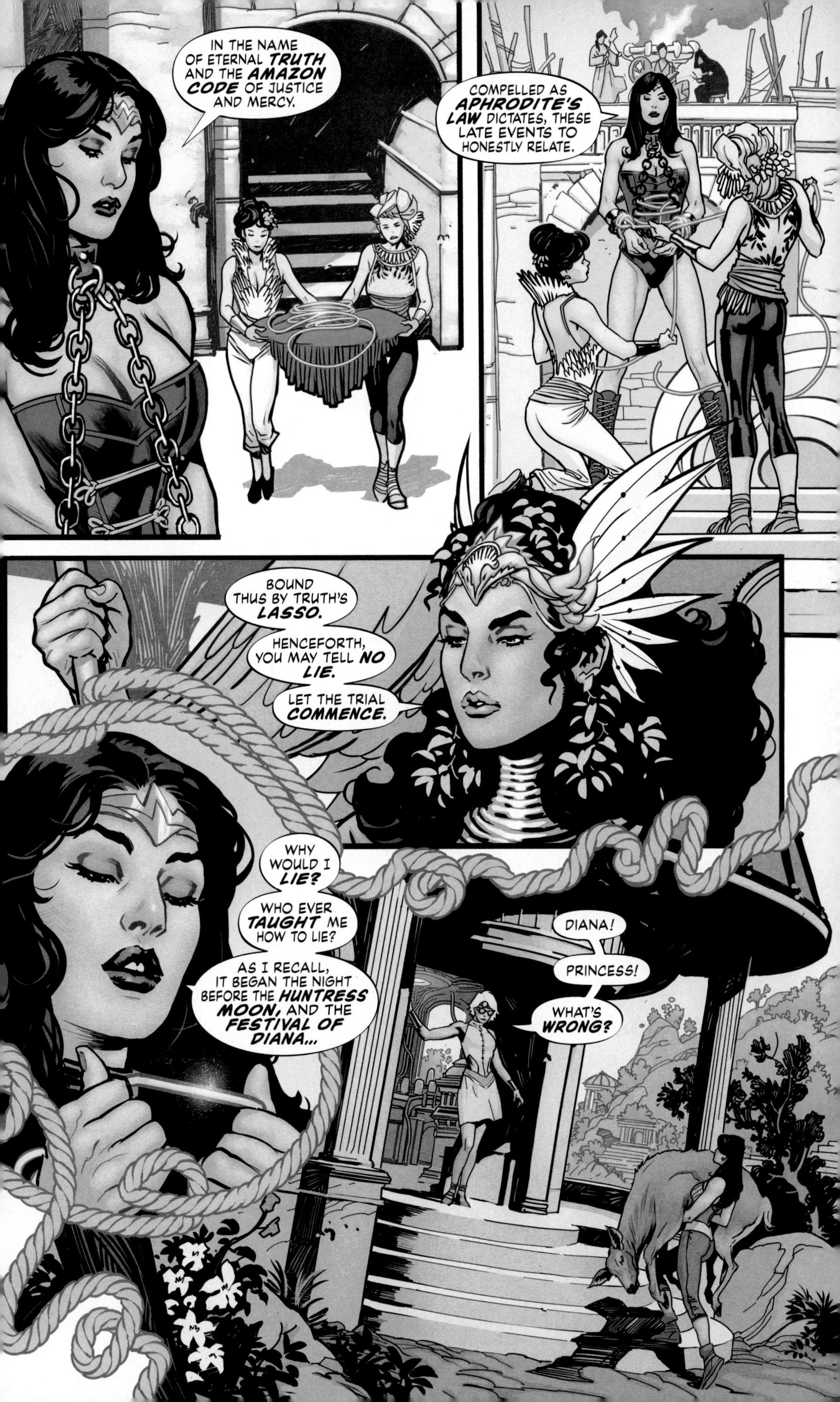
IN THE NAME OF ETERNAL TRUTH AND THE AMAZON CODE OF JUSTICE AND MERCY.
COMPELLED AS APHRODITE'S LAW DICTATES, THESE LATE EVENTS TO HONESTLY RELATE.
BOUND THUS BY TRUTH'S LASSO.
HENCEFORTH, YOU MAY TELL NO LIE.
LET THE TRIAL COMMENCE.
WHY WOULD I LIE?
WHO EVER TAUGHT ME HOW TO LIE?
AS I RECALL, IT BEGAN THE NIGHT BEFORE THE HUNTRESS MOON, AND THE FESTIVAL OF DIANA...
DIANA!
PRINCESS!
WHAT'S WRONG?

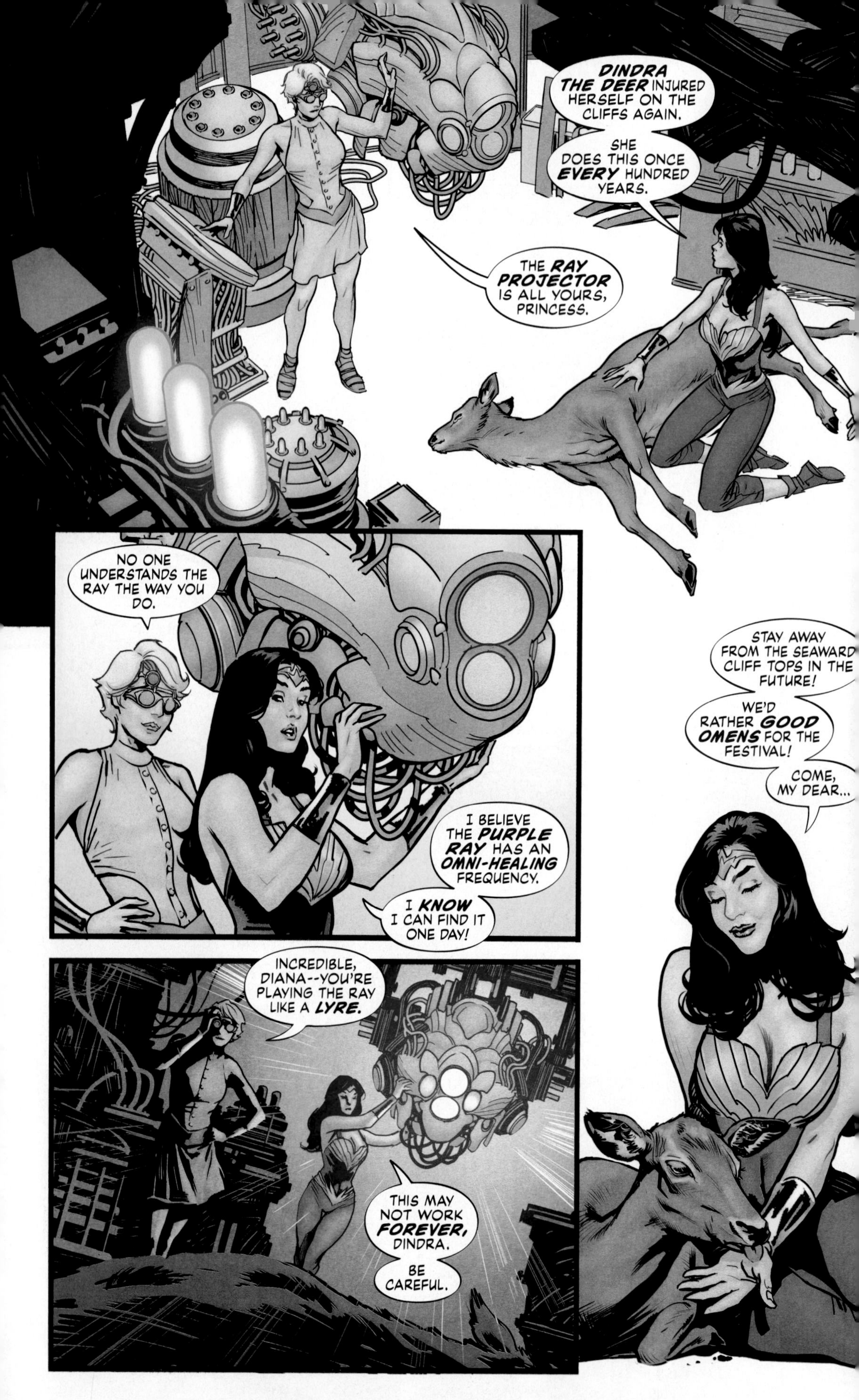

DINDRA THE DEER INJURED HERSELF ON THE CLIFFS AGAIN.
SHE DOES THIS ONCE EVERY HUNDRED YEARS.
THE RAY PROJECTOR IS ALL YOURS, PRINCESS.
NO ONE UNDERSTANDS THE RAY THE WAY YOU DO.
I BELIEVE THE PURPLE RAY HAS AN OMNI-HEALING FREQUENCY.
I KNOW I CAN FIND IT ONE DAY!
INCREDIBLE, DIANA--YOU'RE PLAYING THE RAY LIKE A LYRE.
THIS MAY NOT WORK FOREVER, DINDRA.
BE CAREFUL.
STAY AWAY FROM THE SEAWARD CLIFF TOPS IN THE FUTURE!
WE'D RATHER GOOD OMENS FOR THE FESTIVAL!
COME, MY DEAR...

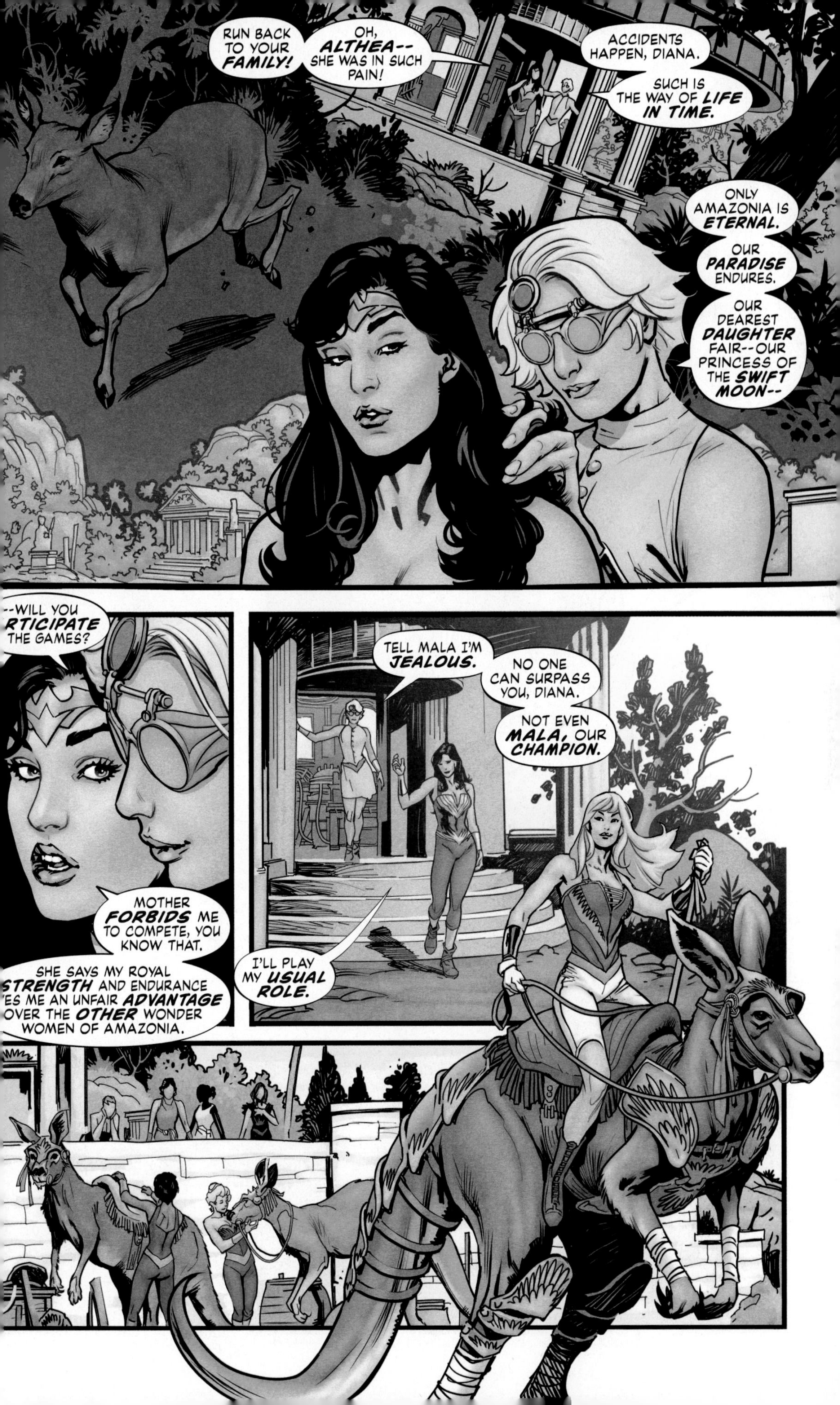

RUN BACK TO YOUR FAMILY!
OH, ALTHEA-- SHE WAS IN SUCH PAIN!
ACCIDENTS HAPPEN, DIANA.
SUCH IS THE WAY OF LIFE IN TIME.
ONLY AMAZONIA IS ETERNAL.
OUR PARADISE ENDURES.
OUR DEAREST DAUGHTER FAIR--OUR PRINCESS OF THE SWIFT MOON--
--WILL YOU RTICIPATE THE GAMES?
MOTHER FORBIDS ME TO COMPETE, YOU KNOW THAT.
SHE SAYS MY ROYAL STRENGTH AND ENDURANCE 'ES ME AN UNFAIR ADVANTAGE OVER THE OTHER WONDER WOMEN OF AMAZONIA.
TELL MALA I'M JEALOUS.
NO ONE CAN SURPASS YOU, DIANA.
NOT EVEN MALA, OUR CHAMPION.
I'LL PLAY MY USUAL ROLE.

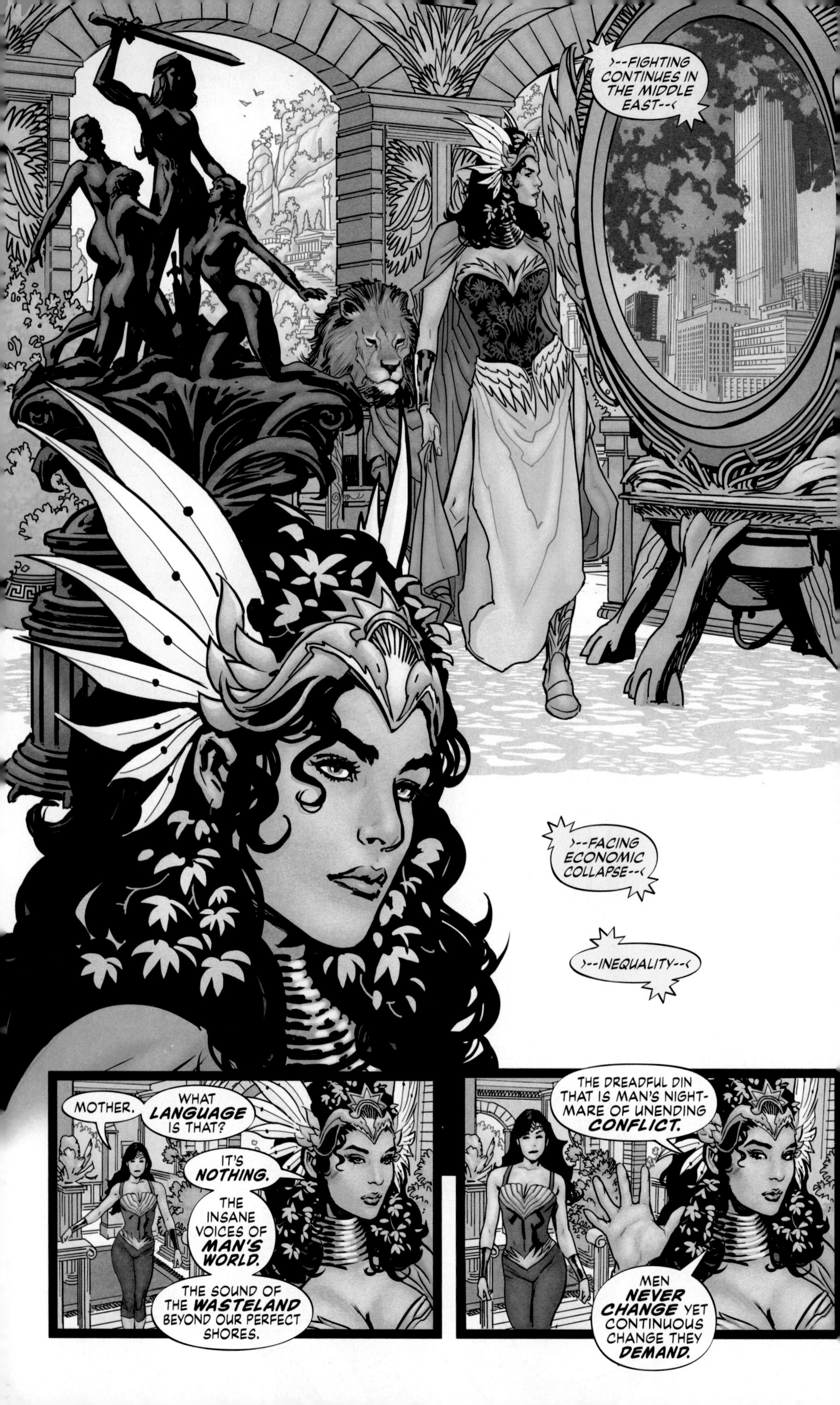
>--FIGHTING CONTINUES IN THE MIDDLE EAST--<
>--FACING ECONOMIC COLLAPSE--<
>--INEQUALITY--<
MOTHER.
WHAT LANGUAGE IS THAT?
IT'S NOTHING.
THE INSANE VOICES OF MAN'S WORLD.
THE SOUND OF THE WASTELAND BEYOND OUR PERFECT SHORES.
THE DREADFUL DIN THAT IS MAN'S NIGHT-MARE OF UNENDING CONFLICT.
MEN NEVER CHANGE YET CONTINUOUS CHANGE THEY DEMAND.

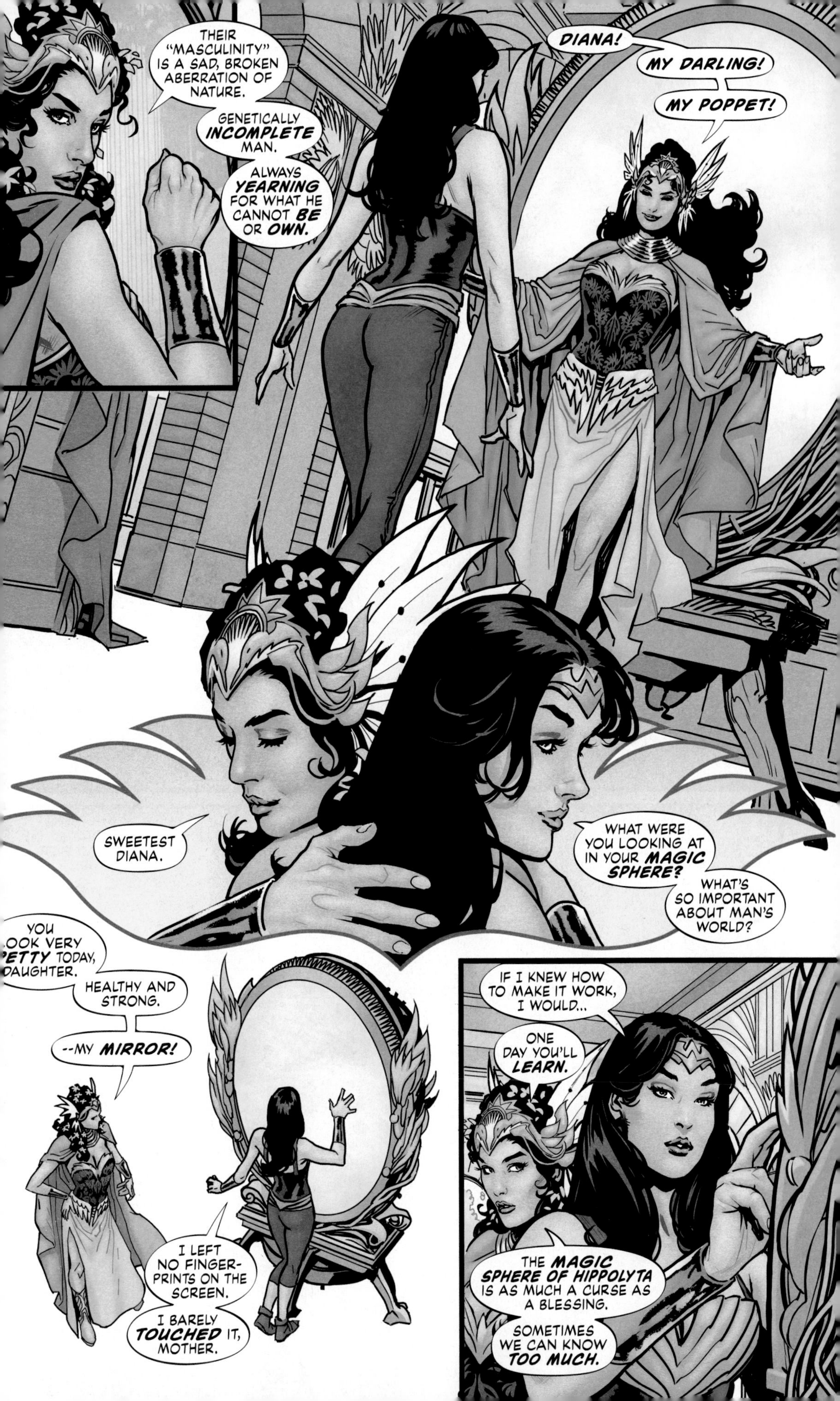

THEIR "MASCULINITY" IS A SAD, BROKEN ABERRATION OF NATURE.
GENETICALLY INCOMPLETE MAN.
ALWAYS YEARNING FOR WHAT HE CANNOT BE OR OWN.
DIANA!
MY DARLING!
MY POPPET!
SWEETEST DIANA.
WHAT WERE YOU LOOKING AT IN YOUR MAGIC SPHERE?
WHAT'S SO IMPORTANT ABOUT MAN'S WORLD?
YOU LOOK VERY PETTY TODAY, DAUGHTER.
HEALTHY AND STRONG.
--MY MIRROR!
I LEFT NO FINGER-PRINTS ON THE SCREEN.
I BARELY TOUCHED IT, MOTHER.
IF I KNEW HOW TO MAKE IT WORK, I WOULD...
ONE DAY YOU'LL LEARN.
THE MAGIC SPHERE OF HIPPOLYTA IS AS MUCH A CURSE AS A BLESSING.
SOMETIMES WE CAN KNOW TOO MUCH.

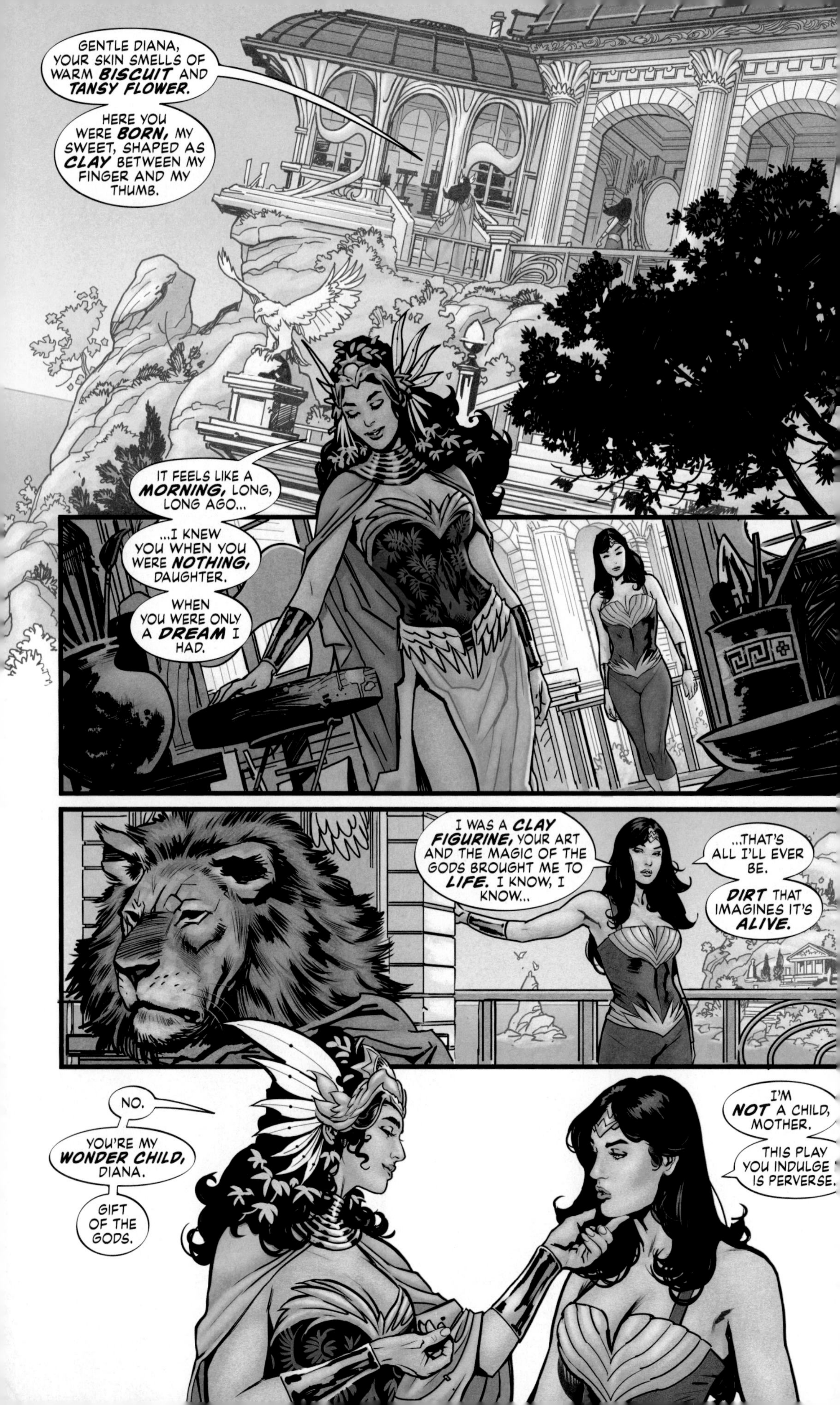
GENTLE DIANA, YOUR SKIN SMELLS OF WARM BISCUIT AND TANSY FLOWER.
HERE YOU WERE BORN, MY SWEET, SHAPED AS CLAY BETWEEN MY FINGER AND MY THUMB.
IT FEELS LIKE A MORNING, LONG, LONG AGO...
...I KNEW YOU WHEN YOU WERE NOTHING, DAUGHTER.
WHEN YOU WERE ONLY A DREAM I HAD.
I WAS A CLAY FIGURINE, YOUR ART AND THE MAGIC OF THE GODS BROUGHT ME TO LIFE. I KNOW, I KNOW...
...THAT'S ALL I'LL EVER BE.
DIRT THAT IMAGINES IT'S ALIVE.
NO.
YOU'RE MY WONDER CHILD, DIANA.
GIFT OF THE GODS.
I'M NOT A CHILD, MOTHER.
THIS PLAY YOU INDULGE IS PERVERSE.

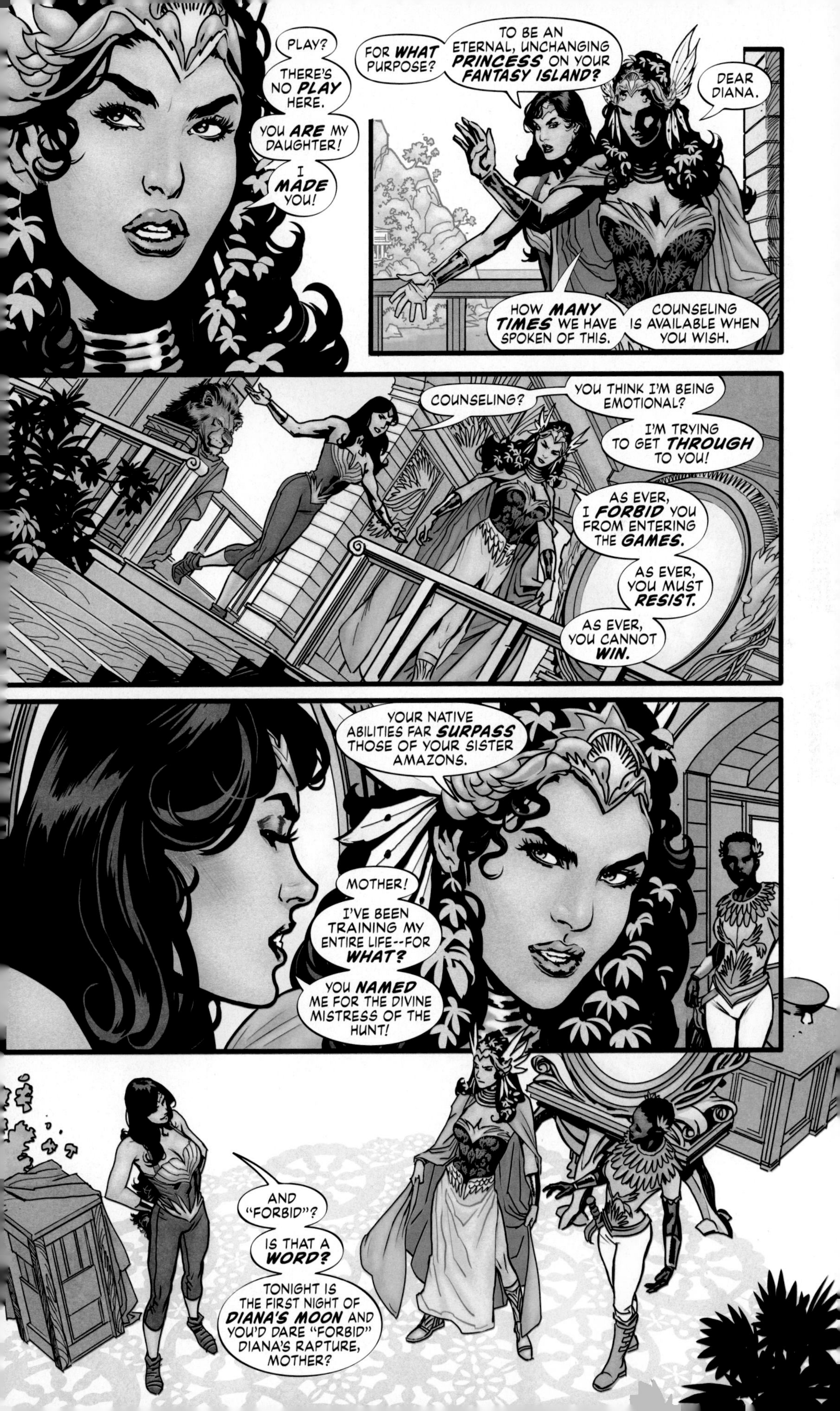
PLAY?
THERE'S NO PLAY HERE.
YOU ARE MY DAUGHTER!
I MADE YOU!
FOR WHAT PURPOSE?
TO BE AN ETERNAL, UNCHANGING PRINCESS ON YOUR FANTASY ISLAND?
DEAR DIANA.
HOW MANY TIMES WE HAVE SPOKEN OF THIS.
COUNSELING IS AVAILABLE WHEN YOU WISH.
COUNSELING?
YOU THINK I'M BEING EMOTIONAL?
I'M TRYING TO GET THROUGH TO YOU!
AS EVER, I FORBID YOU FROM ENTERING THE GAMES.
AS EVER, YOU MUST RESIST.
AS EVER, YOU CANNOT WIN.
YOUR NATIVE ABILITIES FAR SURPASS THOSE OF YOUR SISTER AMAZONS.
MOTHER!
I'VE BEEN TRAINING MY ENTIRE LIFE--FOR WHAT?
YOU NAMED ME FOR THE DIVINE MISTRESS OF THE HUNT!
AND "FORBID"?
IS THAT A WORD?
TONIGHT IS THE FIRST NIGHT OF DIANA'S MOON AND YOU'D DARE "FORBID" DIANA'S RAPTURE, MOTHER?

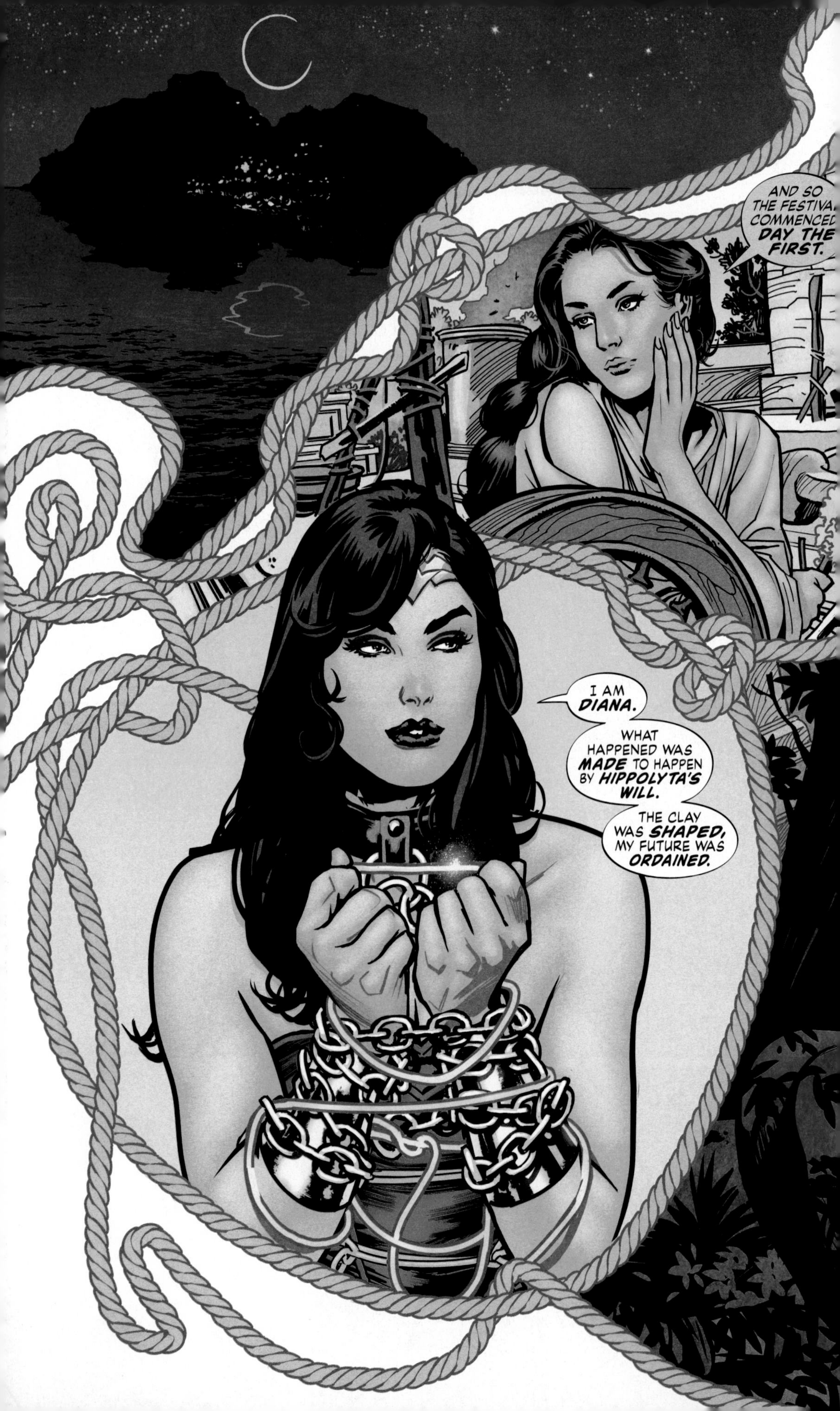

AND SO THE FESTIVAL COMMENCED. DAY THE FIRST.
I AM DIANA.
WHAT HAPPENED WAS MADE TO HAPPEN BY HIPPOLYTA'S WILL.
THE CLAY WAS SHAPED, MY FUTURE WAS ORDAINED.

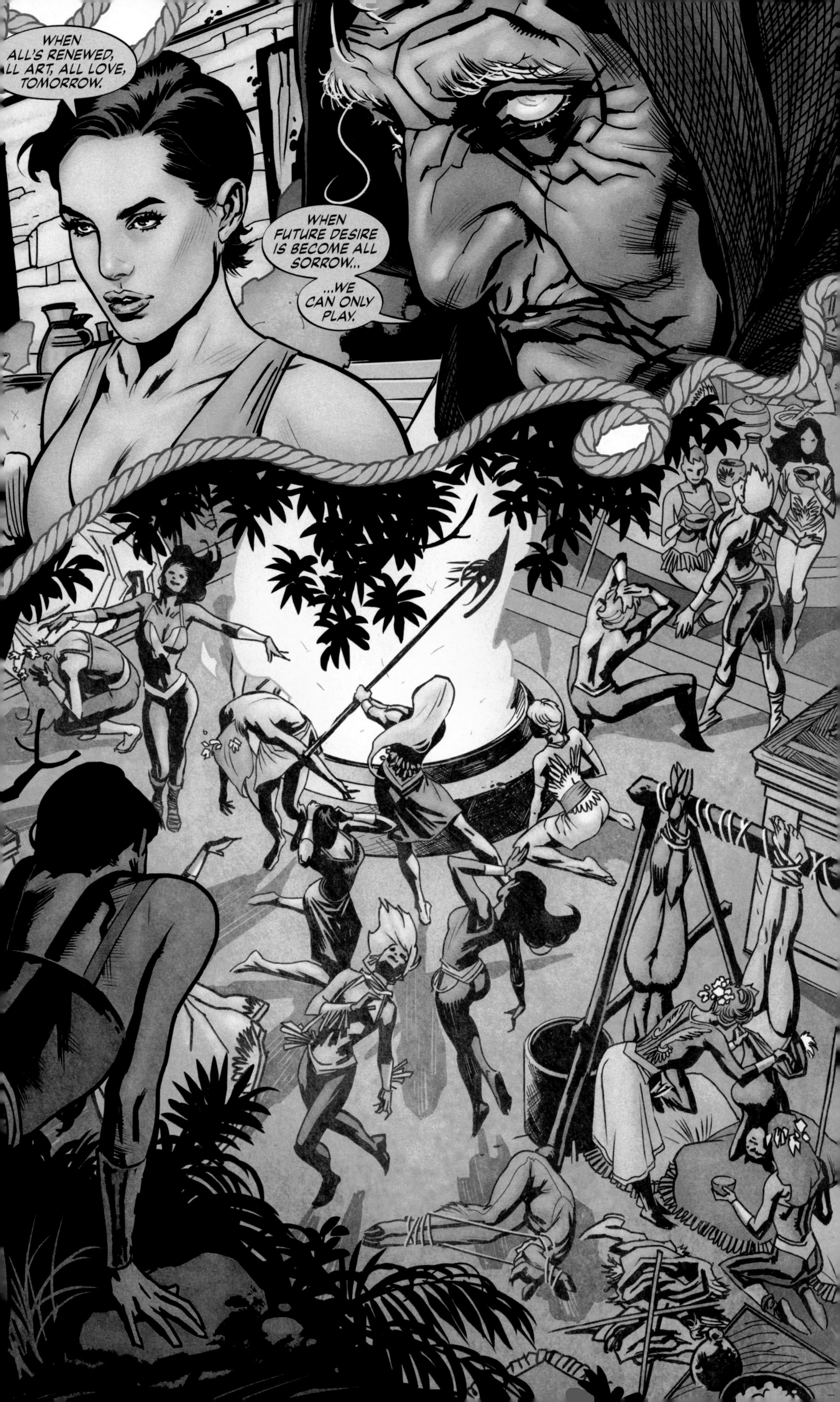
WHEN ALL'S RENEWED, LL ART, ALL LOVE, TOMORROW.
WHEN FUTURE DESIRE IS BECOME ALL SORROW...
...WE CAN ONLY PLAY.

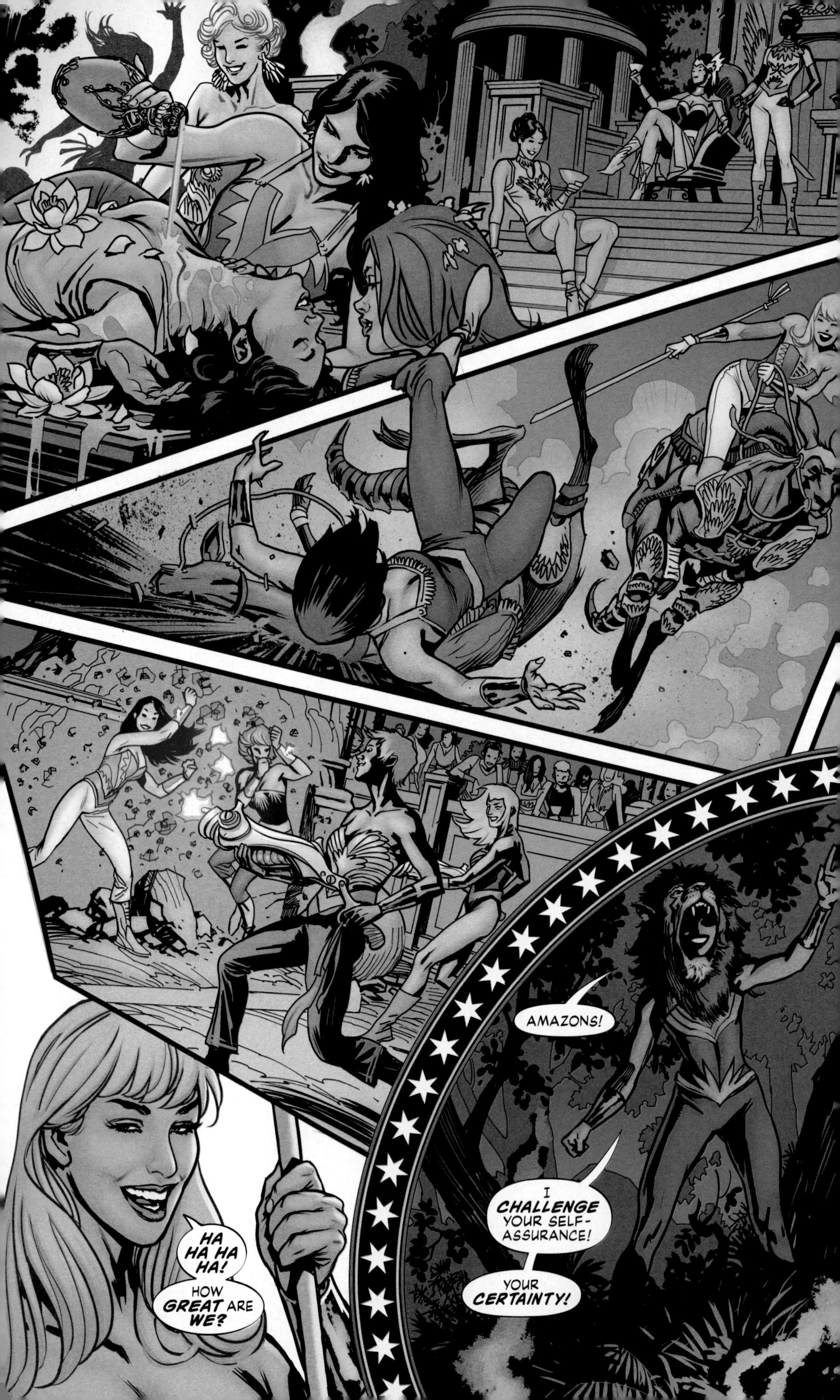
AMAZONS!
I CHALLENGE YOUR SELF-ASSURANCE!
YOUR CERTAINTY!
HA HA HA HA!
HOW GREAT ARE WE?

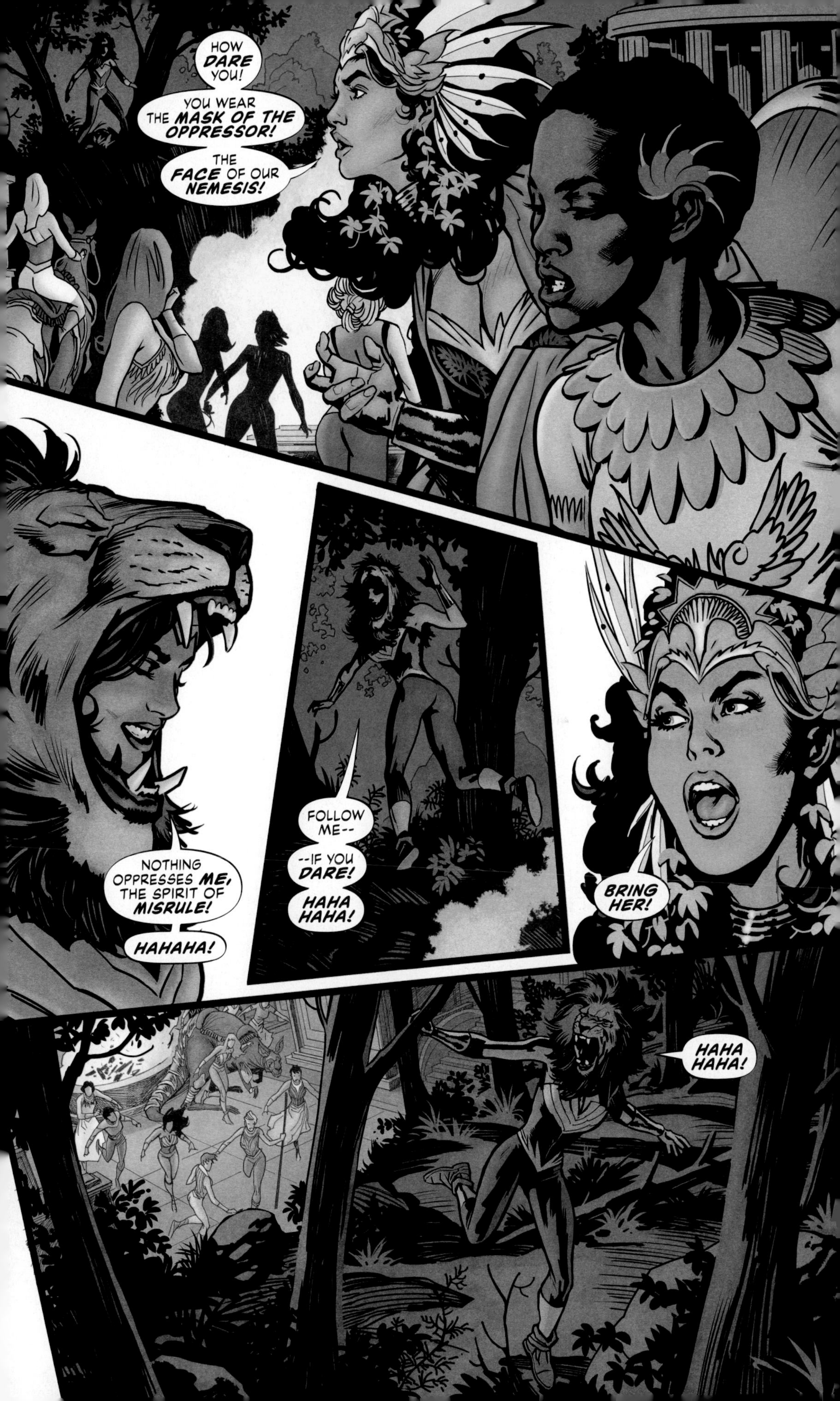
HOW DARE YOU!
YOU WEAR THE MASK OF THE OPPRESSOR!
THE FACE OF OUR NEMESIS!
NOTHING OPPRESSES ME, THE SPIRIT OF MISRULE!
HAHAHA!
FOLLOW ME--
--IF YOU DARE!
HAHA HAHA!
BRING HER!
HAHA HAHA!

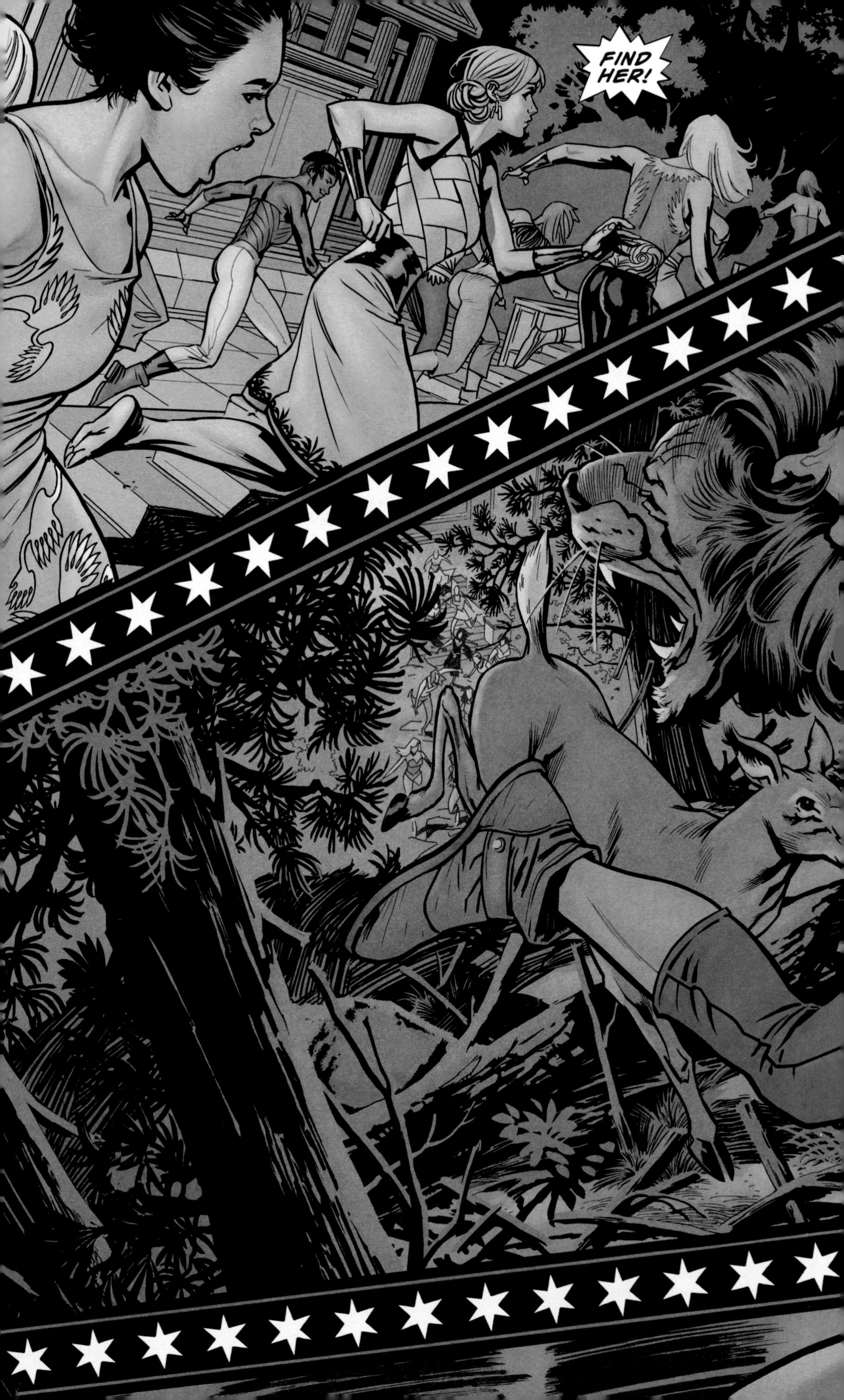
FIND HER!

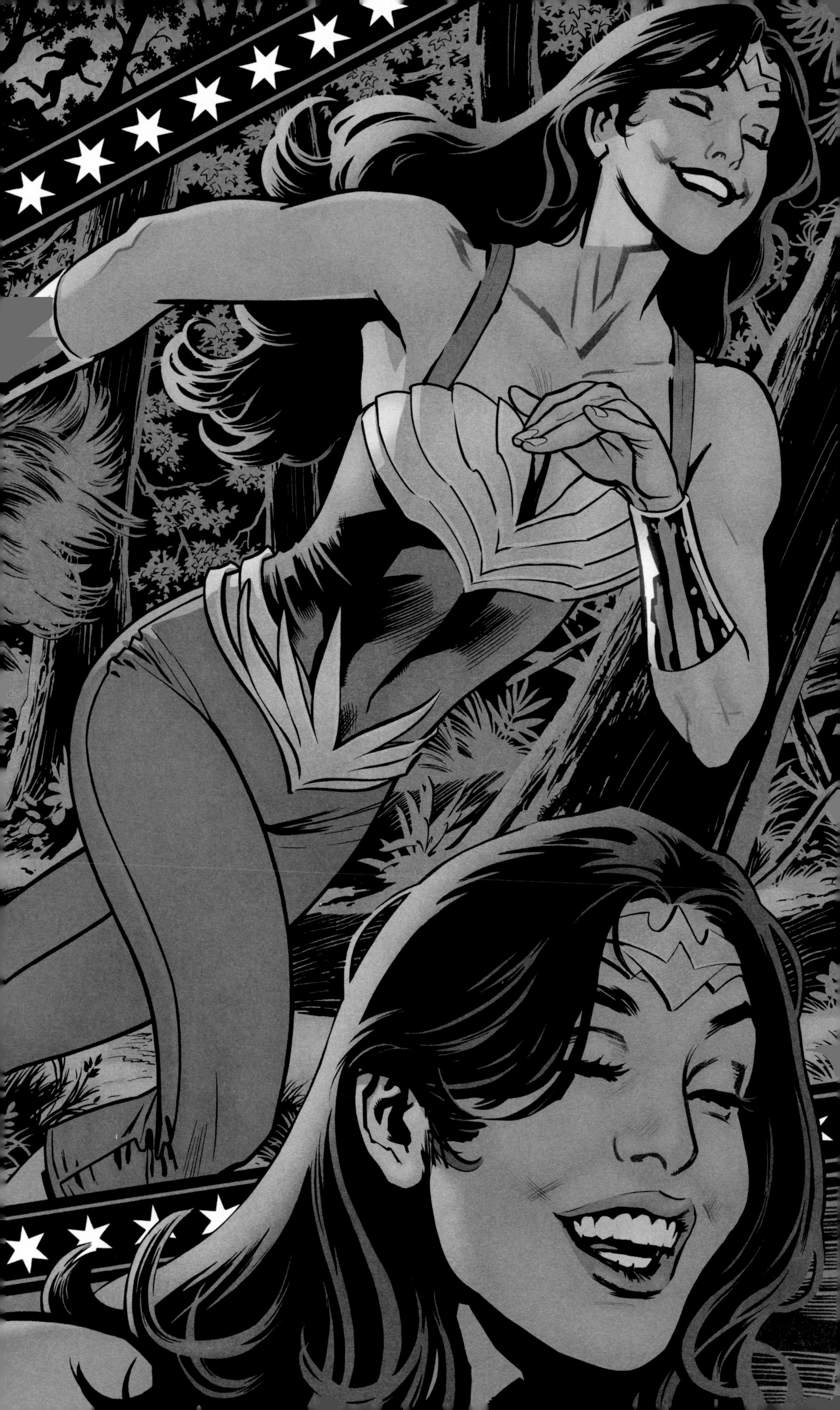

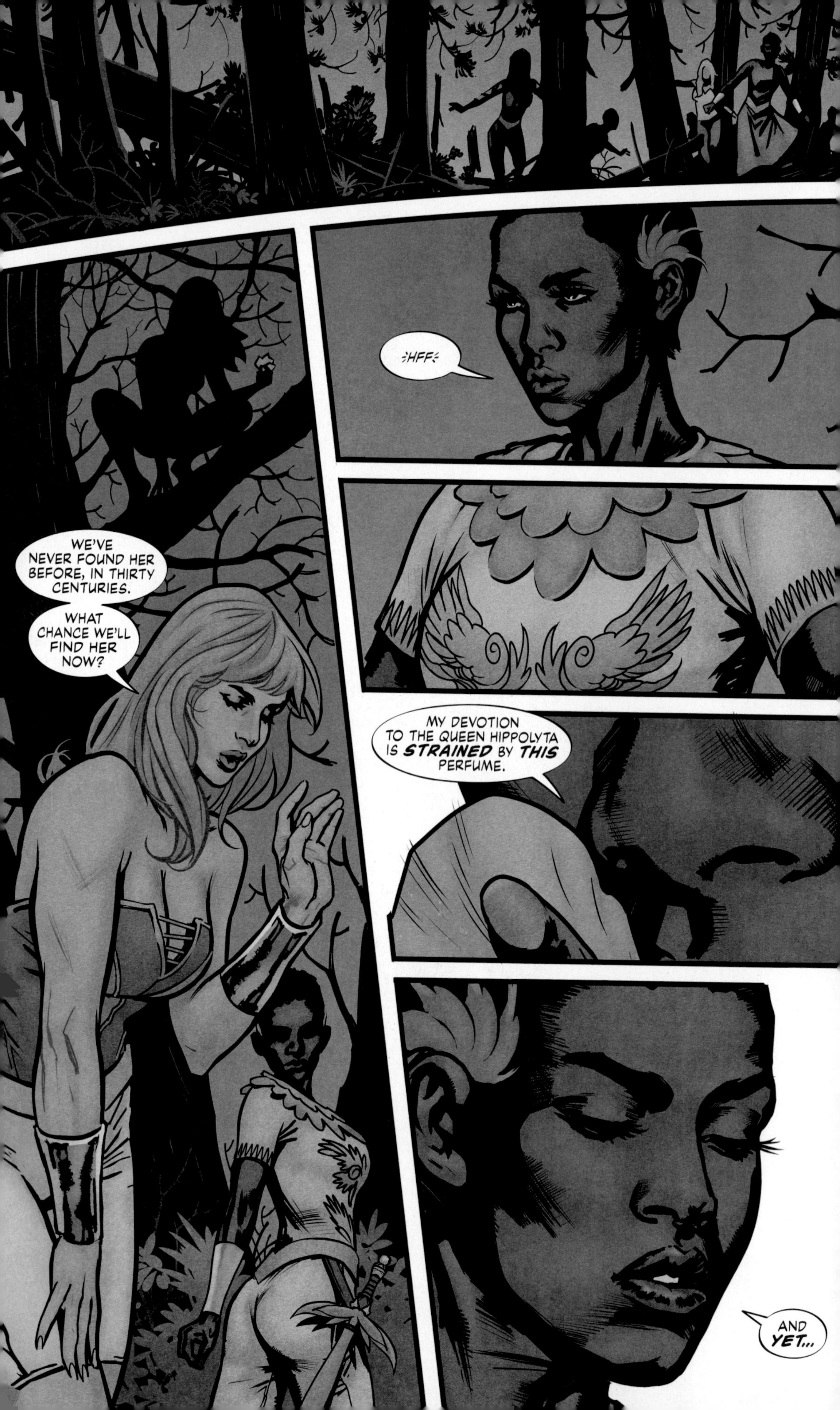
HFF
WE'VE NEVER FOUND HER BEFORE, IN THIRTY CENTURIES.
WHAT CHANCE WE'LL FIND HER NOW?
MY DEVOTION TO THE QUEEN HIPPOLYTA IS STRAINED BY THIS PERFUME.
AND YET...

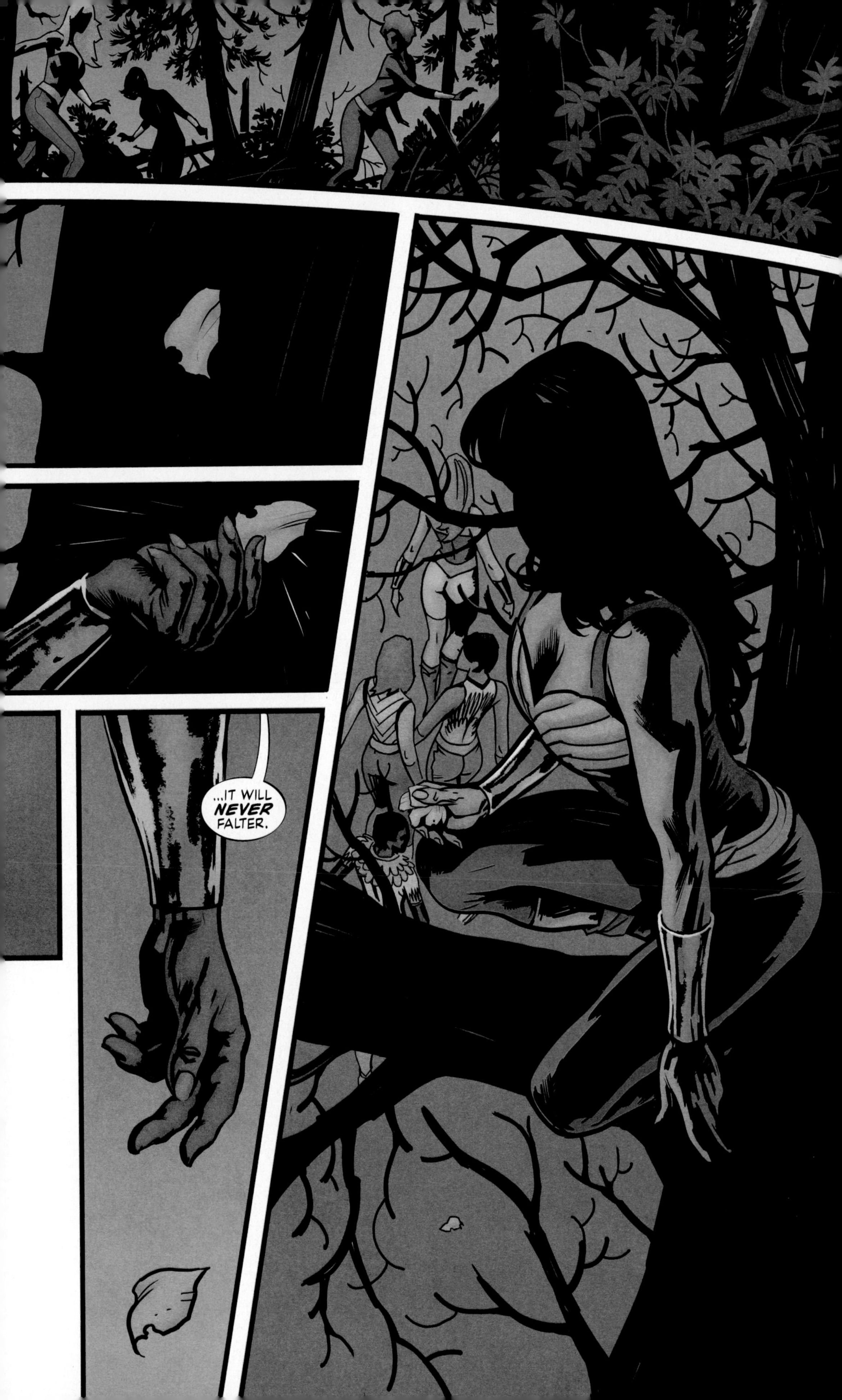
...IT WILL NEVER FALTER.

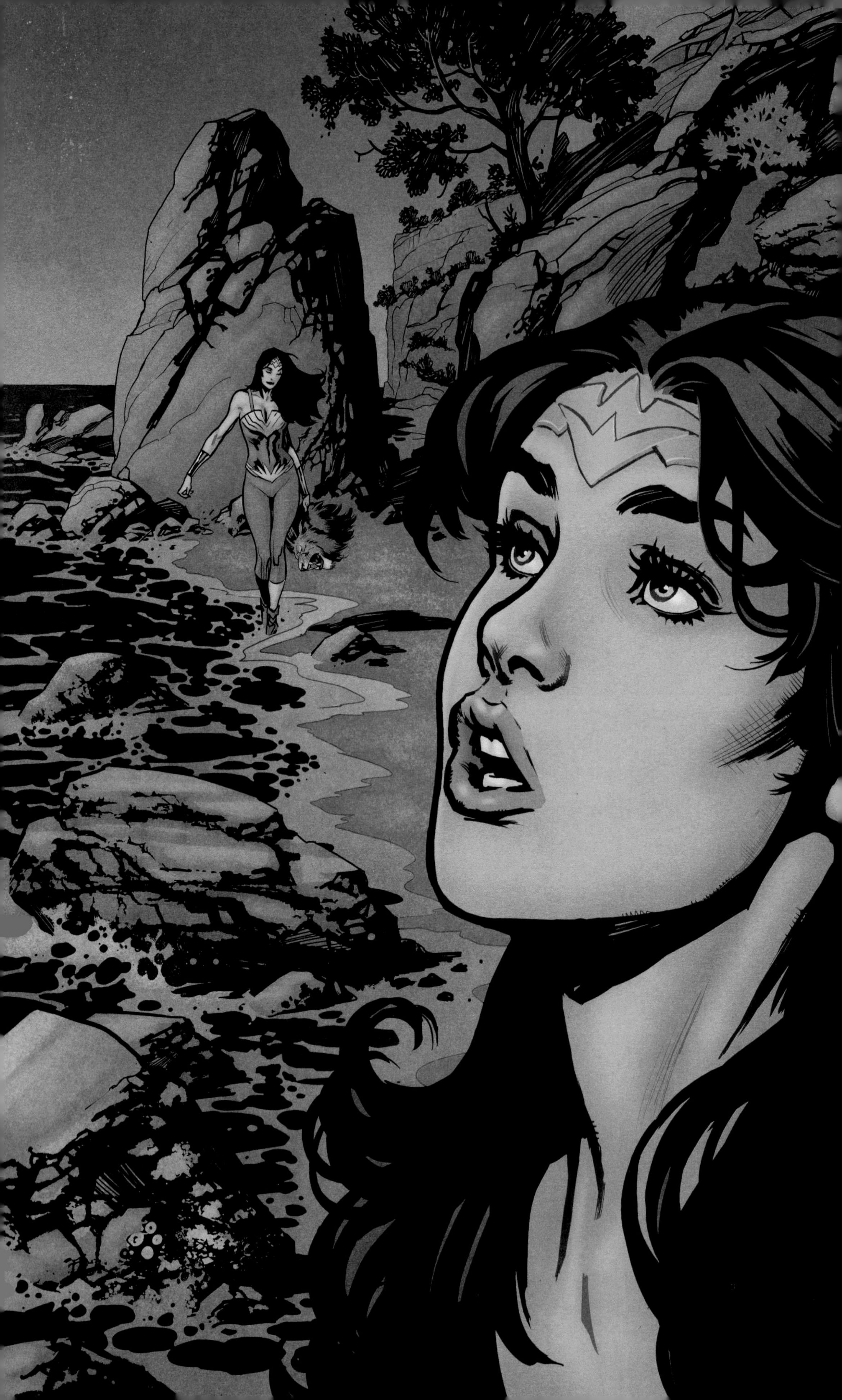

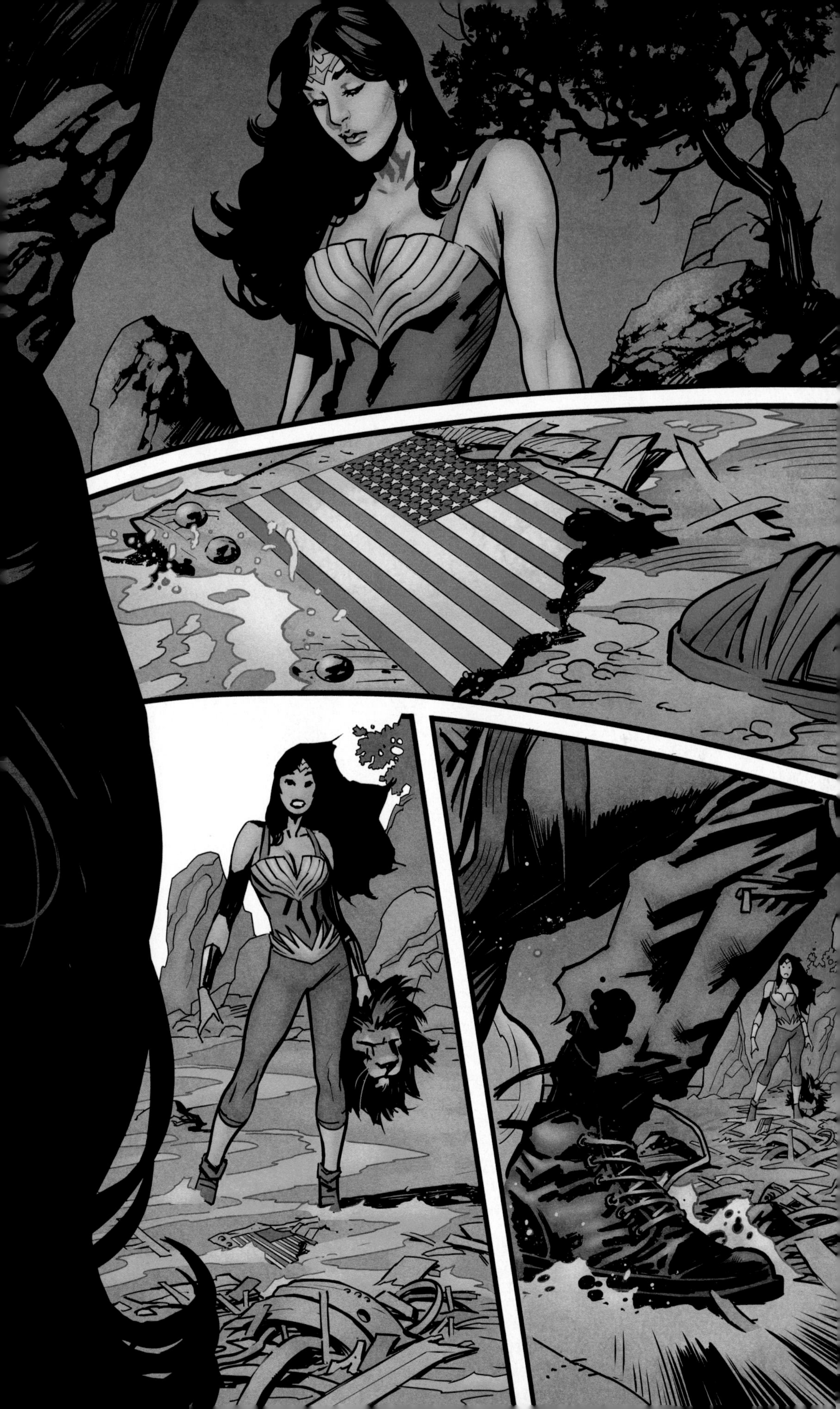

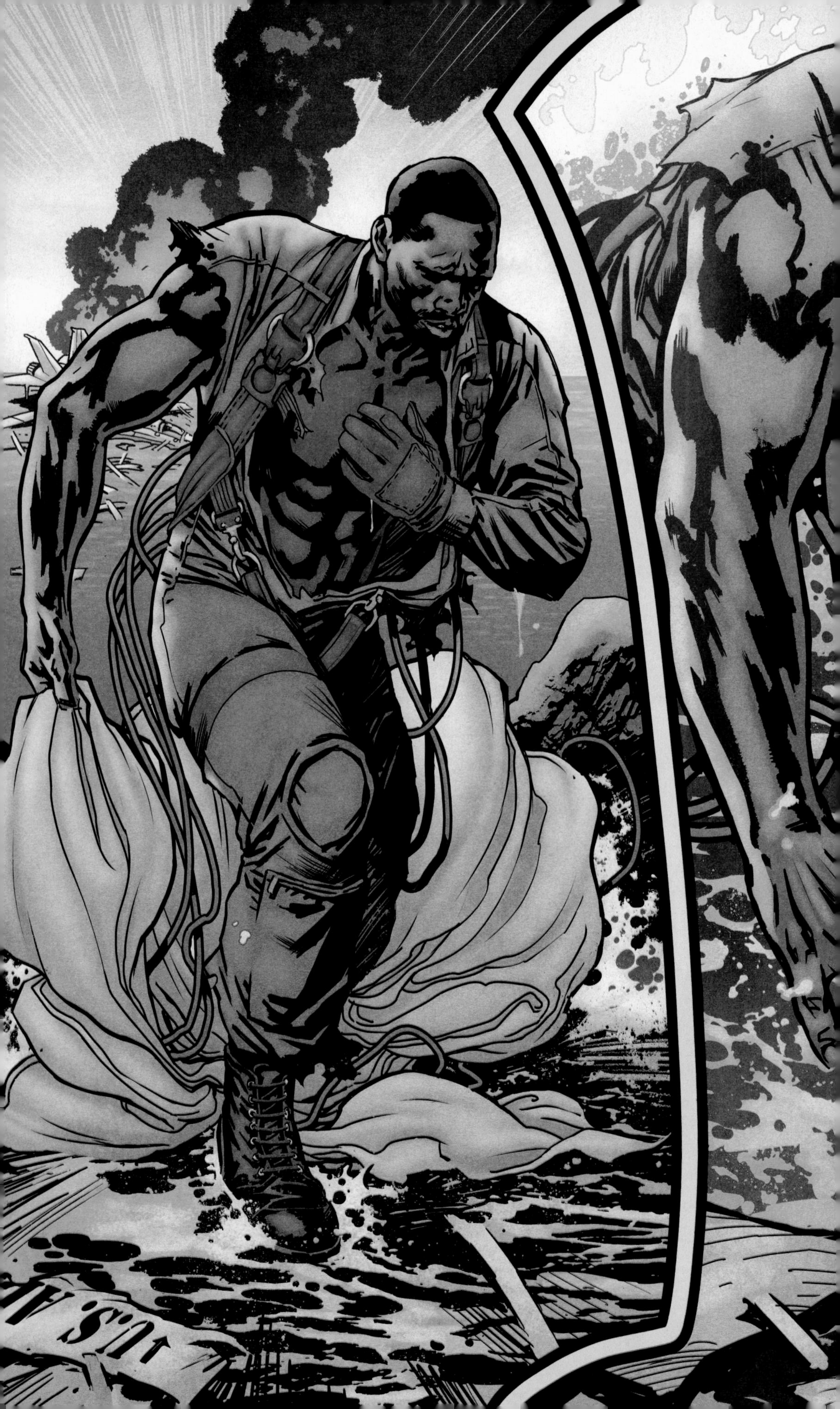

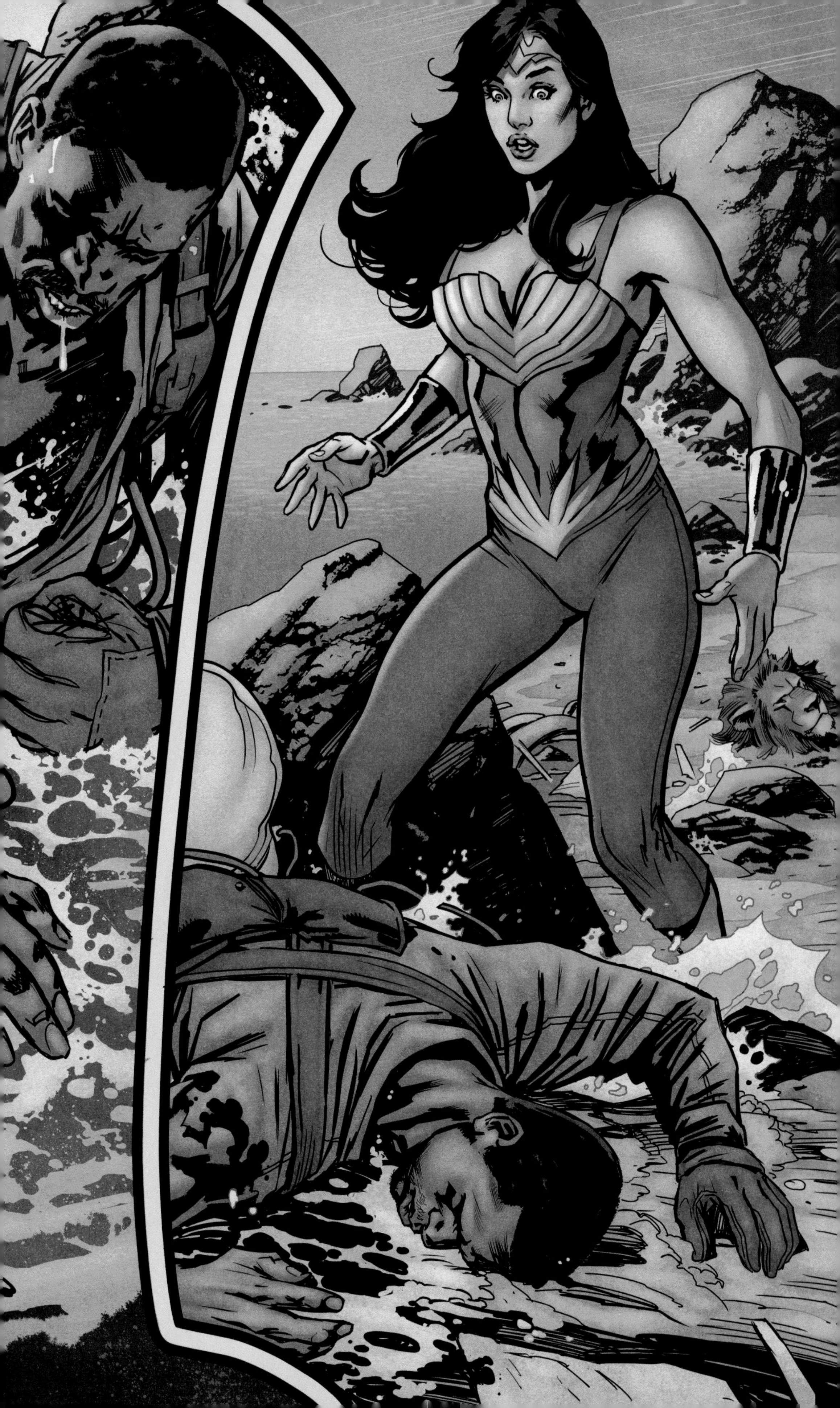

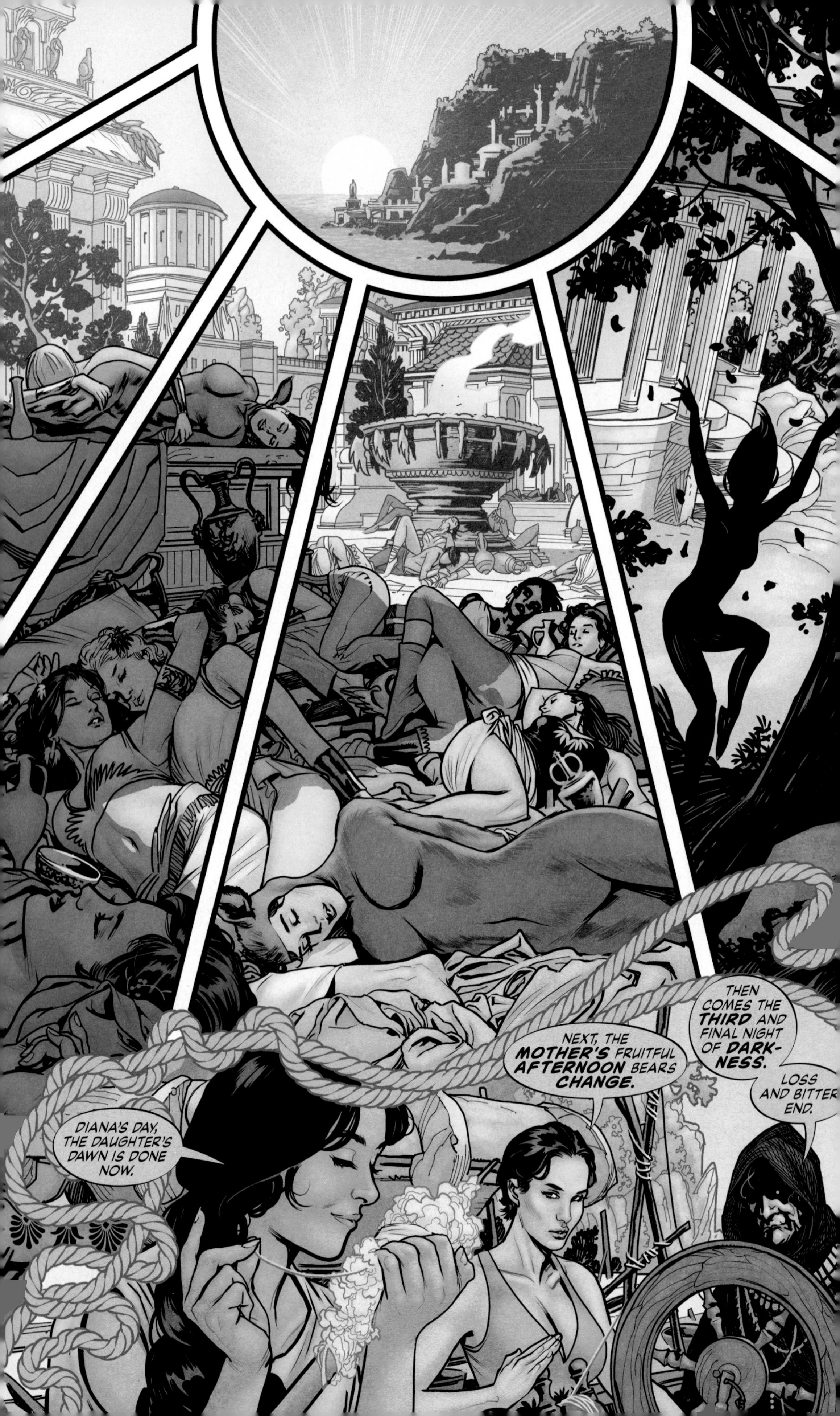
DIANA'S DAY, THE DAUGHTER'S DAWN IS DONE NOW.
NEXT, THE **MOTHER'S** FRUITFUL **AFTERNOON** BEARS **CHANGE.**
THEN COMES THE **THIRD** AND FINAL NIGHT OF **DARK-NESS.**
LOSS AND BITTER END.

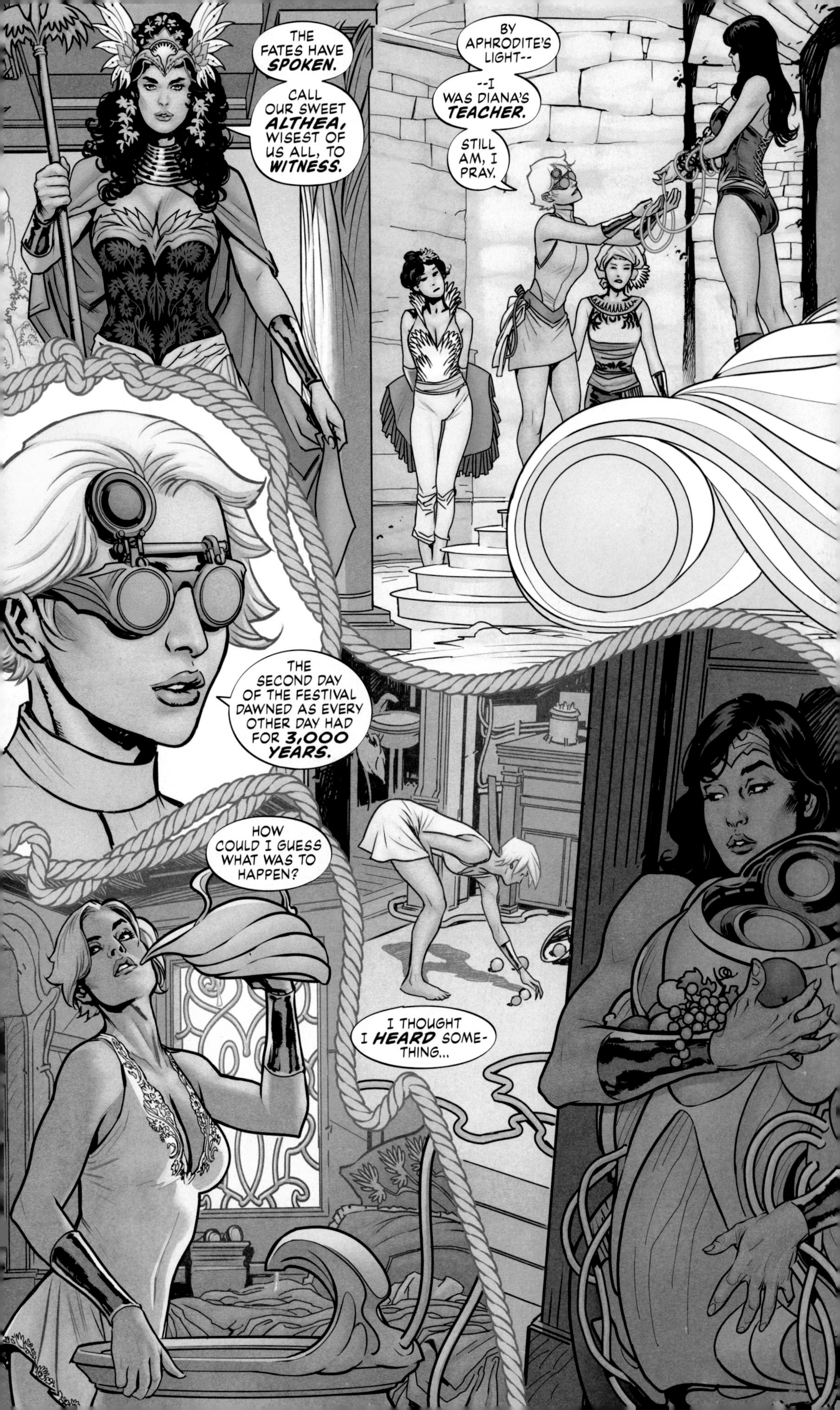
THE FATES HAVE SPOKEN.
CALL OUR SWEET ALTHEA, WISEST OF US ALL, TO WITNESS.
BY APHRODITE'S LIGHT--
--I WAS DIANA'S TEACHER.
STILL AM, I PRAY.
THE SECOND DAY OF THE FESTIVAL DAWNED AS EVERY OTHER DAY HAD FOR 3,000 YEARS.
HOW COULD I GUESS WHAT WAS TO HAPPEN?
I THOUGHT I HEARD SOME-THING...

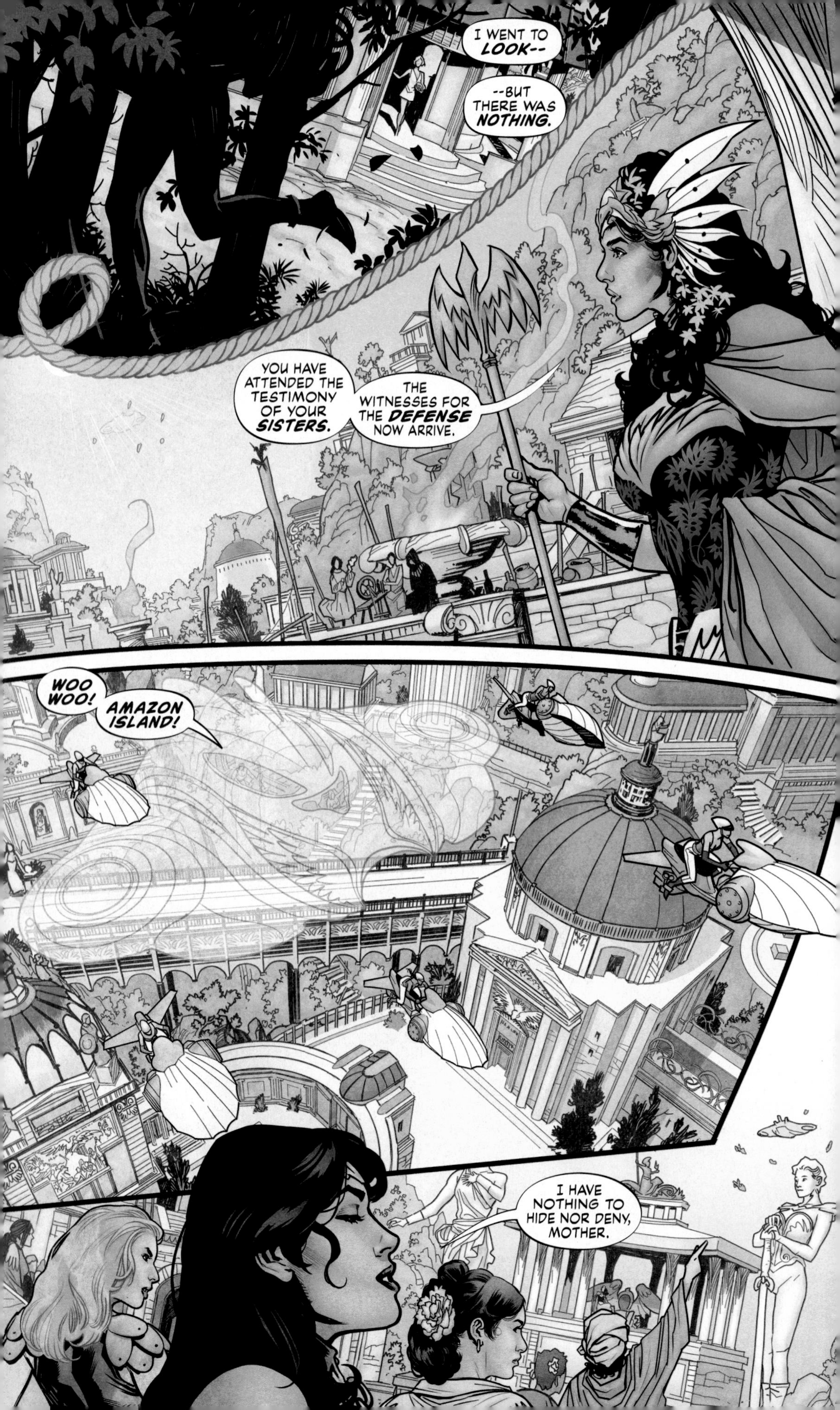
I WENT TO LOOK--
--BUT THERE WAS NOTHING.
YOU HAVE ATTENDED THE TESTIMONY OF YOUR SISTERS.
THE WITNESSES FOR THE DEFENSE NOW ARRIVE.
WOO WOO!
AMAZON ISLAND!
I HAVE NOTHING TO HIDE NOR DENY, MOTHER.

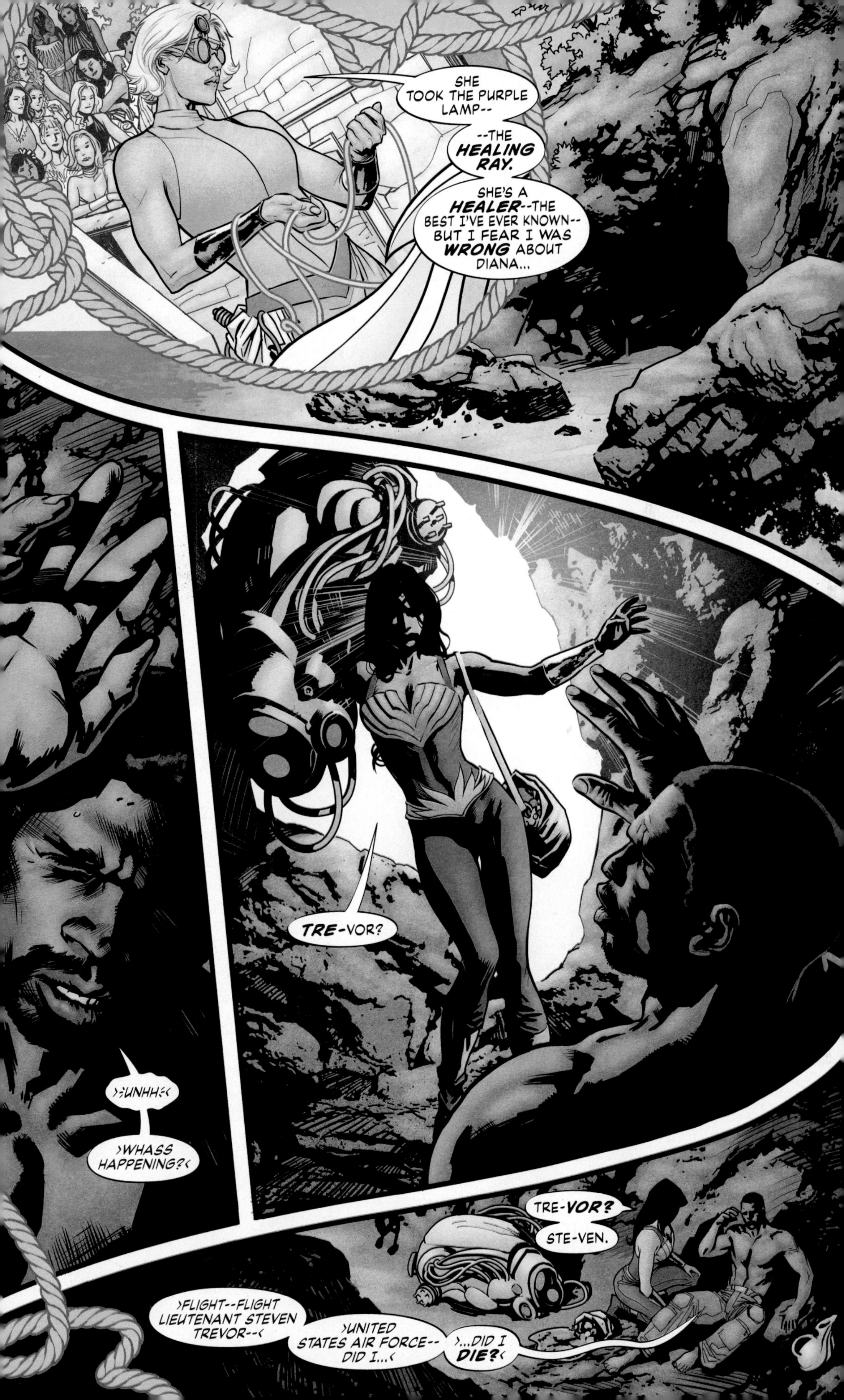
SHE TOOK THE PURPLE LAMP--
--THE HEALING RAY.
SHE'S A HEALER--THE BEST I'VE EVER KNOWN--BUT I FEAR I WAS WRONG ABOUT DIANA...
TRE-VOR?
›UNHH‹
›WHASS HAPPENING?‹
TRE-VOR?
STE-VEN.
›FLIGHT--FLIGHT LIEUTENANT STEVEN TREVOR--‹
›UNITED STATES AIR FORCE--DID I...‹
›...DID I DIE?‹

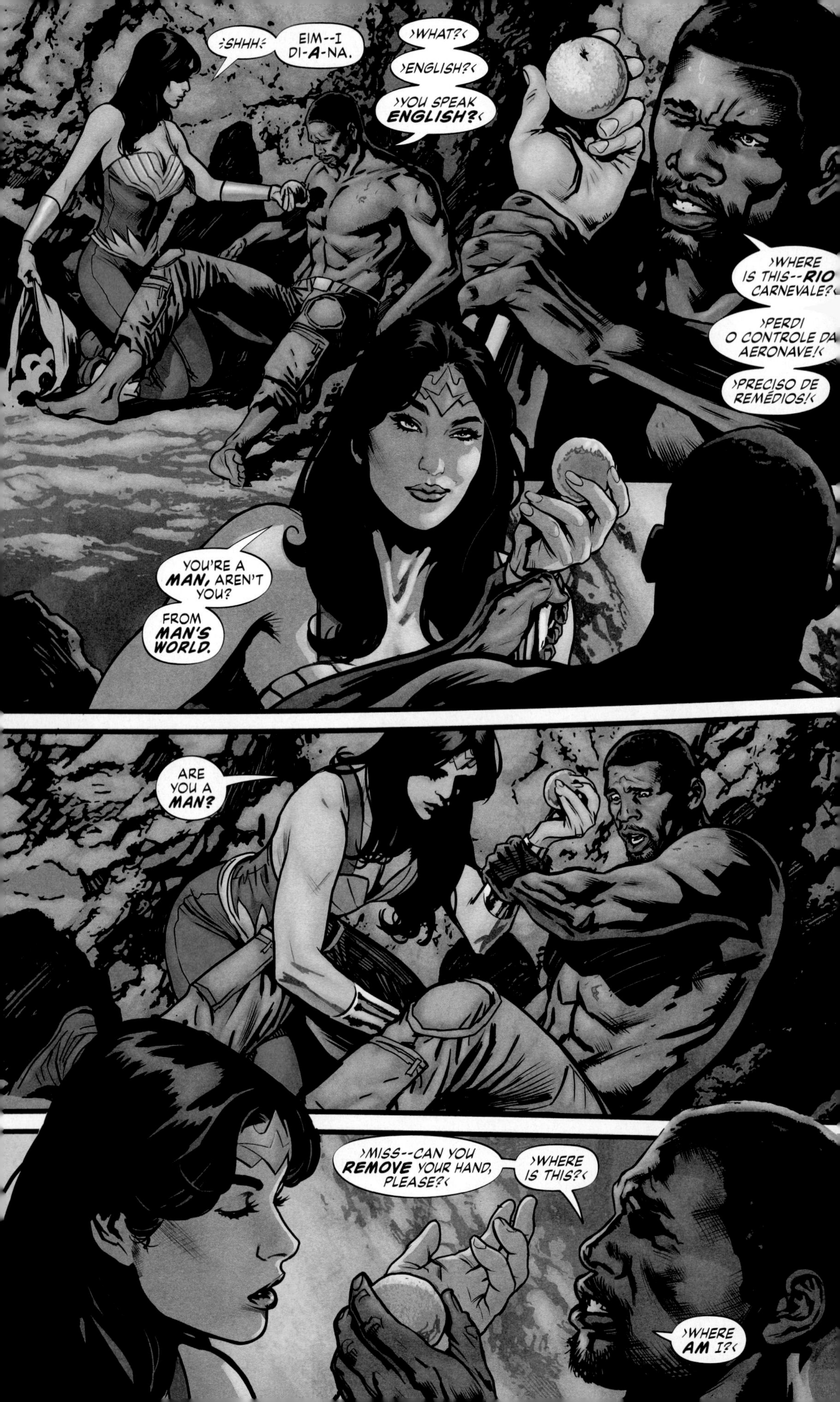
›SHHH‹
EIM--I DI-**A**-NA.
›WHAT?‹
›ENGLISH?‹
›YOU SPEAK **ENGLISH?**‹
›WHERE IS THIS--**RIO** CARNEVALE?‹
›PERDI O CONTROLE DA AERONAVE!‹
›PRECISO DE REMÉDIOS!‹
YOU'RE A **MAN,** AREN'T YOU?
FROM **MAN'S WORLD.**
ARE YOU A **MAN?**
›MISS--CAN YOU **REMOVE** YOUR HAND, PLEASE?‹
›WHERE IS THIS?‹
›WHERE **AM** I?‹

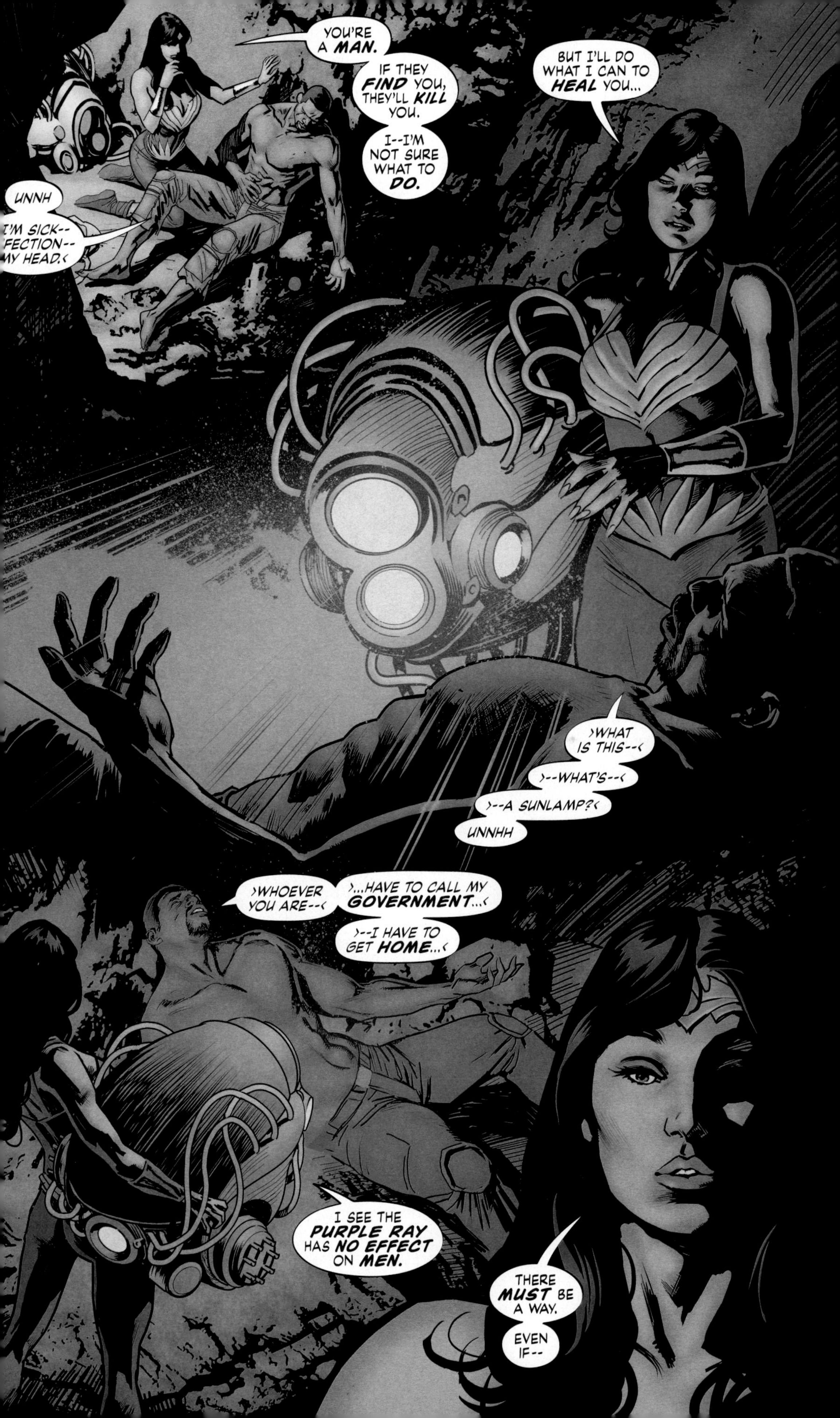
YOU'RE A **MAN.**
IF THEY **FIND** YOU, THEY'LL **KILL** YOU.
I--I'M NOT SURE WHAT TO **DO.**
UNNH
I'M SICK-- FECTION-- MY HEAD.‹
BUT I'LL DO WHAT I CAN TO **HEAL** YOU...
›WHAT IS THIS--‹
›--WHAT'S--‹
›--A SUNLAMP?‹
UNNHH
›WHOEVER YOU ARE--‹
›...HAVE TO CALL MY **GOVERNMENT**...‹
›--I HAVE TO GET **HOME**...‹
I SEE THE **PURPLE RAY** HAS **NO EFFECT** ON **MEN.**
THERE **MUST** BE A WAY.
EVEN IF--

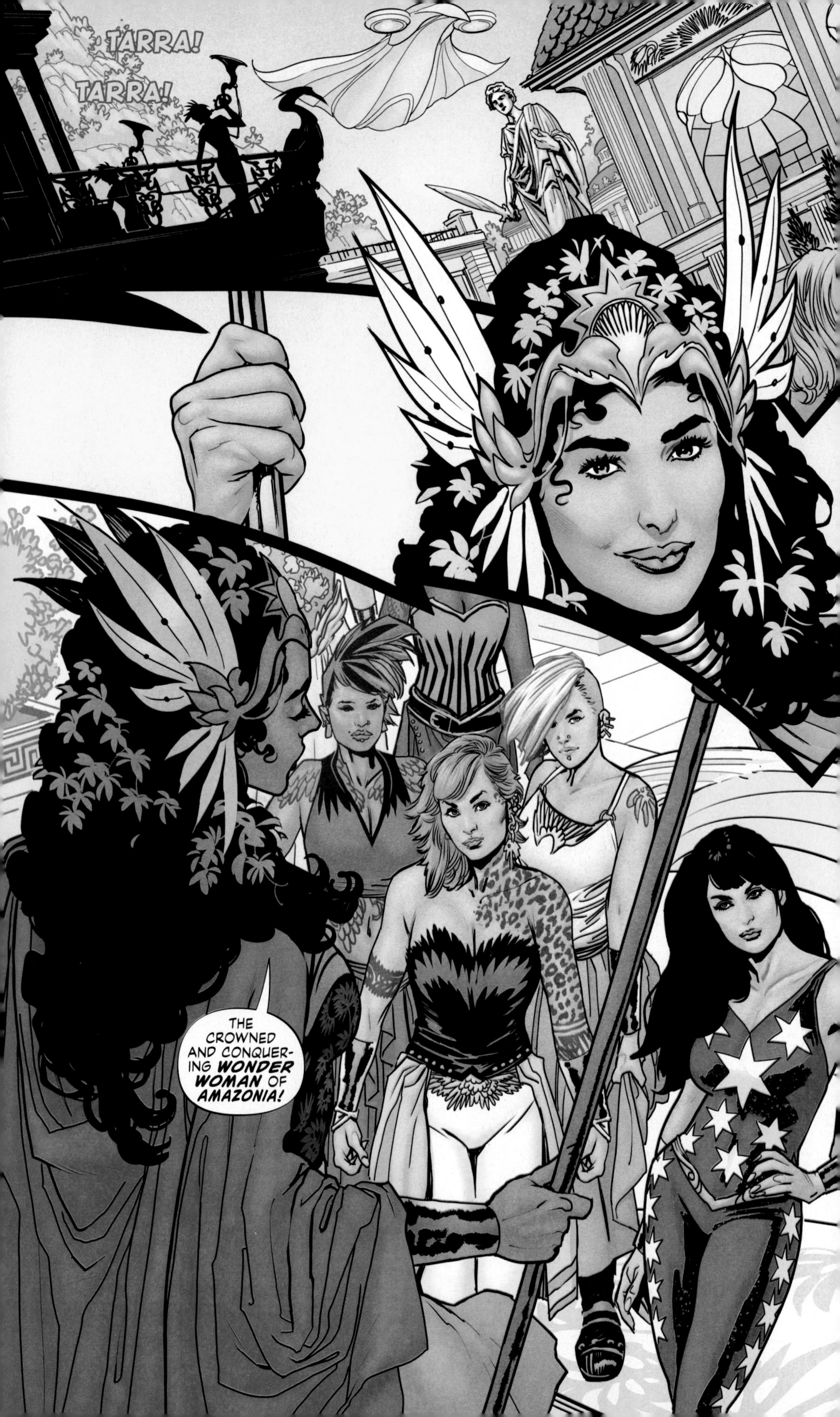
TARRA!
TARRA!
THE CROWNED AND CONQUER-ING WONDER WOMAN OF AMAZONIA!

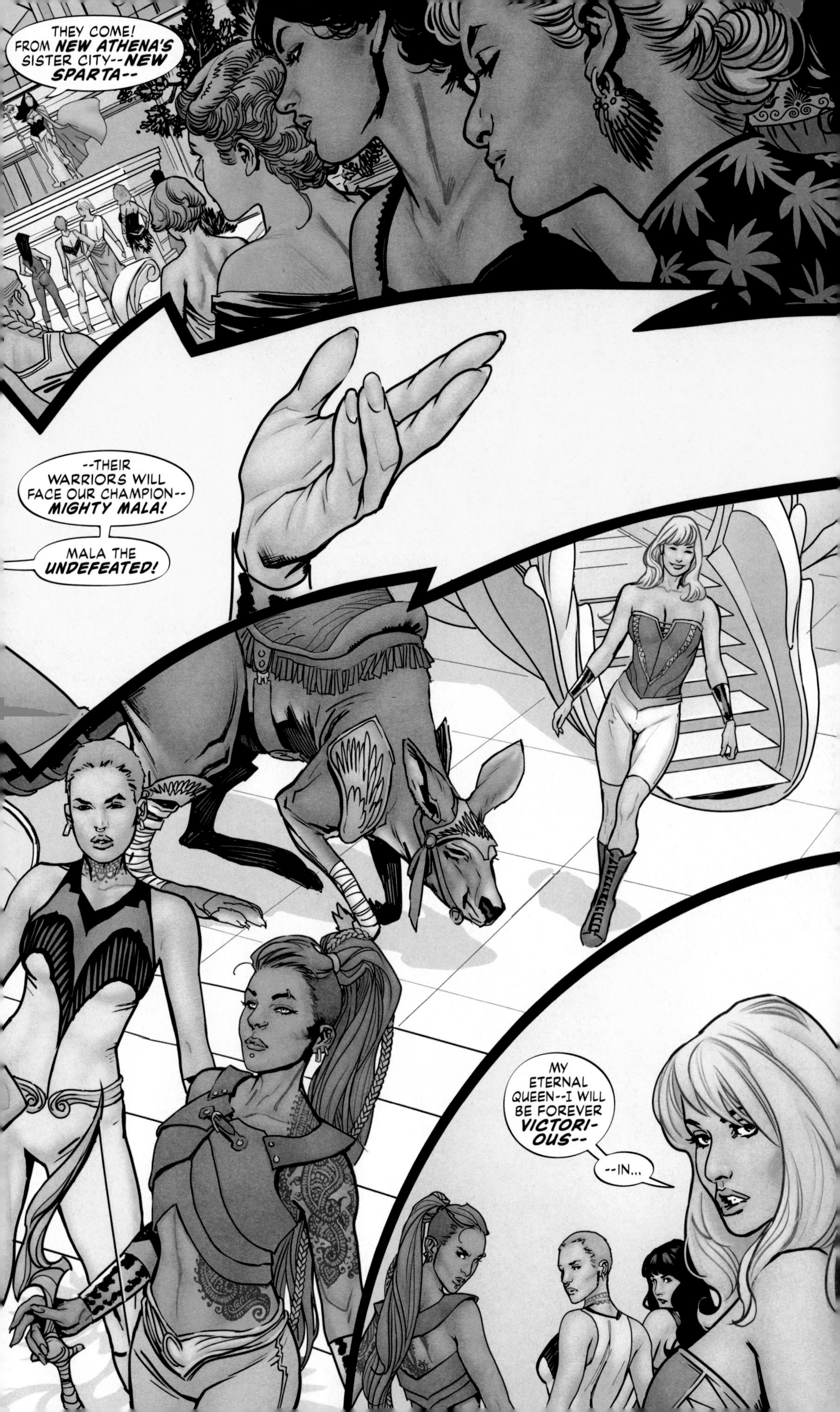
THEY COME! FROM NEW ATHENA'S SISTER CITY--NEW SPARTA--
--THEIR WARRIORS WILL FACE OUR CHAMPION--MIGHTY MALA!
MALA THE UNDEFEATED!
MY ETERNAL QUEEN--I WILL BE FOREVER VICTORI-OUS--
--IN...

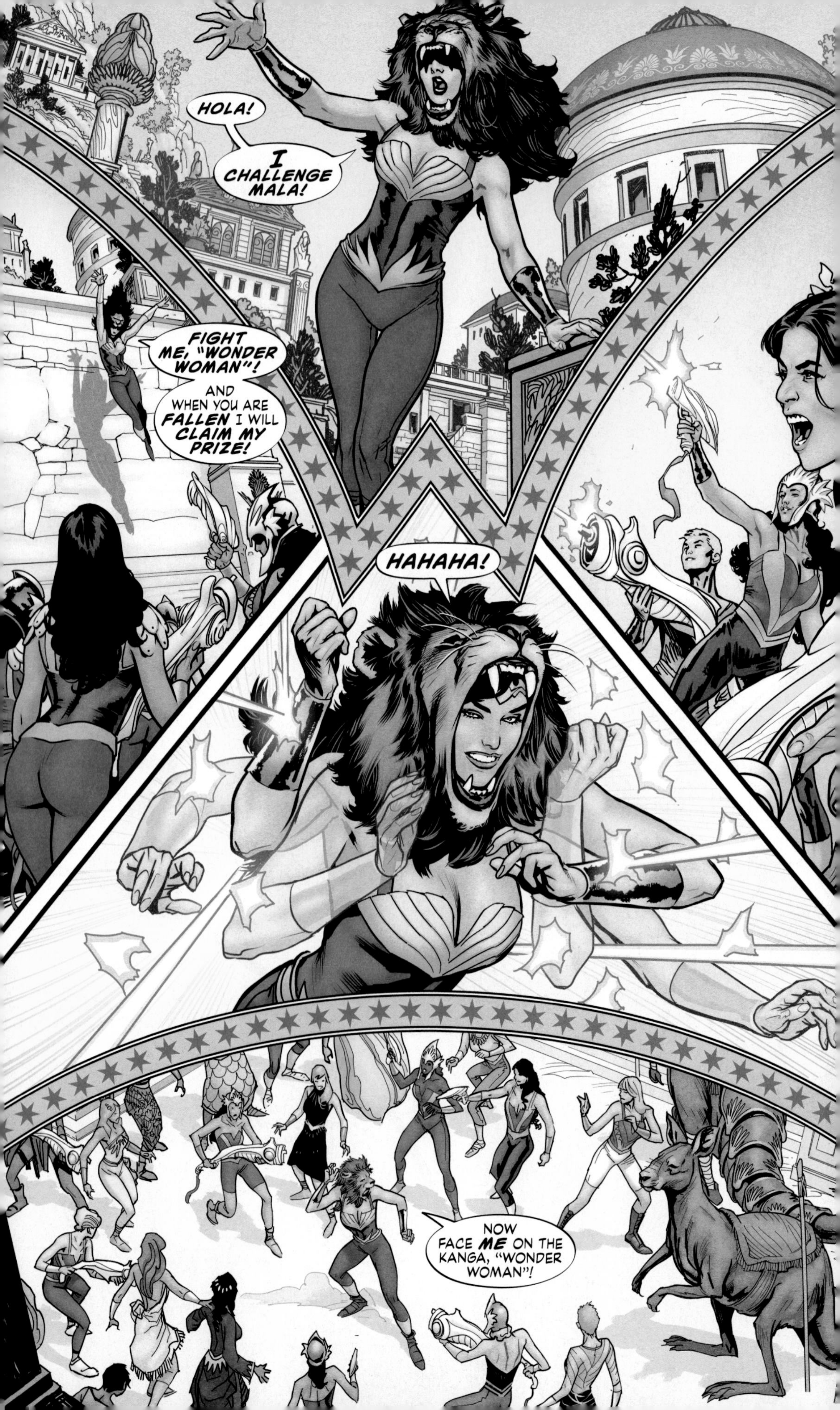
HOLA!
I CHALLENGE MALA!
FIGHT ME, "WONDER WOMAN"!
AND WHEN YOU ARE FALLEN I WILL CLAIM MY PRIZE!
HAHAHA!
NOW FACE ME ON THE KANGA, "WONDER WOMAN"!

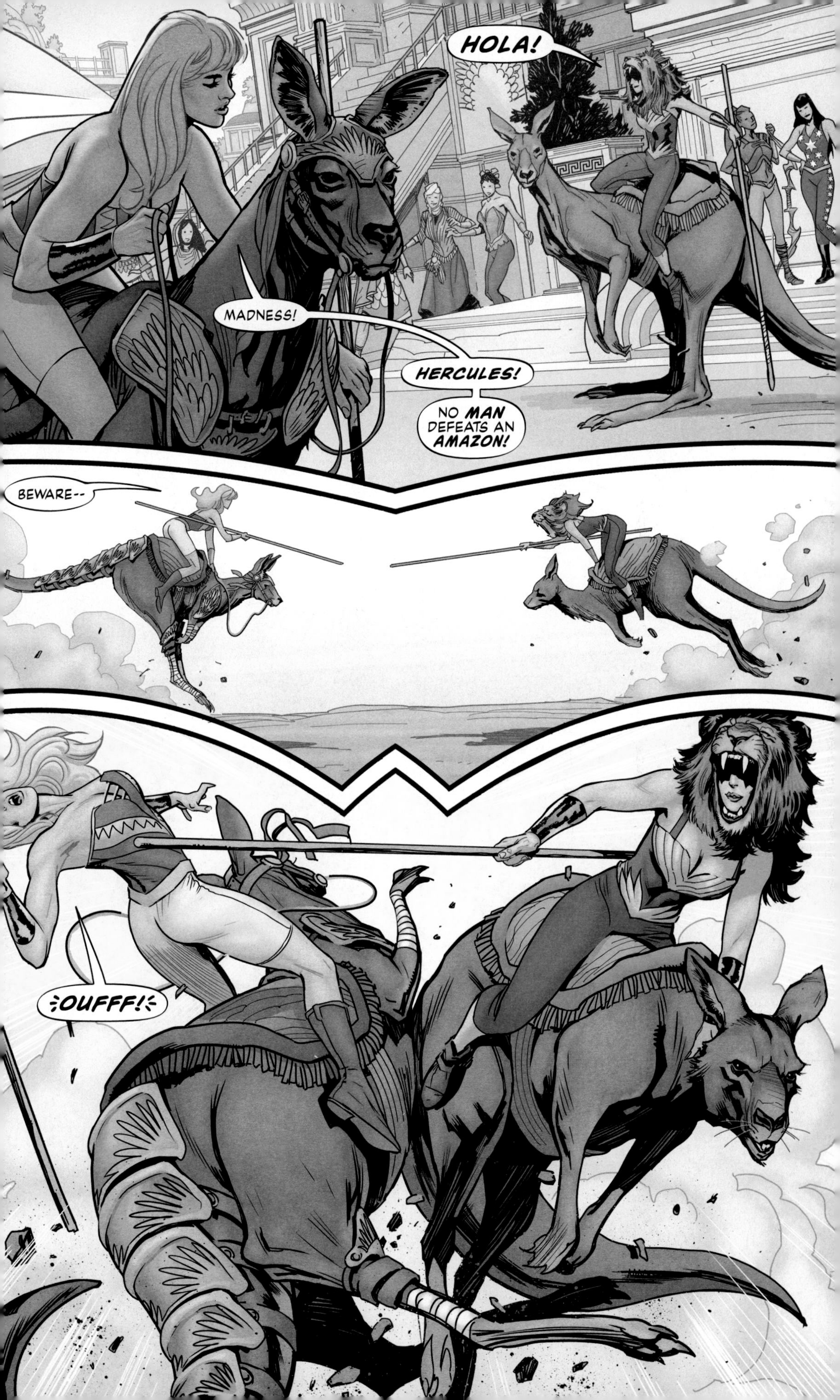
HOLA!
MADNESS!
HERCULES!
NO MAN DEFEATS AN AMAZON!
BEWARE--
¡OUFFF!

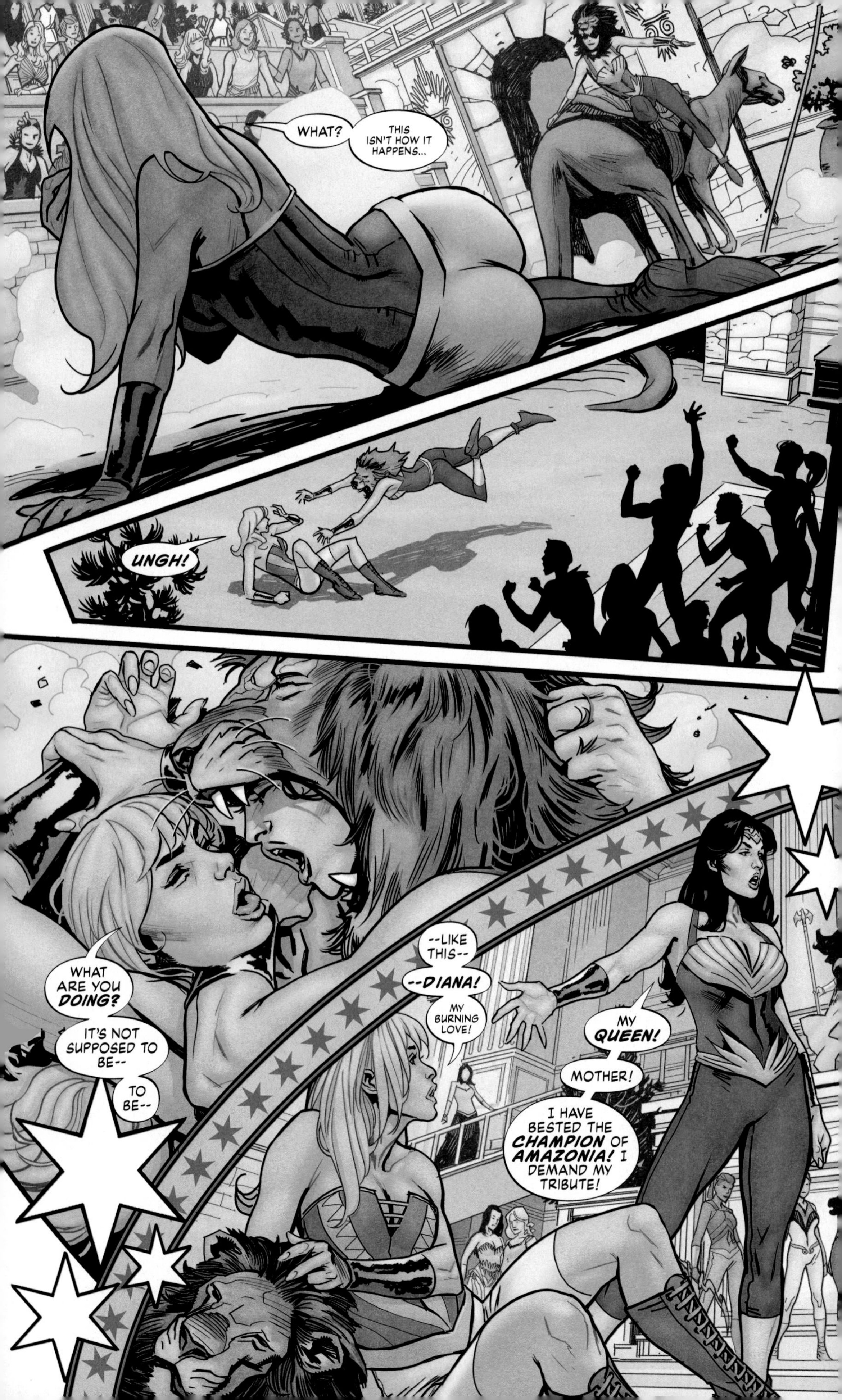

WHAT?
THIS ISN'T HOW IT HAPPENS...
UNGH!
WHAT ARE YOU DOING?
IT'S NOT SUPPOSED TO BE--
TO BE--
--LIKE THIS--
--DIANA!
MY BURNING LOVE!
MY QUEEN!
MOTHER!
I HAVE BESTED THE CHAMPION OF AMAZONIA! I DEMAND MY TRIBUTE!

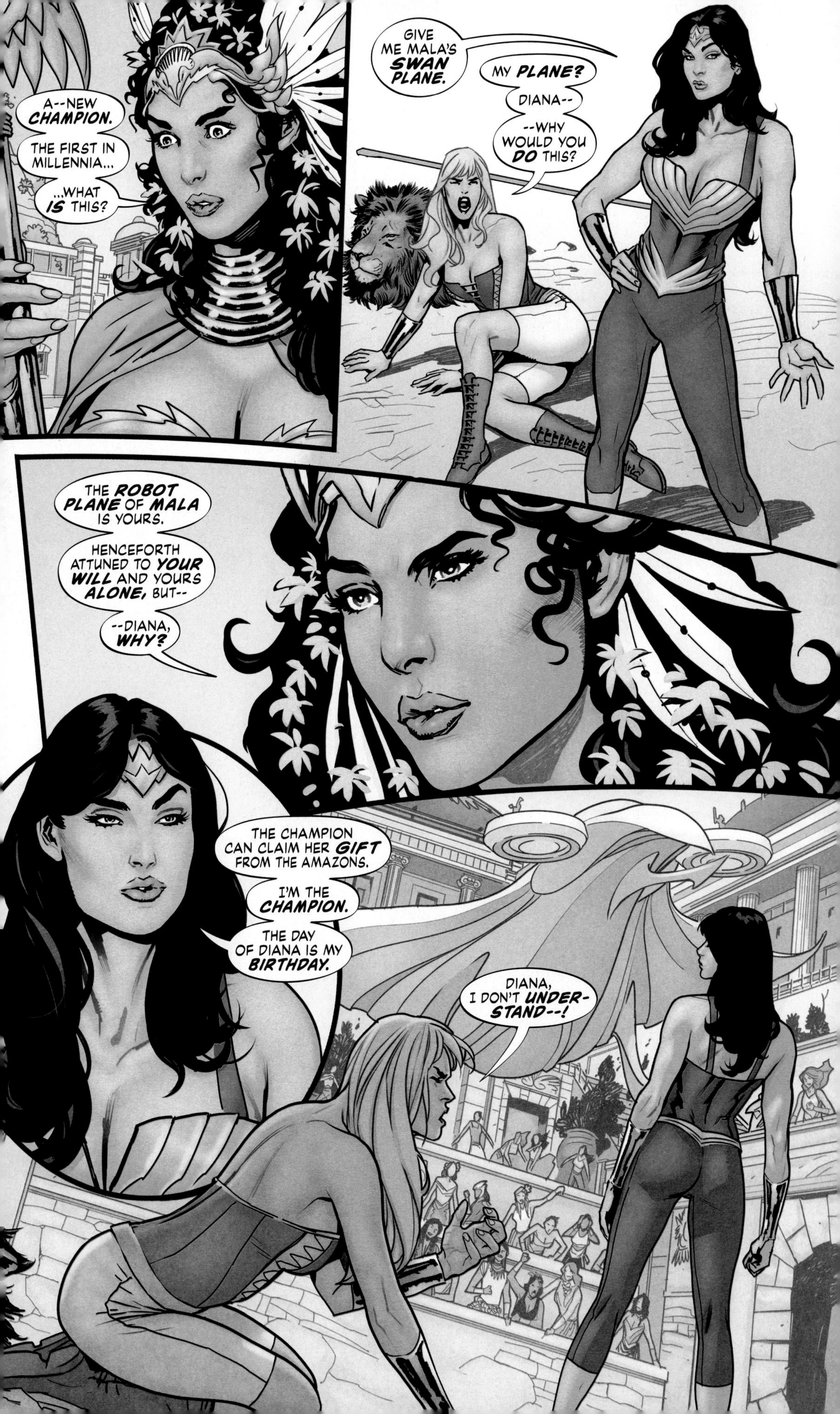
A--NEW CHAMPION.
THE FIRST IN MILLENNIA...
...WHAT IS THIS?
GIVE ME MALA'S SWAN PLANE.
MY PLANE?
DIANA--
--WHY WOULD YOU DO THIS?
THE ROBOT PLANE OF MALA IS YOURS.
HENCEFORTH ATTUNED TO YOUR WILL AND YOURS ALONE, BUT--
--DIANA, WHY?
THE CHAMPION CAN CLAIM HER GIFT FROM THE AMAZONS.
I'M THE CHAMPION.
THE DAY OF DIANA IS MY BIRTHDAY.
DIANA, I DON'T UNDER-STAND--!

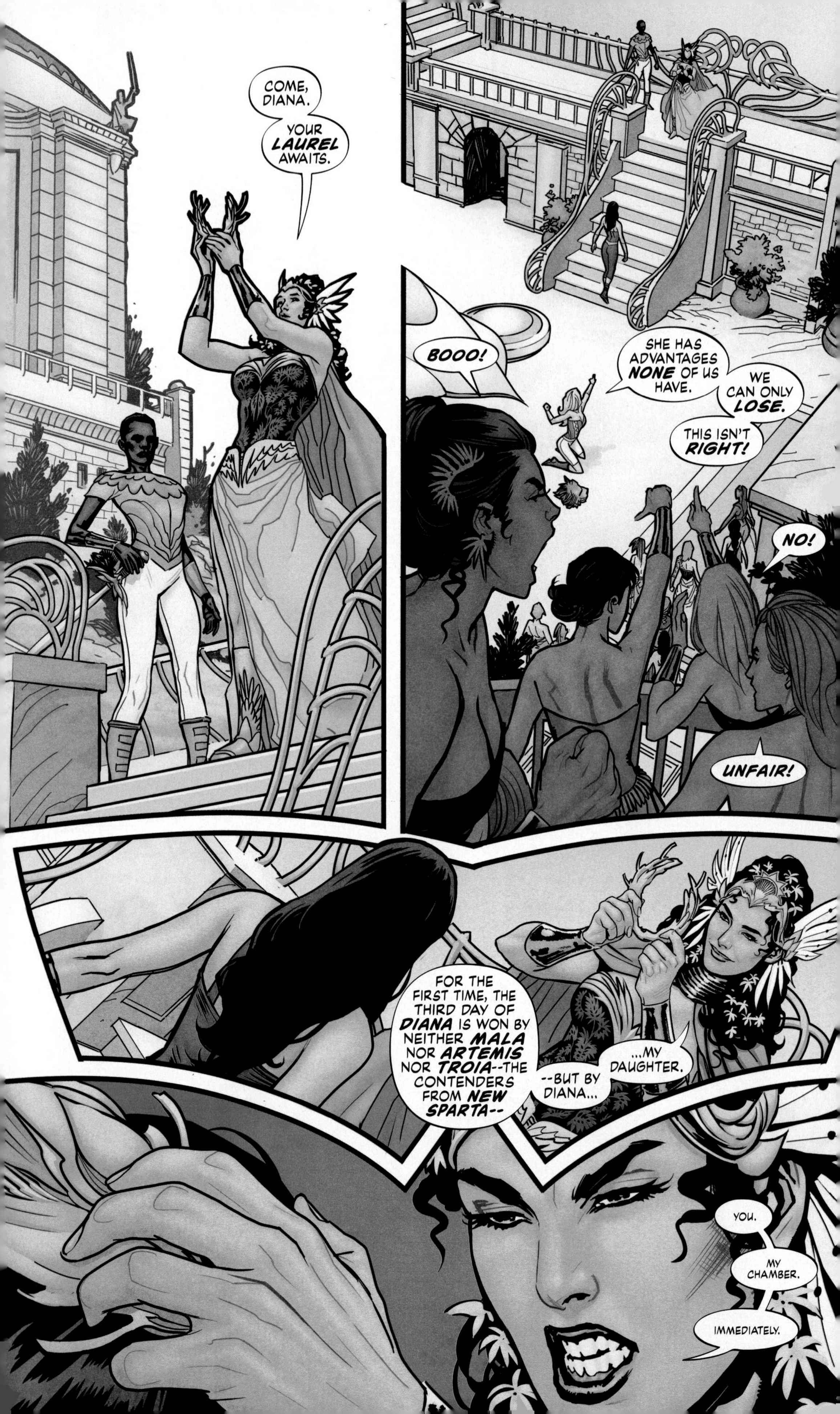
COME, DIANA.
YOUR LAUREL AWAITS.
BOOO!
SHE HAS ADVANTAGES NONE OF US HAVE.
WE CAN ONLY LOSE.
THIS ISN'T RIGHT!
NO!
UNFAIR!
FOR THE FIRST TIME, THE THIRD DAY OF DIANA IS WON BY NEITHER MALA NOR ARTEMIS NOR TROIA--THE CONTENDERS FROM NEW SPARTA--
--BUT BY DIANA...
...MY DAUGHTER.
YOU.
MY CHAMBER.
IMMEDIATELY.

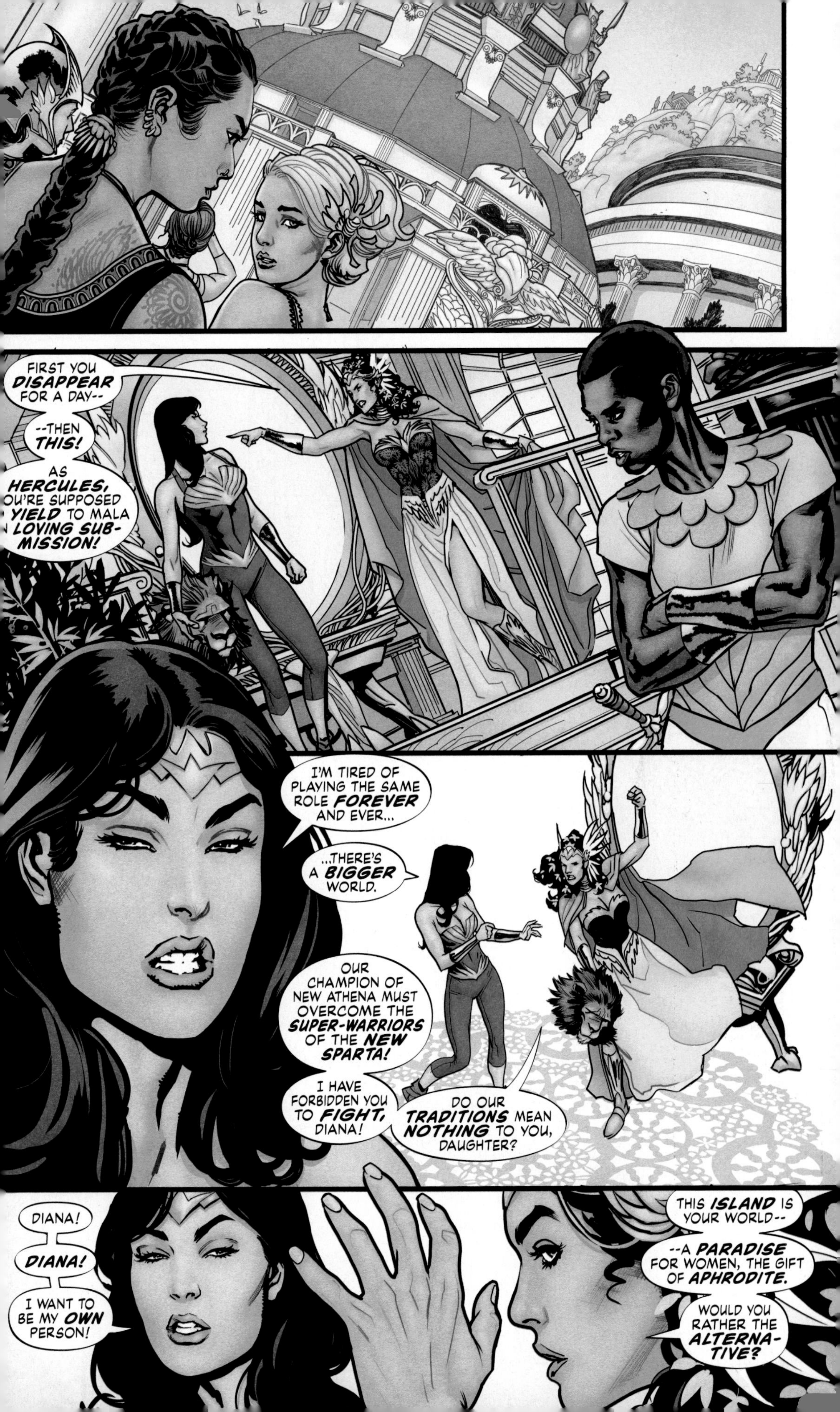

FIRST YOU DISAPPEAR FOR A DAY--
--THEN THIS!
AS HERCULES, OU'RE SUPPOSED YIELD TO MALA N LOVING SUB-MISSION!
I'M TIRED OF PLAYING THE SAME ROLE FOREVER AND EVER...
...THERE'S A BIGGER WORLD.
OUR CHAMPION OF NEW ATHENA MUST OVERCOME THE SUPER-WARRIORS OF THE NEW SPARTA!
I HAVE FORBIDDEN YOU TO FIGHT, DIANA!
DO OUR TRADITIONS MEAN NOTHING TO YOU, DAUGHTER?
DIANA!
DIANA!
I WANT TO BE MY OWN PERSON!
THIS ISLAND IS YOUR WORLD--
--A PARADISE FOR WOMEN, THE GIFT OF APHRODITE.
WOULD YOU RATHER THE ALTERNA-TIVE?

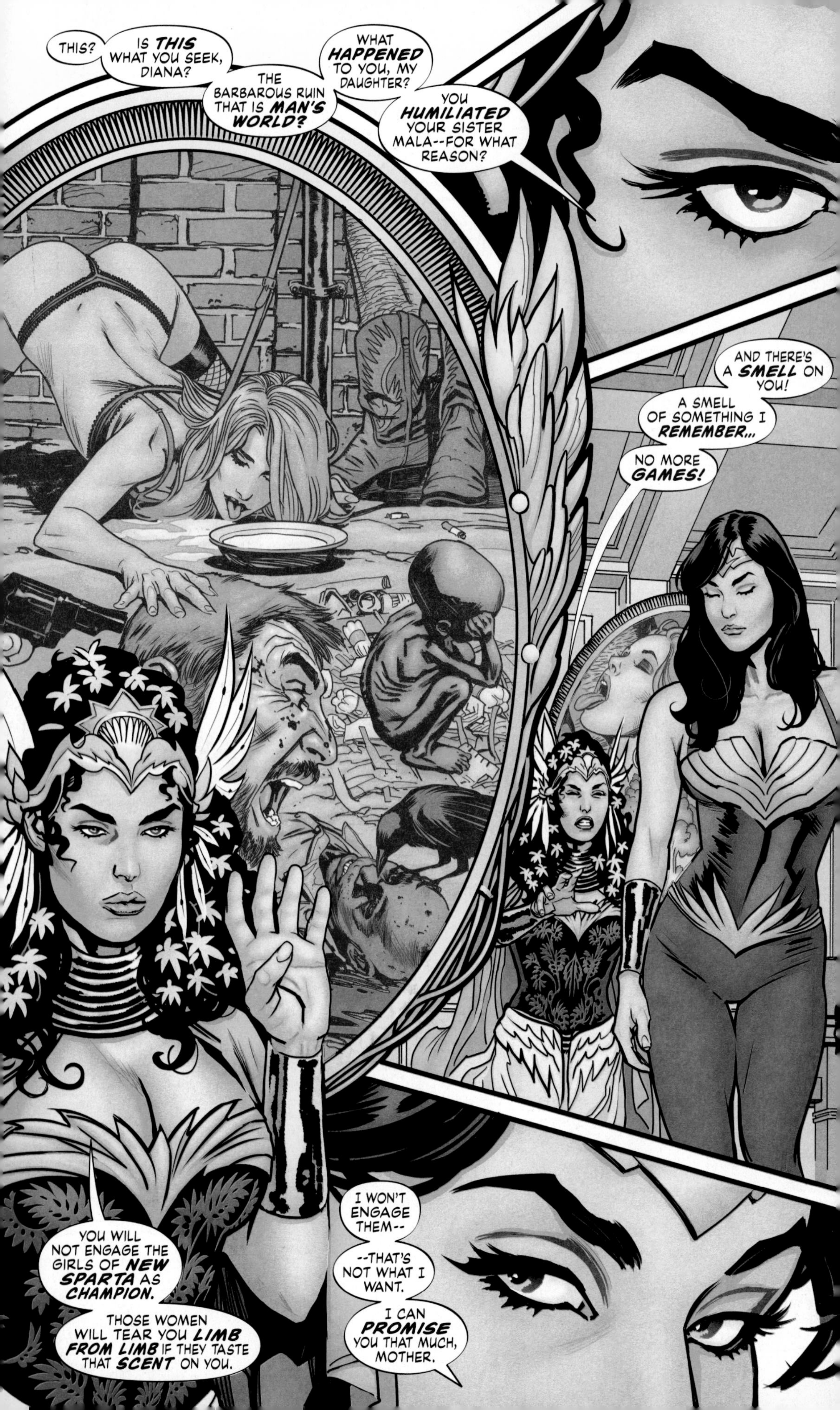

THIS?
IS THIS WHAT YOU SEEK, DIANA?
THE BARBAROUS RUIN THAT IS MAN'S WORLD?
WHAT HAPPENED TO YOU, MY DAUGHTER?
YOU HUMILIATED YOUR SISTER MALA--FOR WHAT REASON?
AND THERE'S A SMELL ON YOU!
A SMELL OF SOMETHING I REMEMBER...
NO MORE GAMES!
YOU WILL NOT ENGAGE THE GIRLS OF NEW SPARTA AS CHAMPION.
THOSE WOMEN WILL TEAR YOU LIMB FROM LIMB IF THEY TASTE THAT SCENT ON YOU.
I WON'T ENGAGE THEM--
--THAT'S NOT WHAT I WANT.
I CAN PROMISE YOU THAT MUCH, MOTHER.

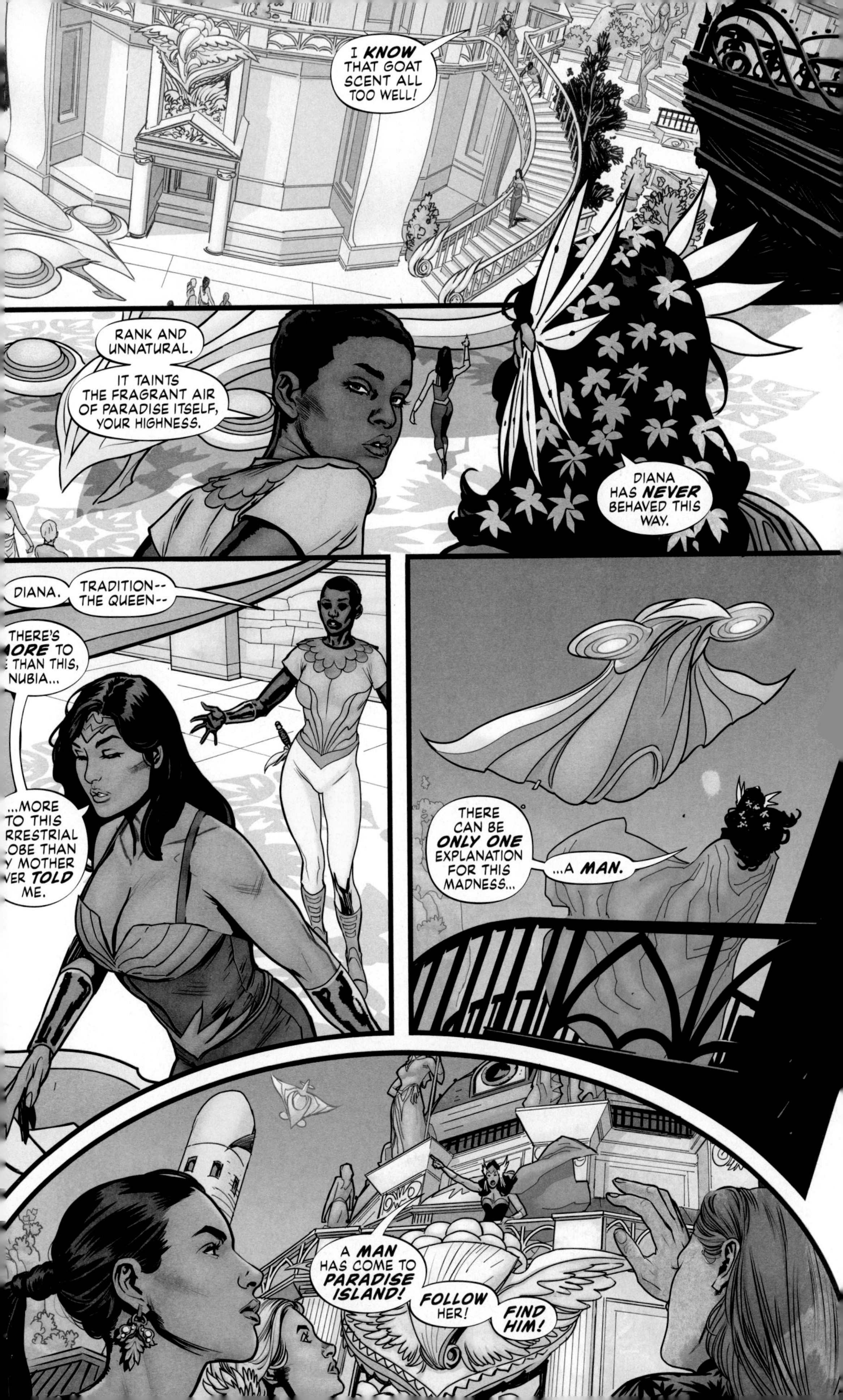
I KNOW THAT GOAT SCENT ALL TOO WELL!
RANK AND UNNATURAL.
IT TAINTS THE FRAGRANT AIR OF PARADISE ITSELF, YOUR HIGHNESS.
DIANA HAS NEVER BEHAVED THIS WAY.
DIANA.
TRADITION-- THE QUEEN--
THERE'S MORE TO THAN THIS, NUBIA...
...MORE TO THIS RRESTRIAL OBE THAN MOTHER VER TOLD ME.
THERE CAN BE ONLY ONE EXPLANATION FOR THIS MADNESS...
...A MAN.
A MAN HAS COME TO PARADISE ISLAND!
FOLLOW HER!
FIND HIM!

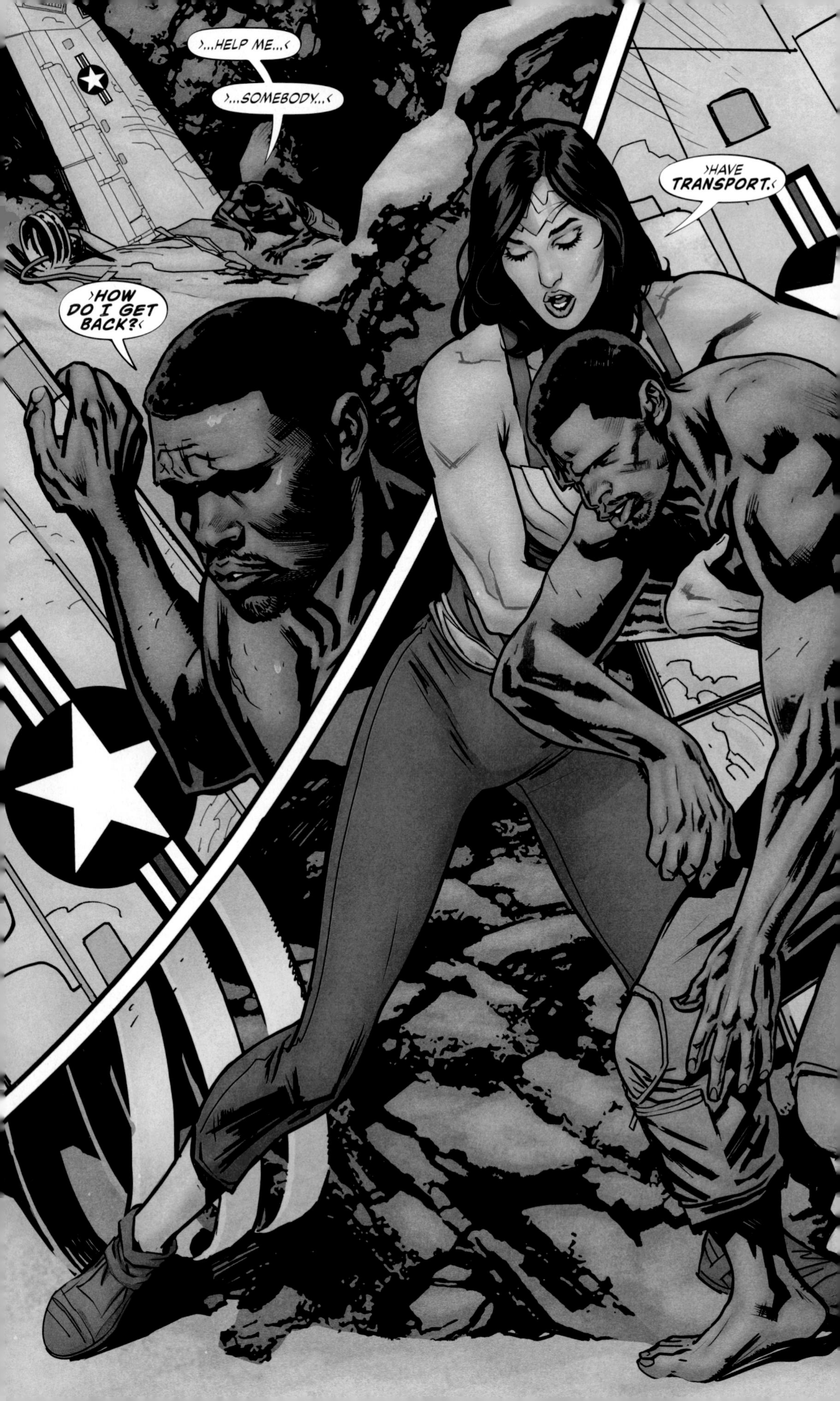
›...HELP ME...‹
›...SOMEBODY...‹
›HOW DO I GET BACK?‹
›HAVE TRANSPORT.‹

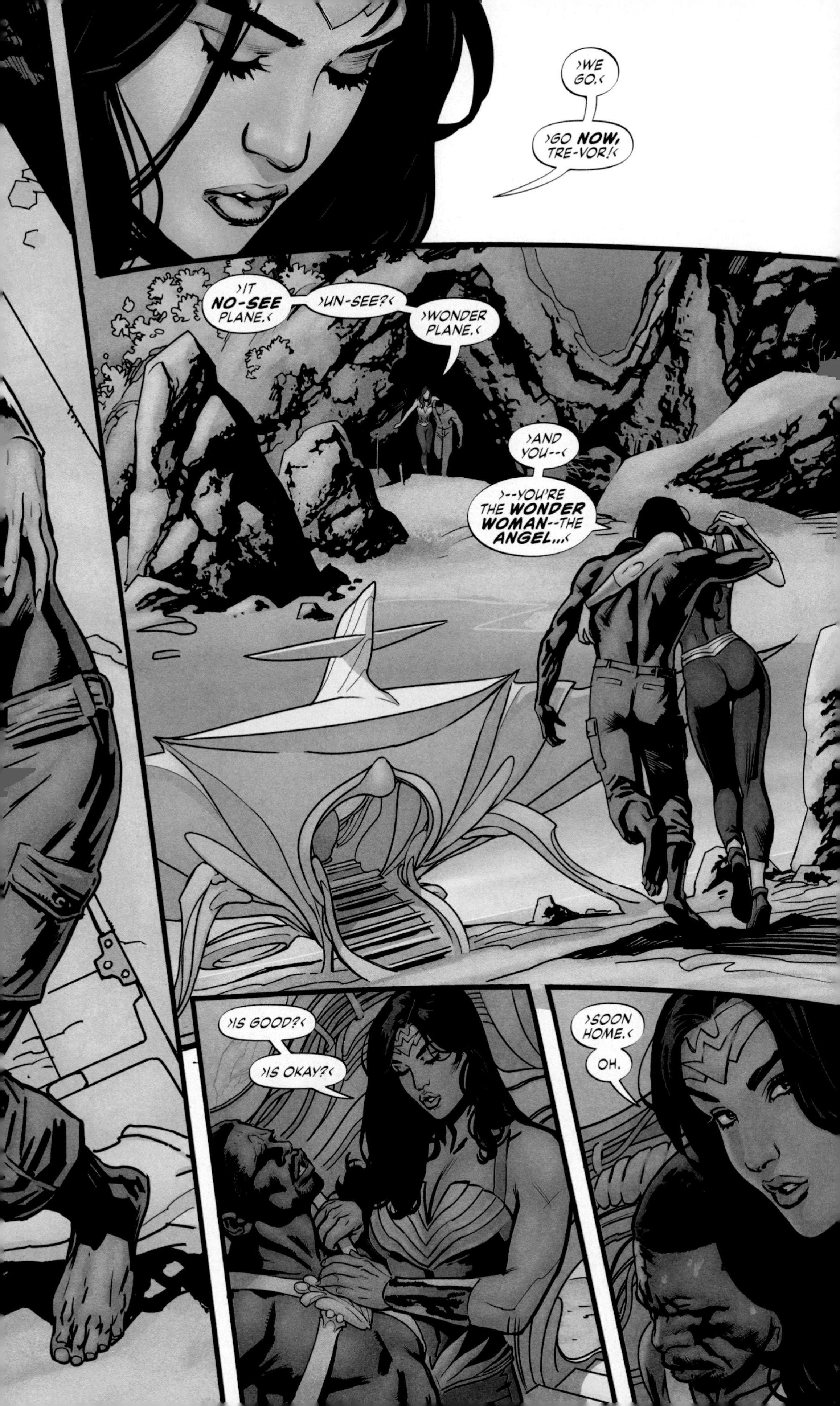

›WE GO.‹
›GO **NOW,** TRE-VOR!‹
›IT **NO-SEE** PLANE.‹
›UN-SEE?‹
›WONDER PLANE.‹
›AND YOU--‹
›--YOU'RE THE **WONDER WOMAN**--THE **ANGEL...**‹
›IS GOOD?‹
›IS OKAY?‹
›SOON HOME.‹
OH.

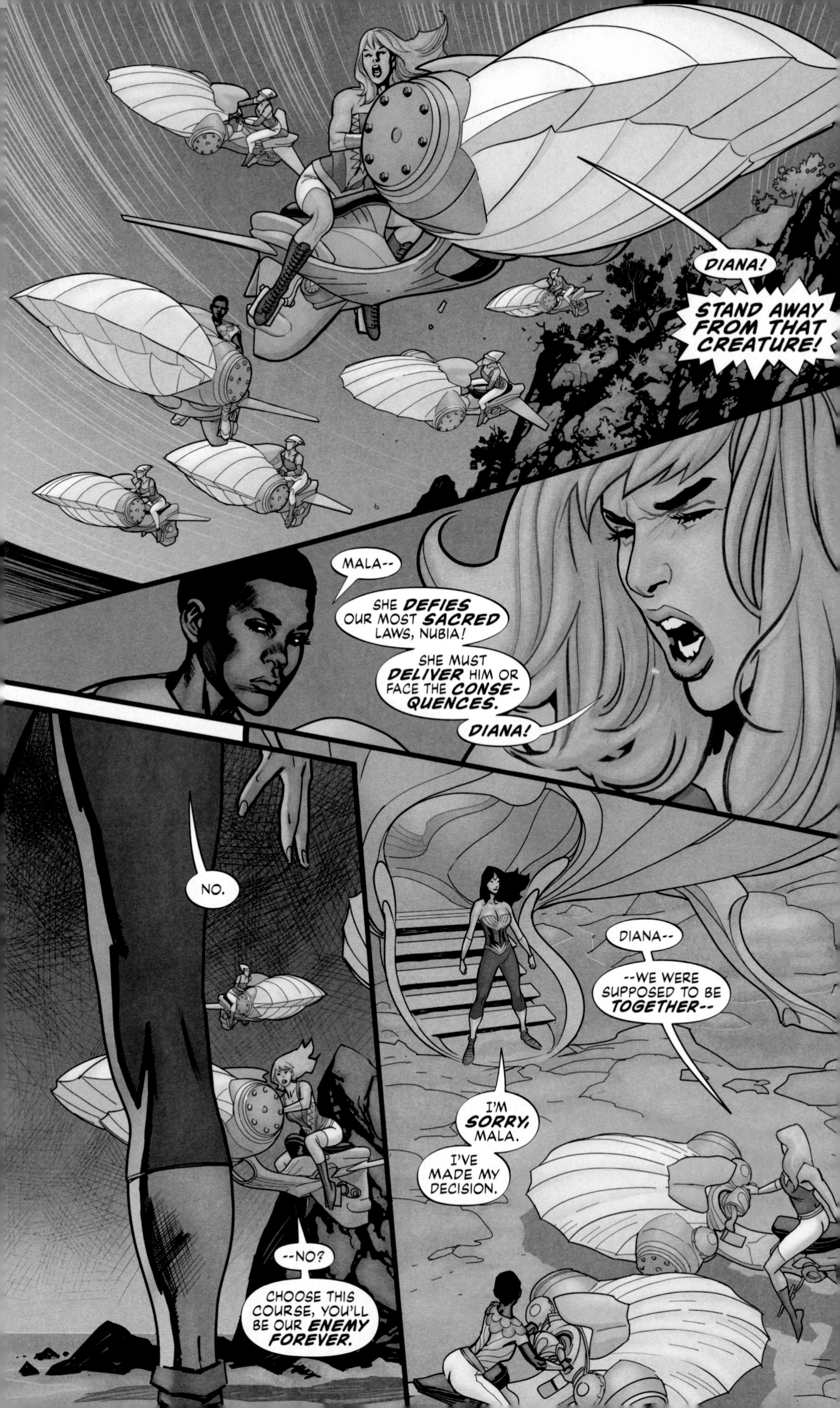
DIANA!
STAND AWAY FROM THAT CREATURE!
MALA--
SHE DEFIES OUR MOST SACRED LAWS, NUBIA!
SHE MUST DELIVER HIM OR FACE THE CONSE-QUENCES.
DIANA!
NO.
DIANA--
--WE WERE SUPPOSED TO BE TOGETHER--
I'M SORRY, MALA.
I'VE MADE MY DECISION.
--NO?
CHOOSE THIS COURSE, YOU'LL BE OUR ENEMY FOREVER.

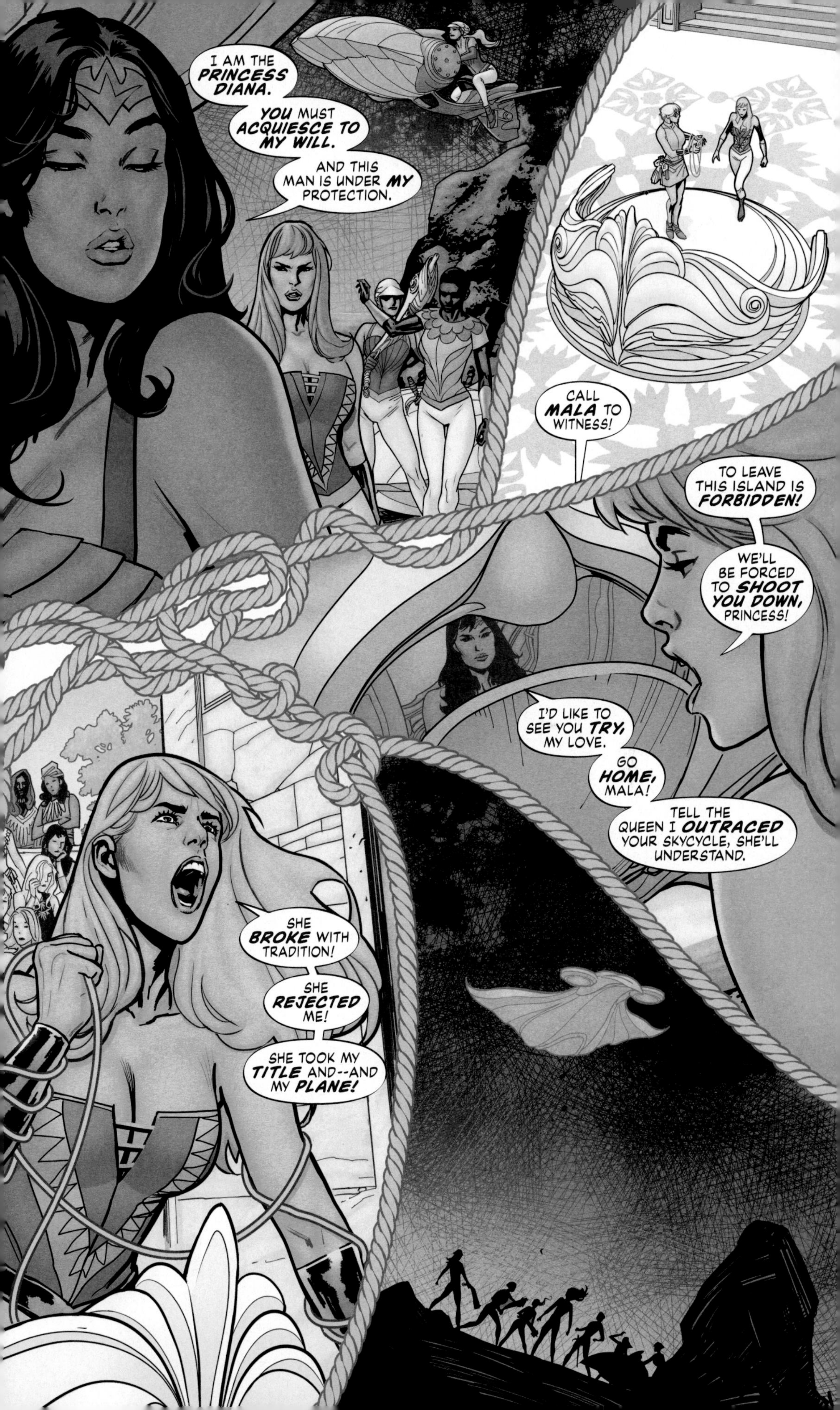
I AM THE PRINCESS DIANA.
YOU MUST ACQUIESCE TO MY WILL.
AND THIS MAN IS UNDER MY PROTECTION.
CALL MALA TO WITNESS!
TO LEAVE THIS ISLAND IS FORBIDDEN!
WE'LL BE FORCED TO SHOOT YOU DOWN, PRINCESS!
I'D LIKE TO SEE YOU TRY, MY LOVE.
GO HOME, MALA!
TELL THE QUEEN I OUTRACED YOUR SKYCYCLE, SHE'LL UNDERSTAND.
SHE BROKE WITH TRADITION!
SHE REJECTED ME!
SHE TOOK MY TITLE AND--AND MY PLANE!

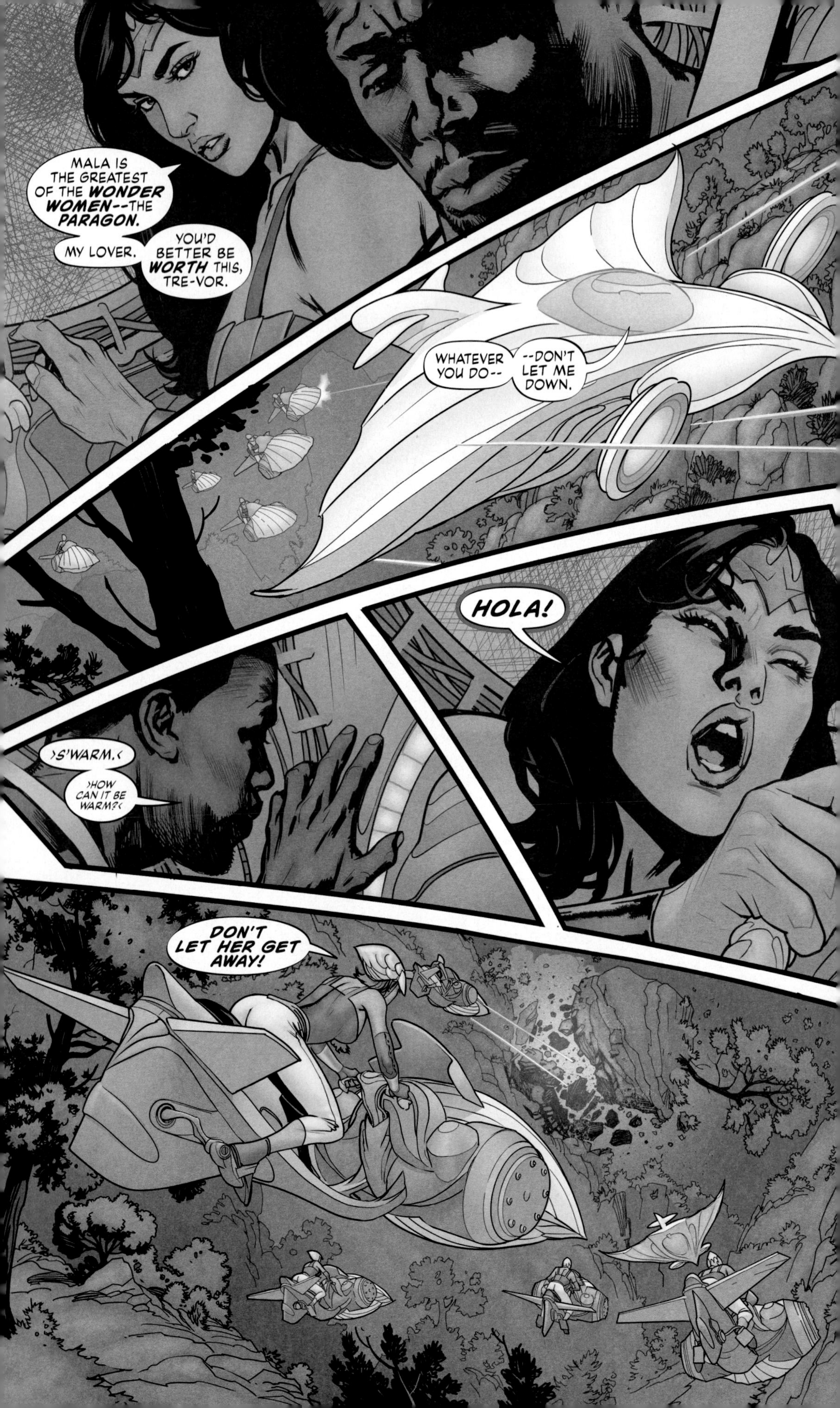

MALA IS THE GREATEST OF THE **WONDER WOMEN**--THE **PARAGON.**
MY LOVER.
YOU'D BETTER BE **WORTH** THIS, TRE-VOR.
WHATEVER YOU DO--
--DON'T LET ME DOWN.
HOLA!
›S'WARM.‹
›HOW CAN IT BE WARM?‹
DON'T LET HER GET AWAY!

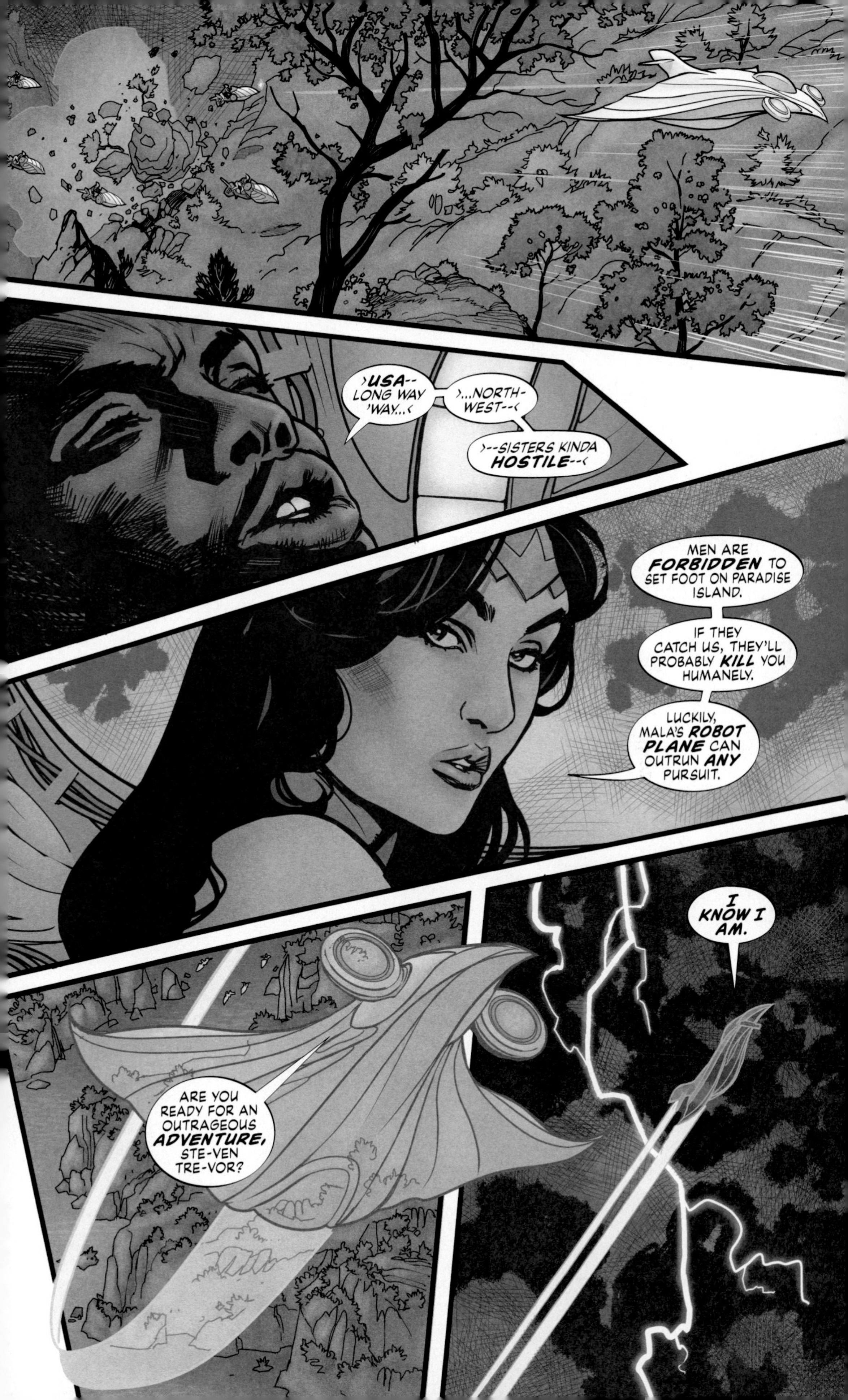
›USA-- LONG WAY 'WAY...‹
›...NORTH-WEST--‹
›--SISTERS KINDA HOSTILE--‹
MEN ARE FORBIDDEN TO SET FOOT ON PARADISE ISLAND.
IF THEY CATCH US, THEY'LL PROBABLY KILL YOU HUMANELY.
LUCKILY, MALA'S ROBOT PLANE CAN OUTRUN ANY PURSUIT.
ARE YOU READY FOR AN OUTRAGEOUS ADVENTURE, STE-VEN TRE-VOR?
I KNOW I AM.

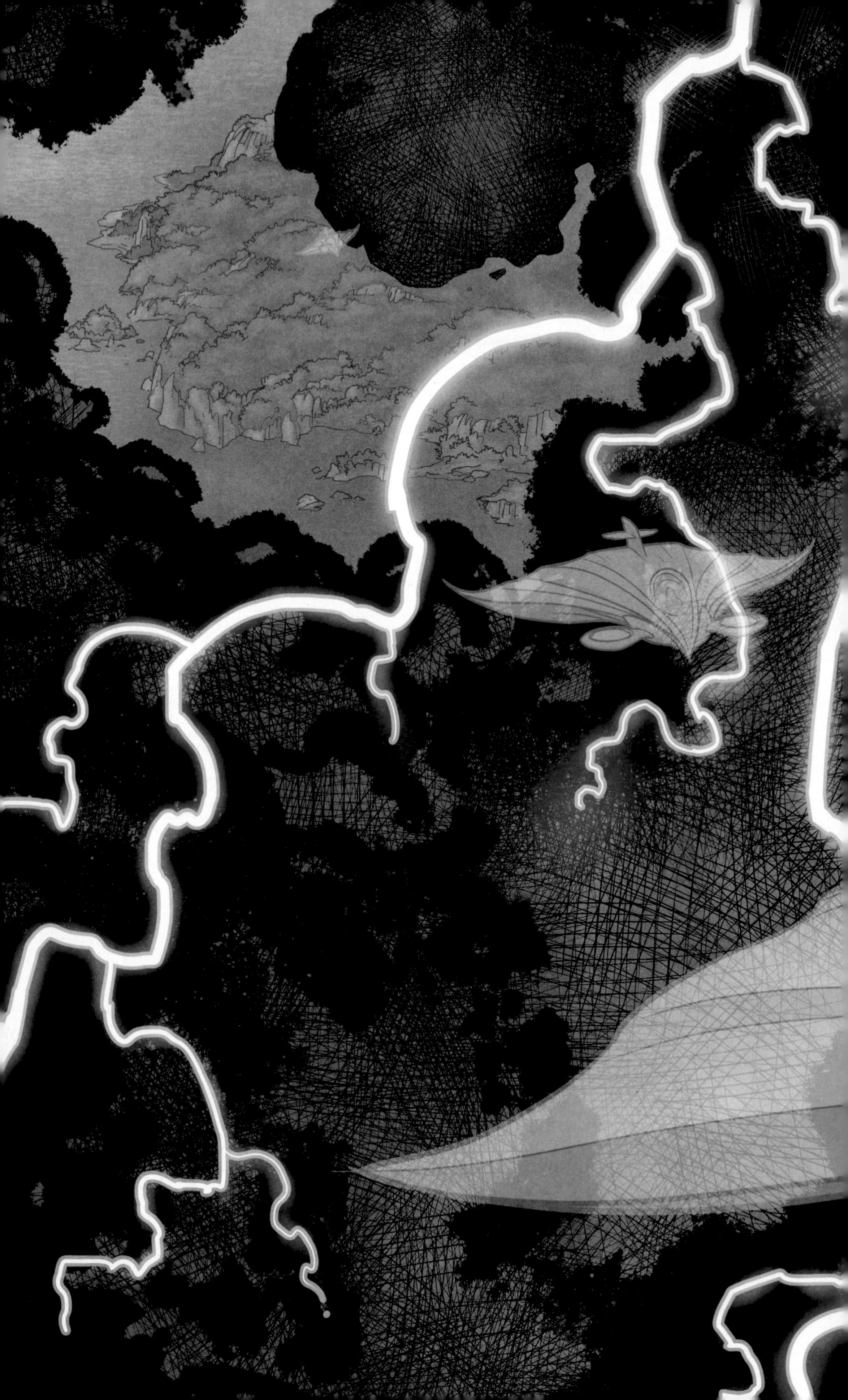

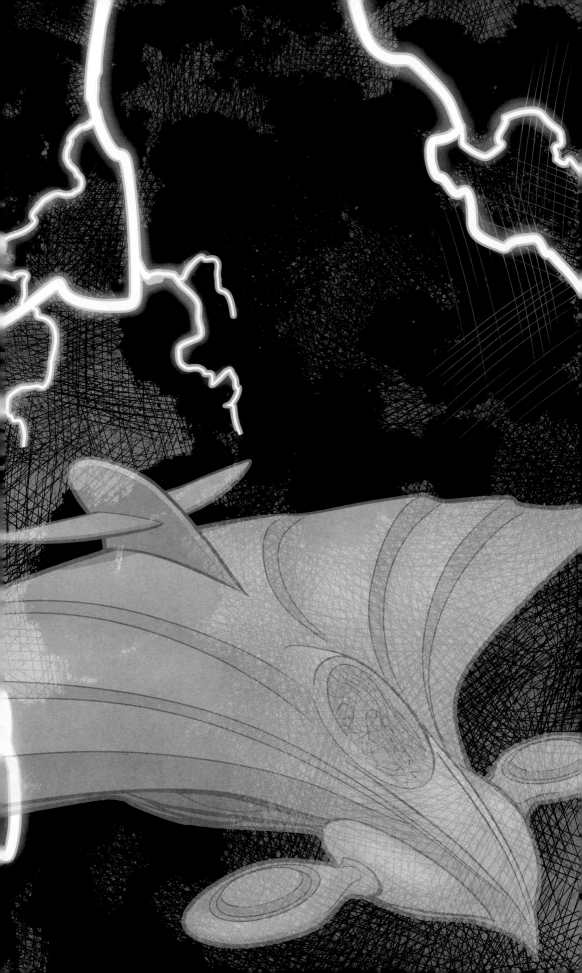

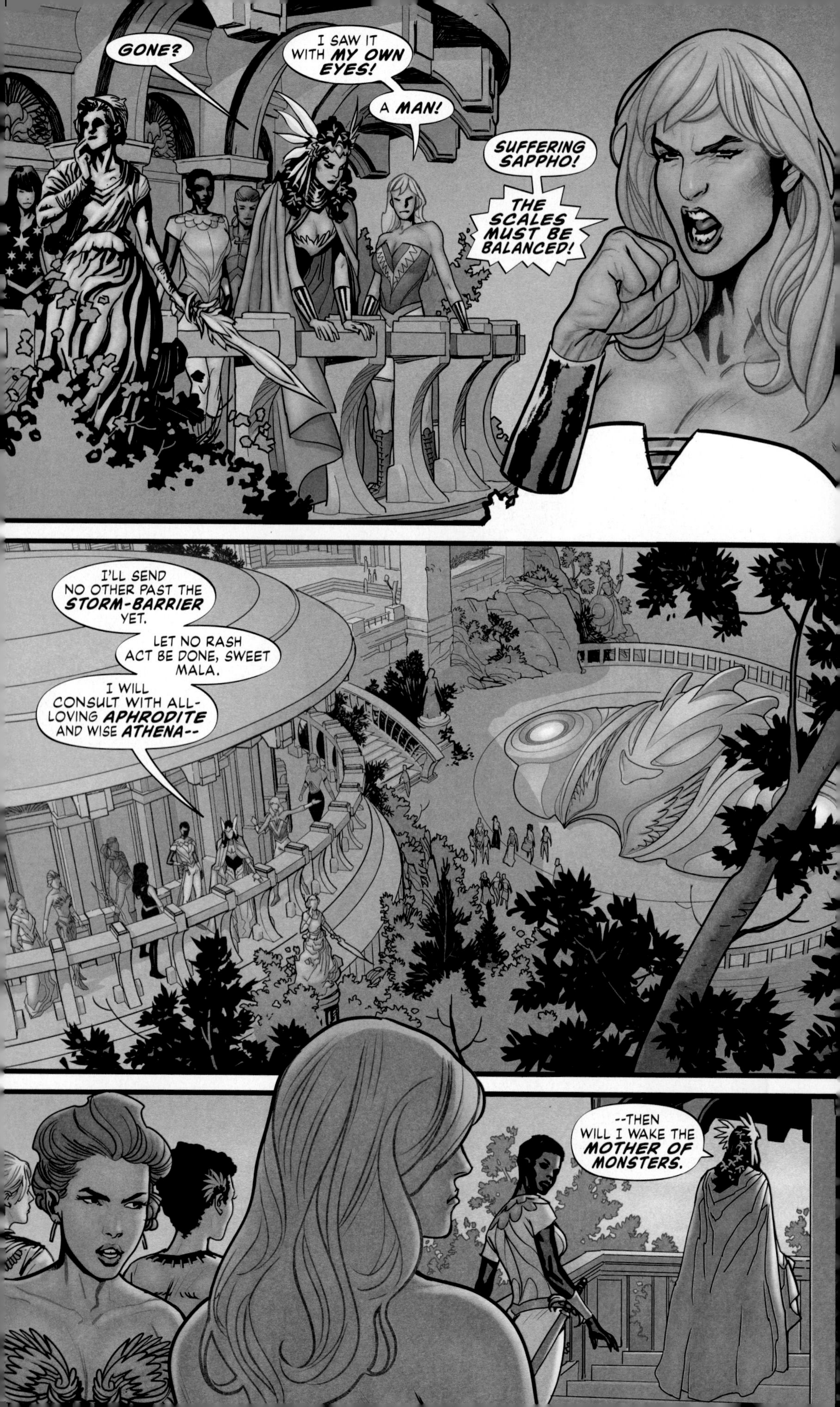
GONE?
I SAW IT WITH MY OWN EYES!
A MAN!
SUFFERING SAPPHO!
THE SCALES MUST BE BALANCED!
I'LL SEND NO OTHER PAST THE STORM-BARRIER YET.
LET NO RASH ACT BE DONE, SWEET MALA.
I WILL CONSULT WITH ALL-LOVING APHRODITE AND WISE ATHENA--
--THEN WILL I WAKE THE MOTHER OF MONSTERS.

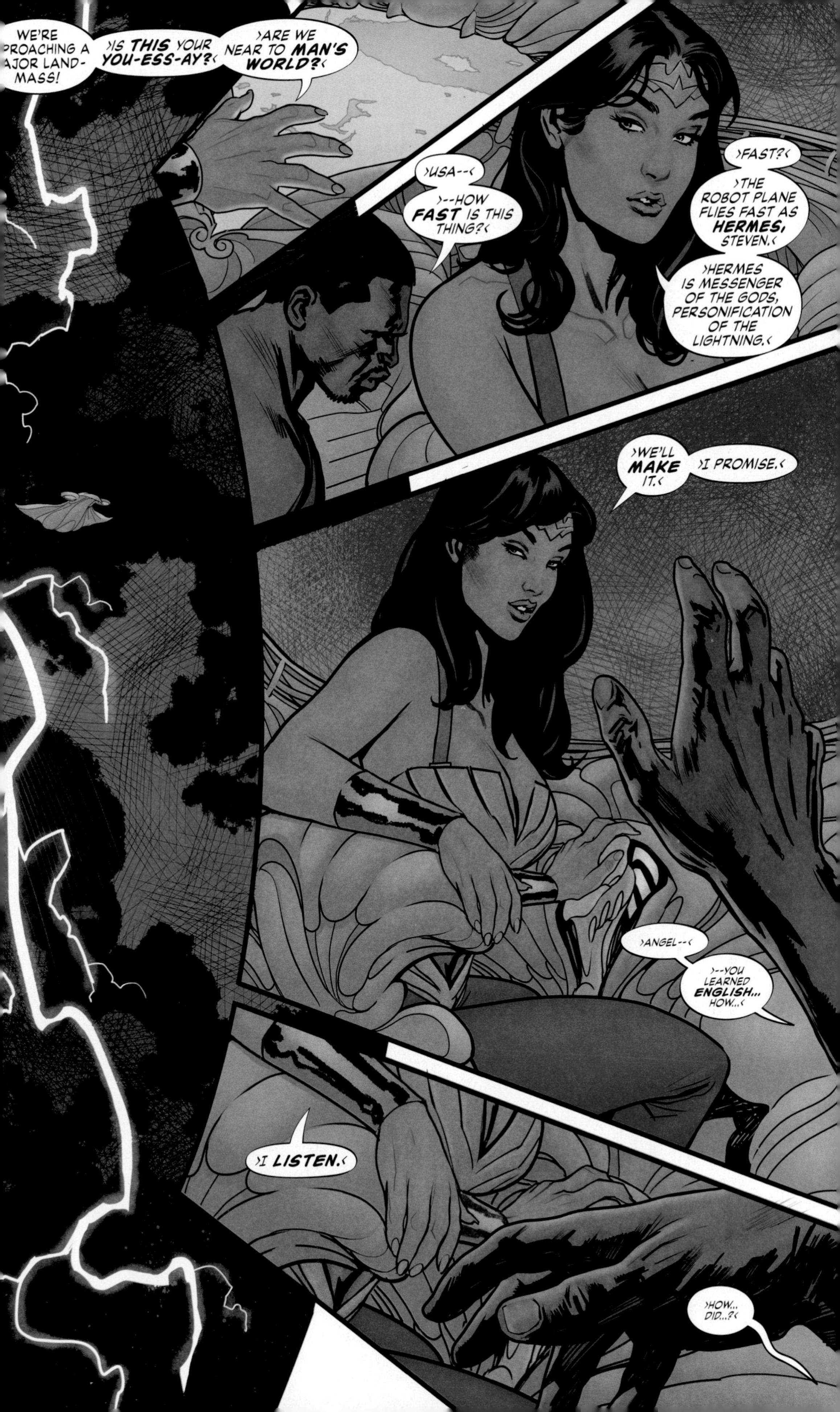

WE'RE PROACHING A AJOR LAND-MASS!
›IS THIS YOUR YOU-ESS-AY?‹
›ARE WE NEAR TO MAN'S WORLD?‹
›USA--‹
›--HOW FAST IS THIS THING?‹
›FAST?‹
›THE ROBOT PLANE FLIES FAST AS HERMES, STEVEN.‹
›HERMES IS MESSENGER OF THE GODS, PERSONIFICATION OF THE LIGHTNING.‹
›WE'LL MAKE IT.‹
›I PROMISE.‹
›ANGEL--‹
›--YOU LEARNED ENGLISH... HOW...‹
›I LISTEN.‹
›HOW... DID...?‹

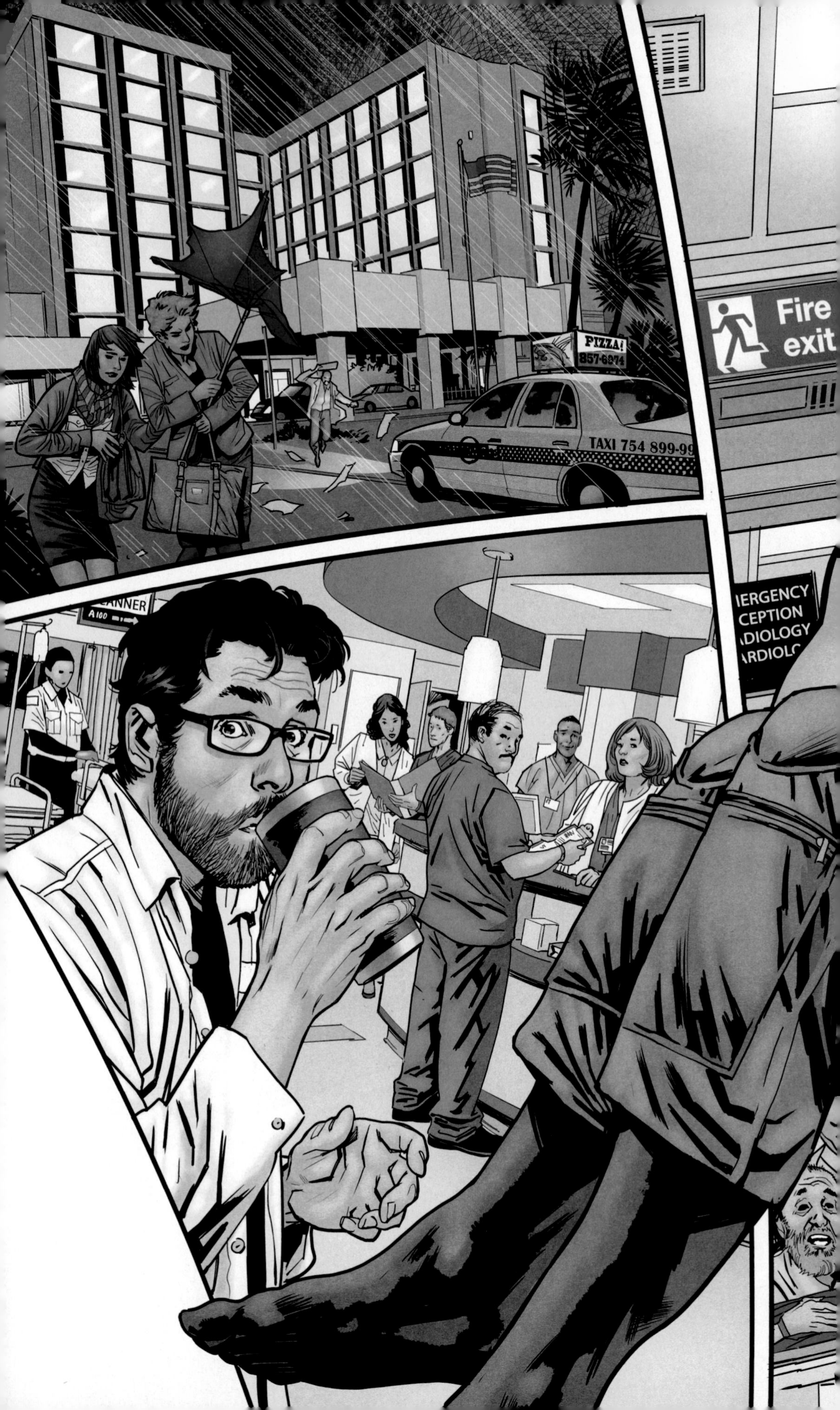
PIZZA!
857-6374
TAXI 754 899-99
Fire
exit
CANNER
A100
IERGENCY
CEPTION
ADIOLOGY
ARDIOLO

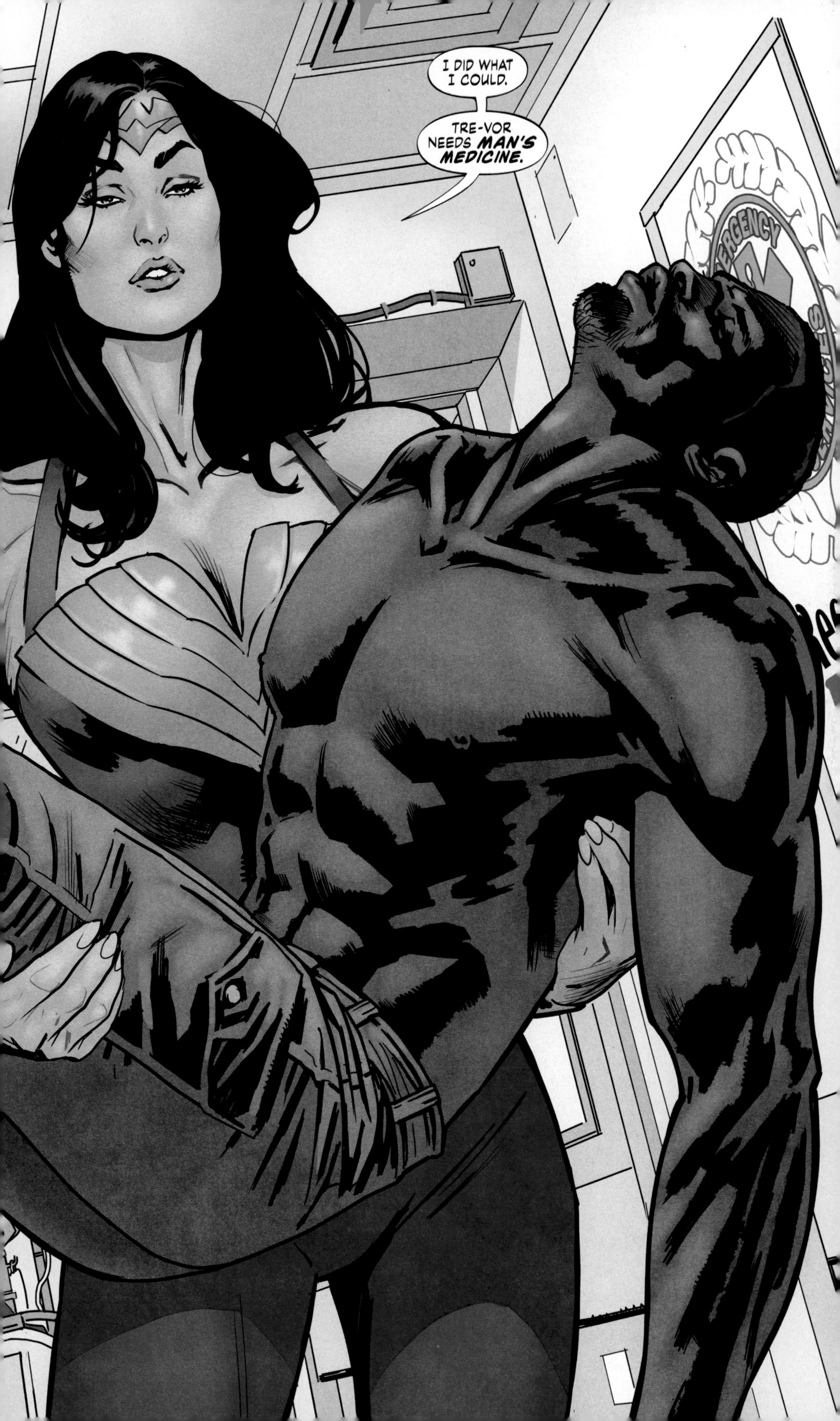
I DID WHAT I COULD.
TRE-VOR NEEDS MAN'S MEDICINE.

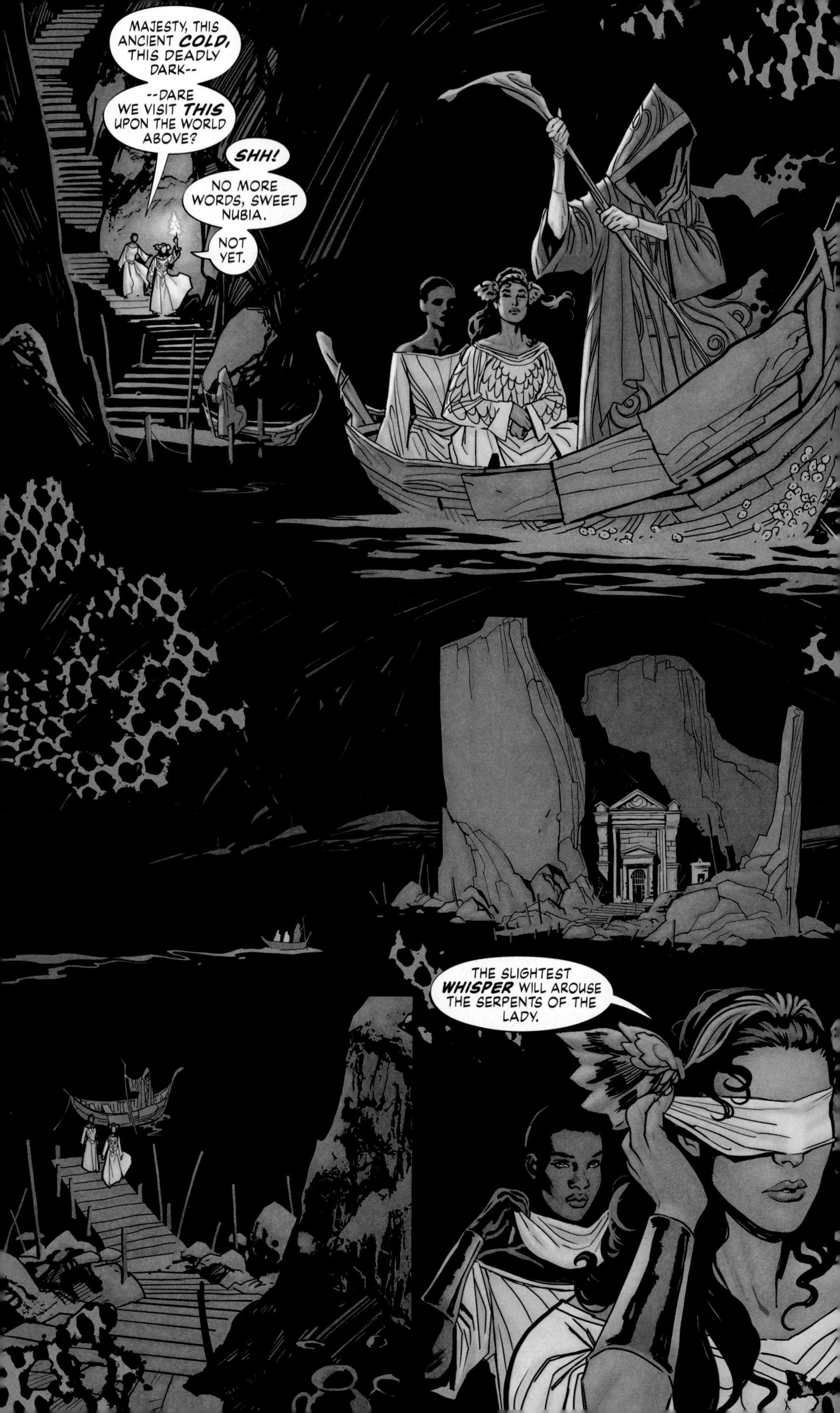
MAJESTY, THIS ANCIENT COLD, THIS DEADLY DARK--
--DARE WE VISIT THIS UPON THE WORLD ABOVE?
SHH!
NO MORE WORDS, SWEET NUBIA.
NOT YET.
THE SLIGHTEST WHISPER WILL AROUSE THE SERPENTS OF THE LADY.

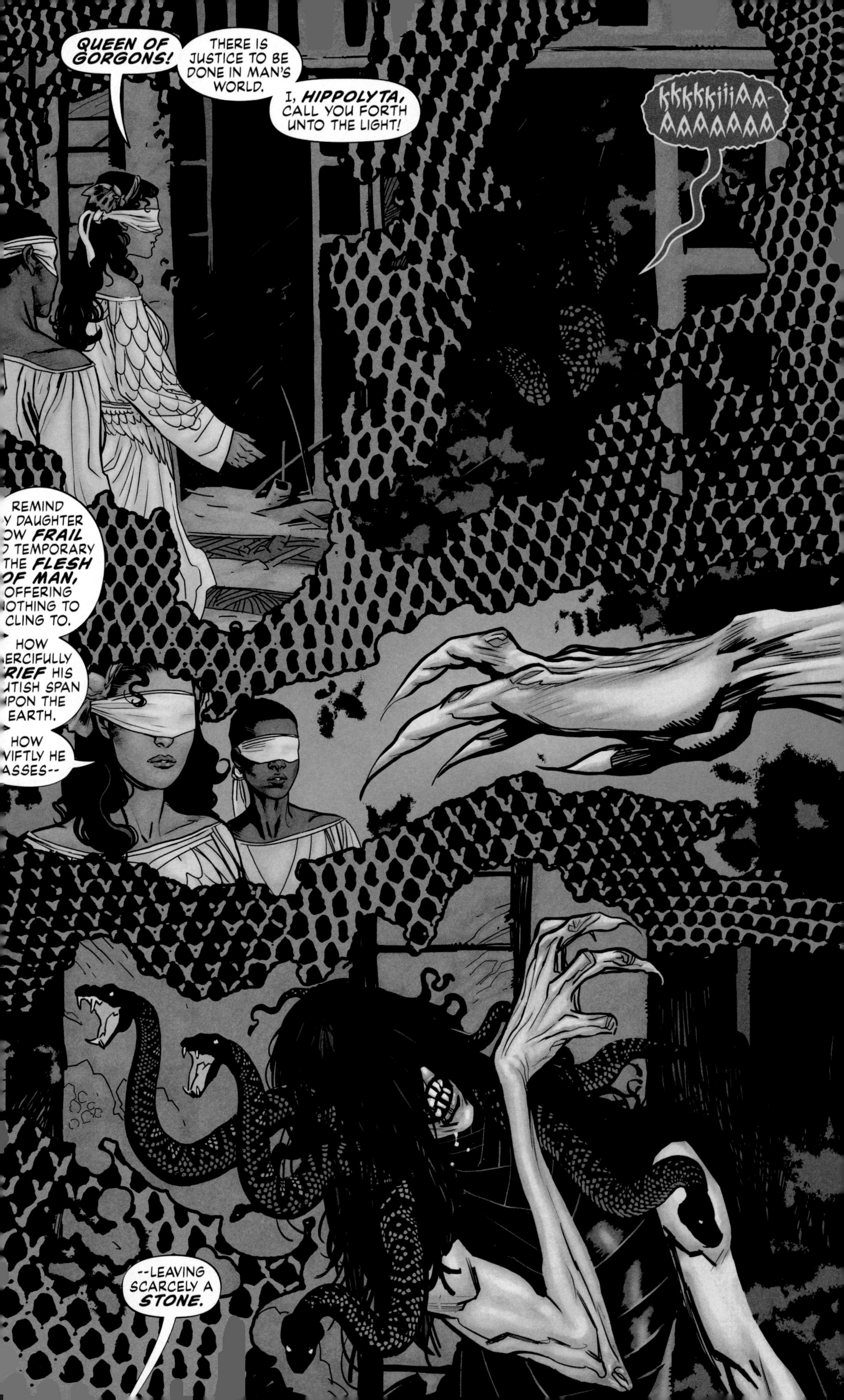
QUEEN OF GORGONS!
THERE IS JUSTICE TO BE DONE IN MAN'S WORLD.
I, HIPPOLYTA, CALL YOU FORTH UNTO THE LIGHT!
KKKKIIIAA-AAAAAAA
REMIND Y DAUGHTER OW FRAIL D TEMPORARY THE FLESH OF MAN, OFFERING OTHING TO CLING TO.
HOW ERCIFULLY RIEF HIS UTISH SPAN PON THE EARTH.
HOW IFTLY HE ASSES--
--LEAVING SCARCELY A STONE.

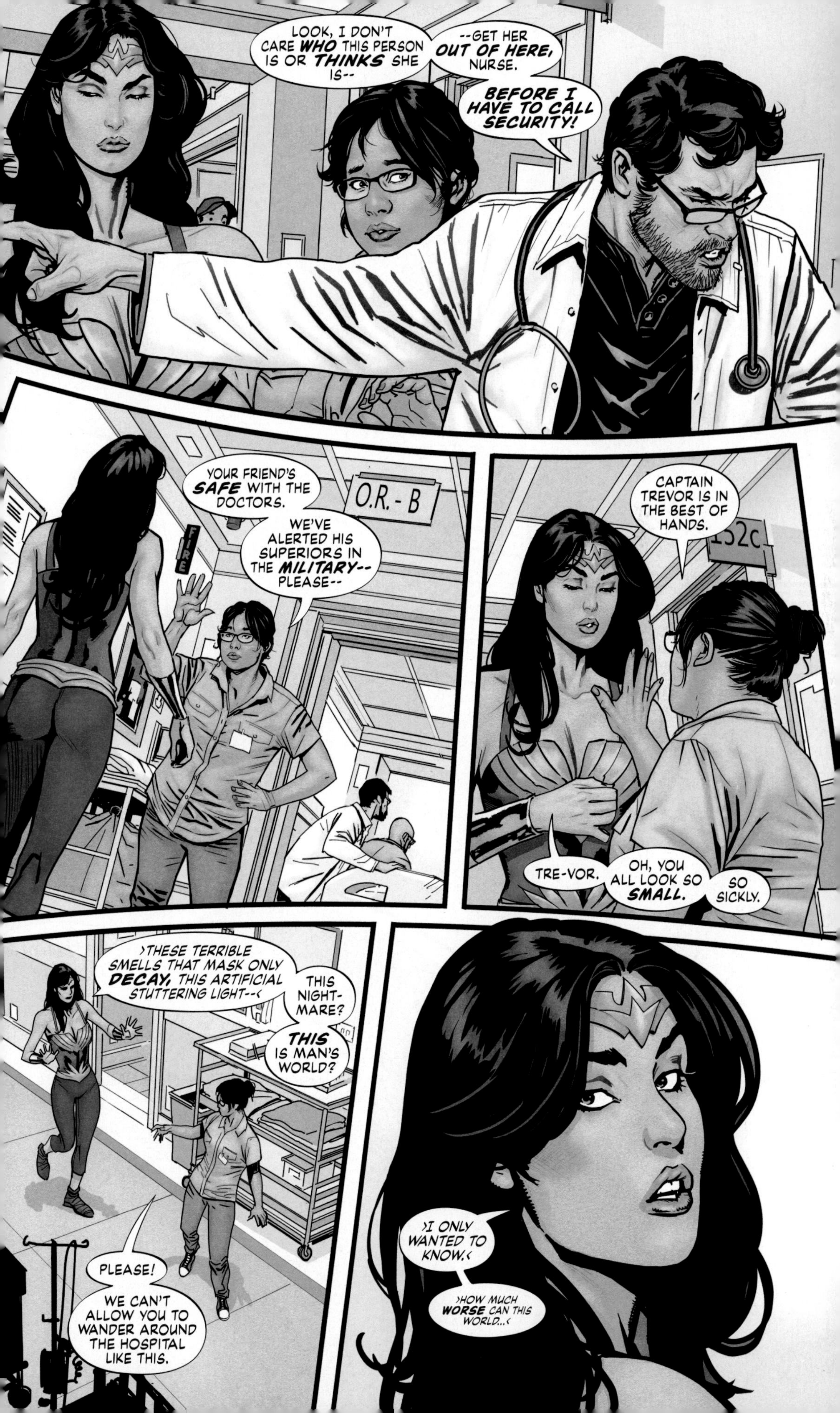

LOOK, I DON'T CARE **WHO** THIS PERSON IS OR **THINKS** SHE IS--
--GET HER **OUT OF HERE,** NURSE.
BEFORE I HAVE TO CALL SECURITY!
YOUR FRIEND'S **SAFE** WITH THE DOCTORS.
WE'VE ALERTED HIS SUPERIORS IN THE **MILITARY--** PLEASE--
O.R. - B
FIRE
CAPTAIN TREVOR IS IN THE BEST OF HANDS.
TRE-VOR.
OH, YOU ALL LOOK SO **SMALL.**
SO SICKLY.
›THESE TERRIBLE SMELLS THAT MASK ONLY **DECAY,** THIS ARTIFICIAL STUTTERING LIGHT--‹
THIS NIGHTMARE?
THIS IS MAN'S WORLD?
PLEASE!
WE CAN'T ALLOW YOU TO WANDER AROUND THE HOSPITAL LIKE THIS.
›I ONLY WANTED TO KNOW.‹
›HOW MUCH **WORSE** CAN THIS WORLD...‹

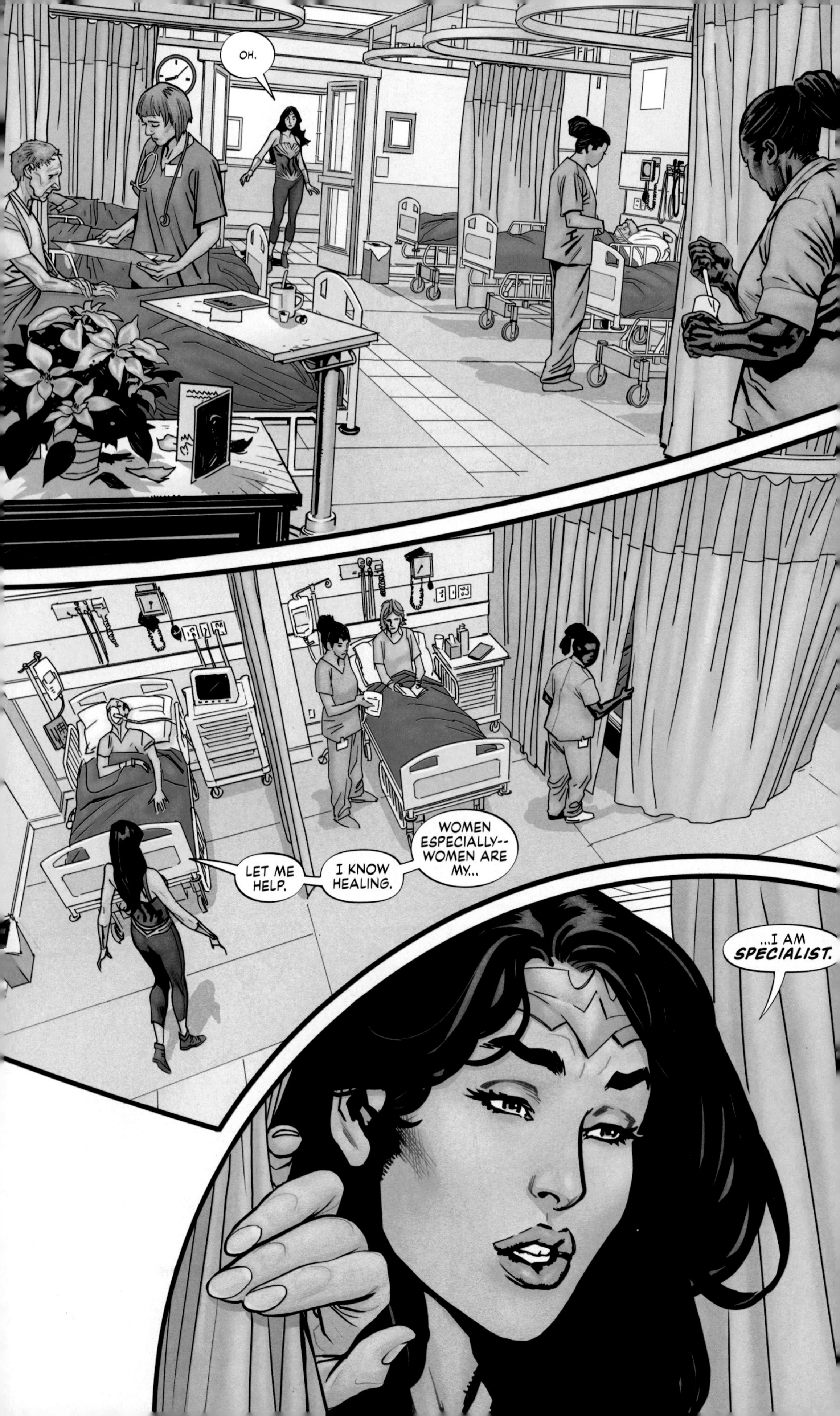
OH.
LET ME HELP.
I KNOW HEALING.
WOMEN ESPECIALLY-- WOMEN ARE MY...
...I AM SPECIALIST.

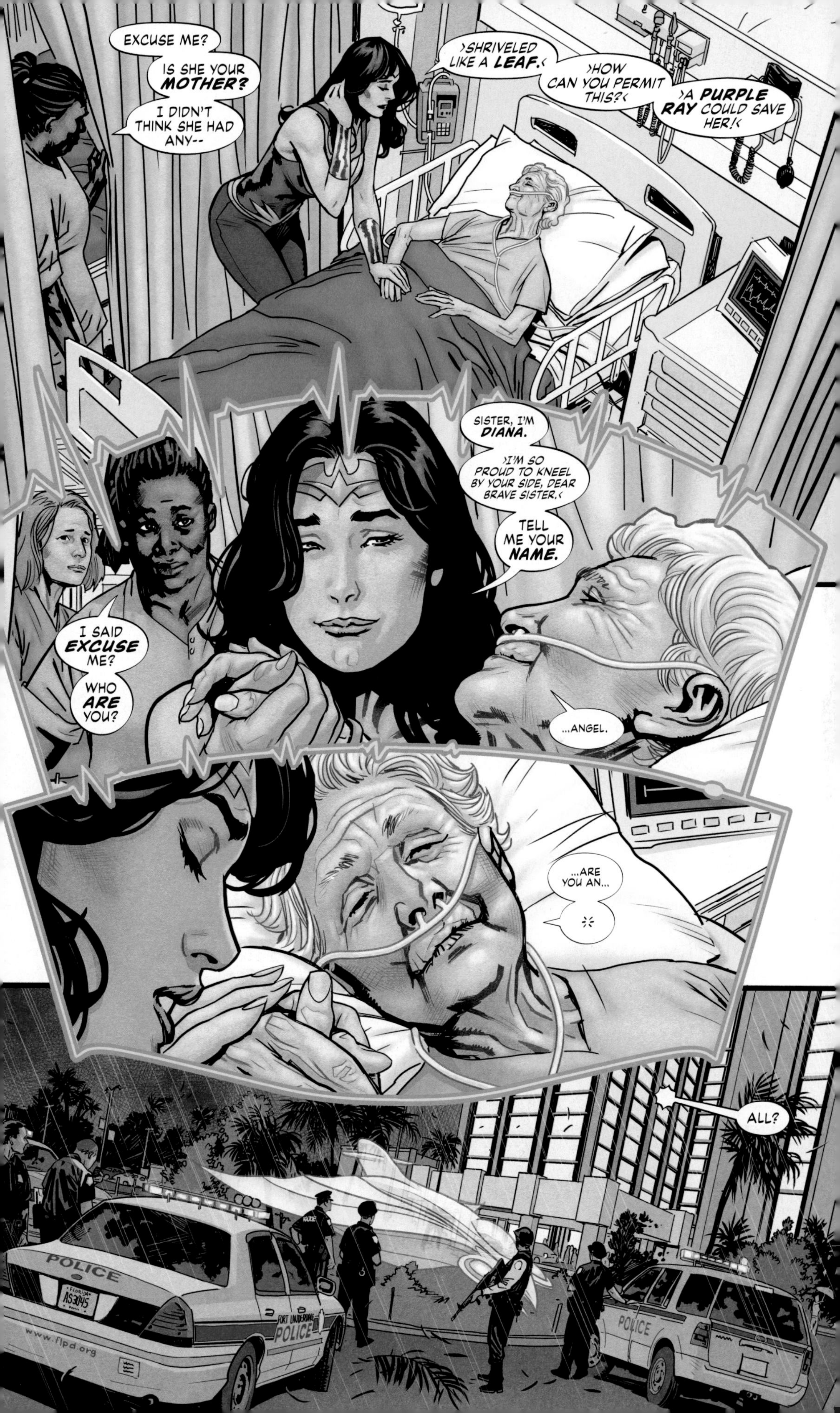
EXCUSE ME?
IS SHE YOUR MOTHER?
I DIDN'T THINK SHE HAD ANY--
›SHRIVELED LIKE A LEAF.‹
›HOW CAN YOU PERMIT THIS?‹
›A PURPLE RAY COULD SAVE HER!‹
SISTER, I'M DIANA.
›I'M SO PROUD TO KNEEL BY YOUR SIDE, DEAR BRAVE SISTER.‹
TELL ME YOUR NAME.
I SAID EXCUSE ME?
WHO ARE YOU?
...ANGEL.
...ARE YOU AN...
ALL?
POLICE
FORT LAUDERDALE POLICE
www.flpd.org
POLICE

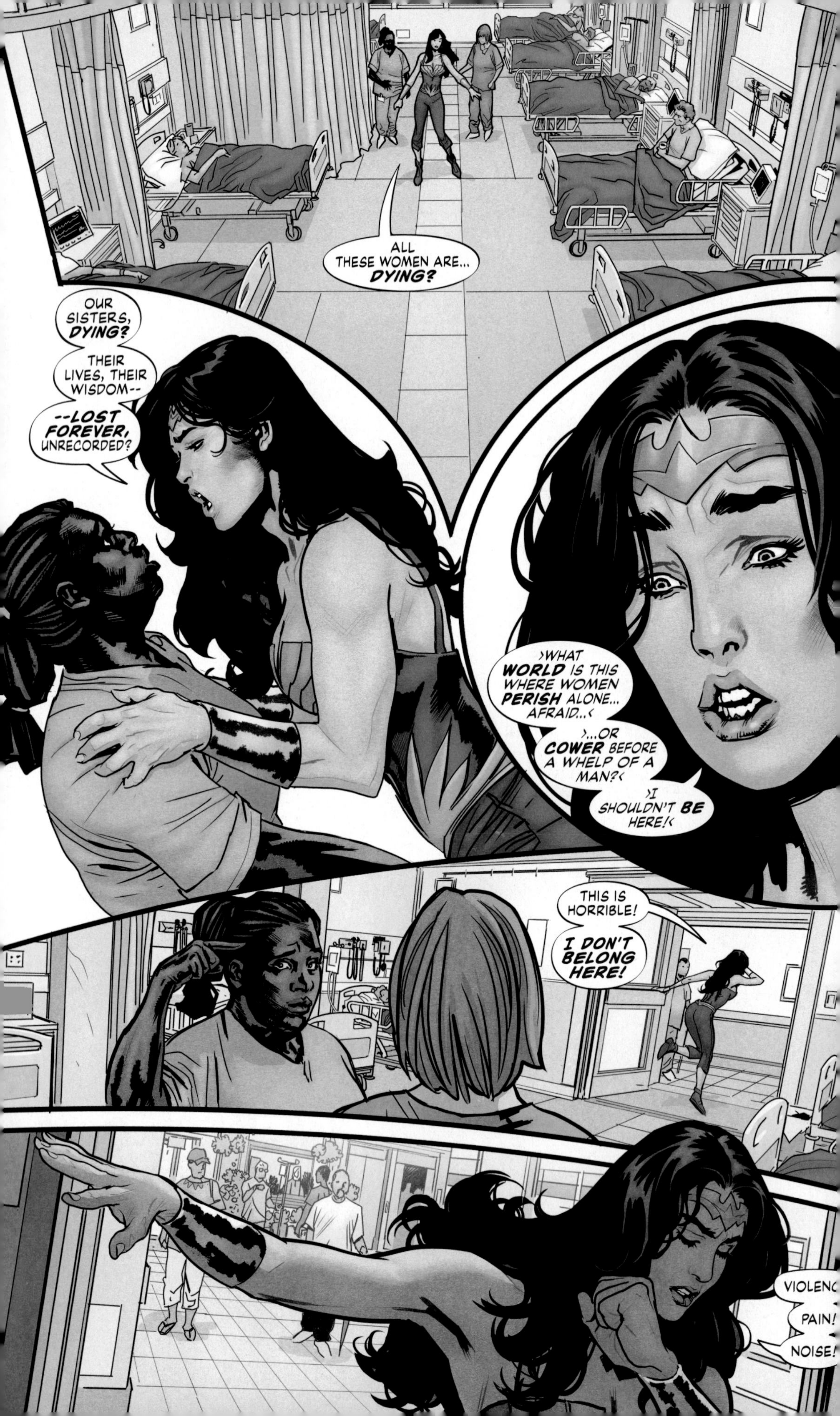
ALL THESE WOMEN ARE... DYING?
OUR SISTERS, DYING?
THEIR LIVES, THEIR WISDOM--
--LOST FOREVER, UNRECORDED?
›WHAT WORLD IS THIS WHERE WOMEN PERISH ALONE... AFRAID...‹
›...OR COWER BEFORE A WHELP OF A MAN?‹
›I SHOULDN'T BE HERE!‹
THIS IS HORRIBLE!
I DON'T BELONG HERE!
VIOLENC
PAIN!
NOISE!

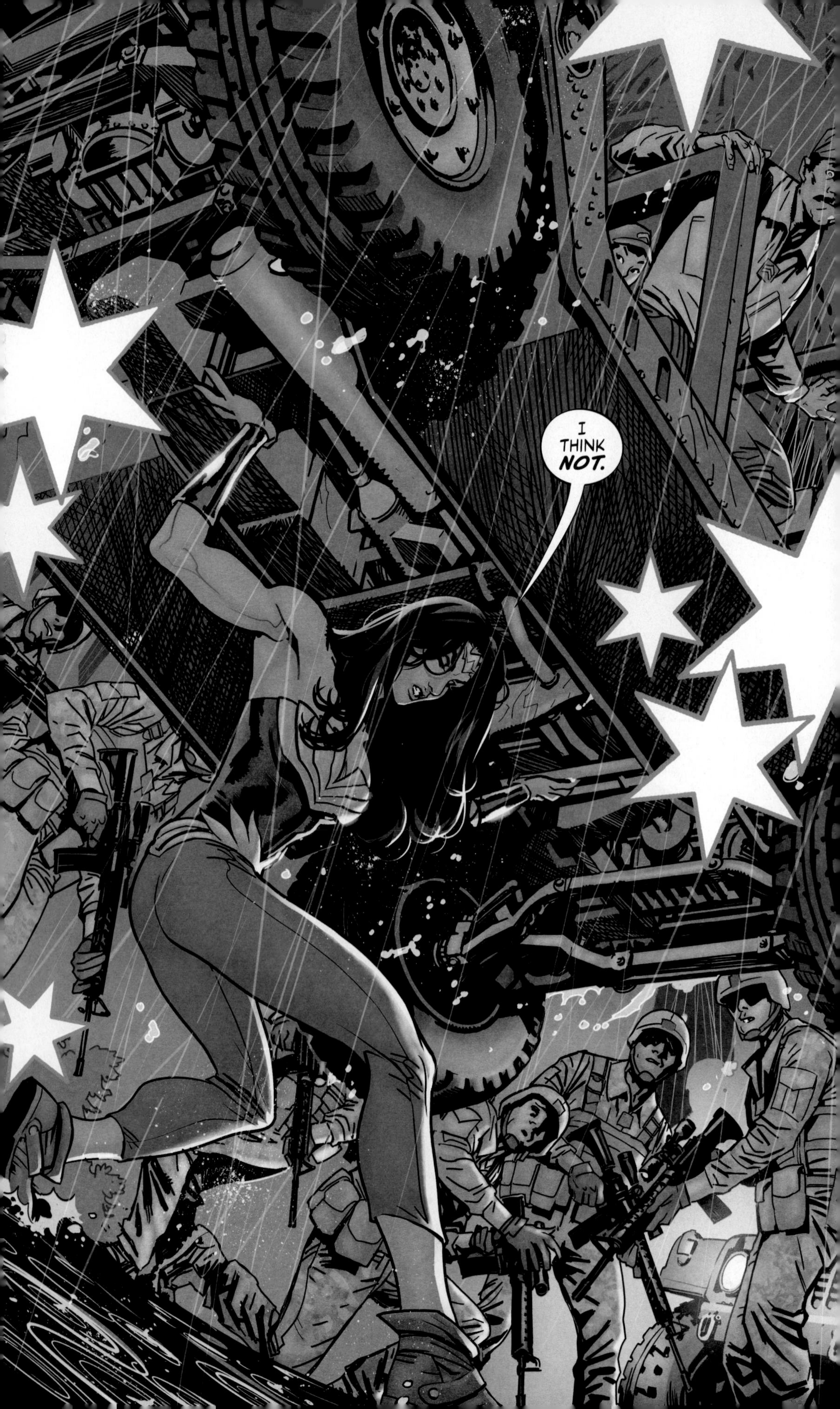
I THINK NOT.

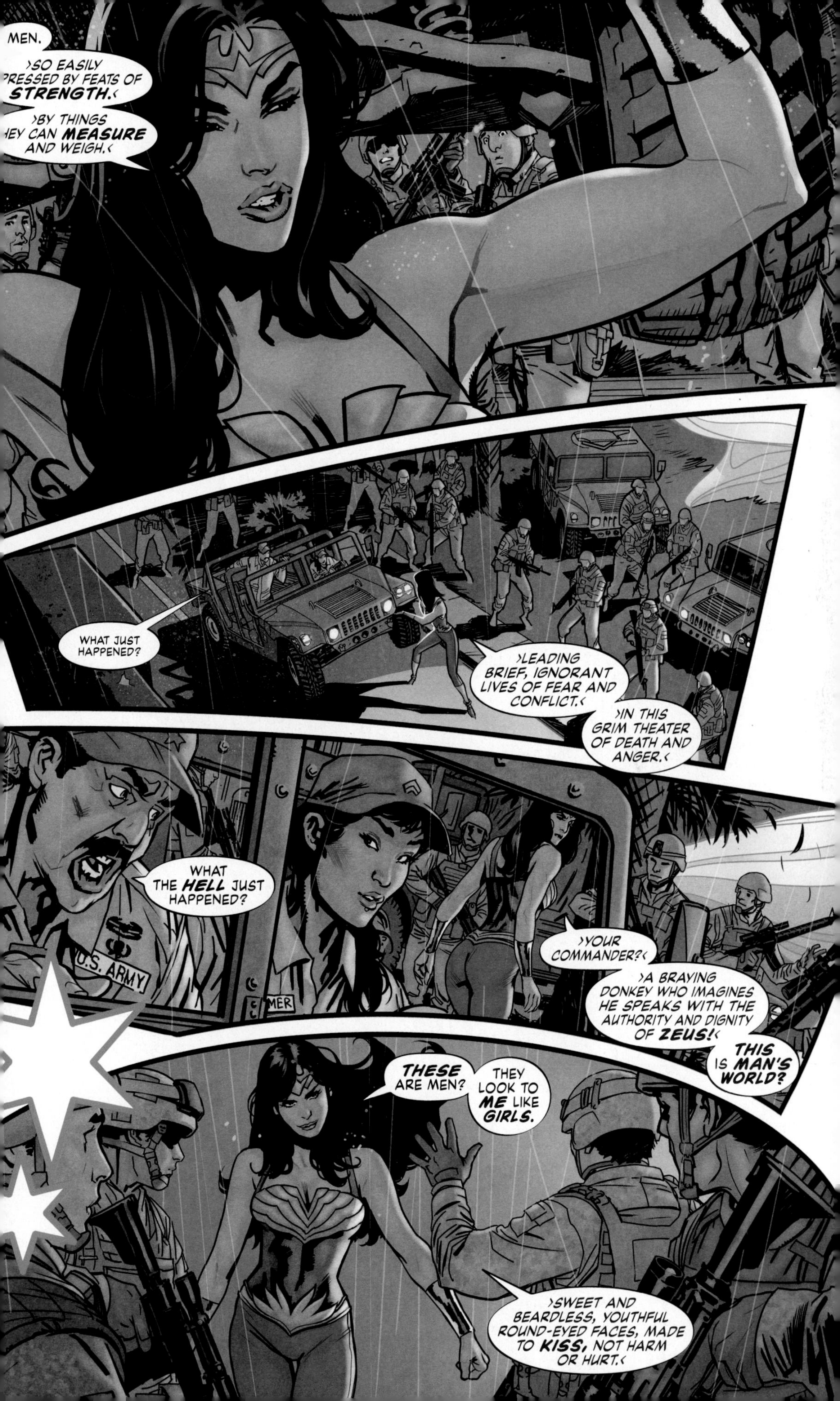
MEN.
›SO EASILY
PRESSED BY FEATS OF
STRENGTH.‹
›BY THINGS
HEY CAN MEASURE
AND WEIGH.‹
WHAT JUST
HAPPENED?
›LEADING
BRIEF, IGNORANT
LIVES OF FEAR AND
CONFLICT.‹
›IN THIS
GRIM THEATER
OF DEATH AND
ANGER.‹
WHAT
THE HELL JUST
HAPPENED?
U.S. ARMY
MER
›YOUR
COMMANDER?‹
›A BRAYING
DONKEY WHO IMAGINES
HE SPEAKS WITH THE
AUTHORITY AND DIGNITY
OF ZEUS!‹
THIS
IS MAN'S
WORLD?
THESE
ARE MEN?
THEY
LOOK TO
ME LIKE
GIRLS.
›SWEET AND
BEARDLESS, YOUTHFUL
ROUND-EYED FACES, MADE
TO KISS, NOT HARM
OR HURT.‹

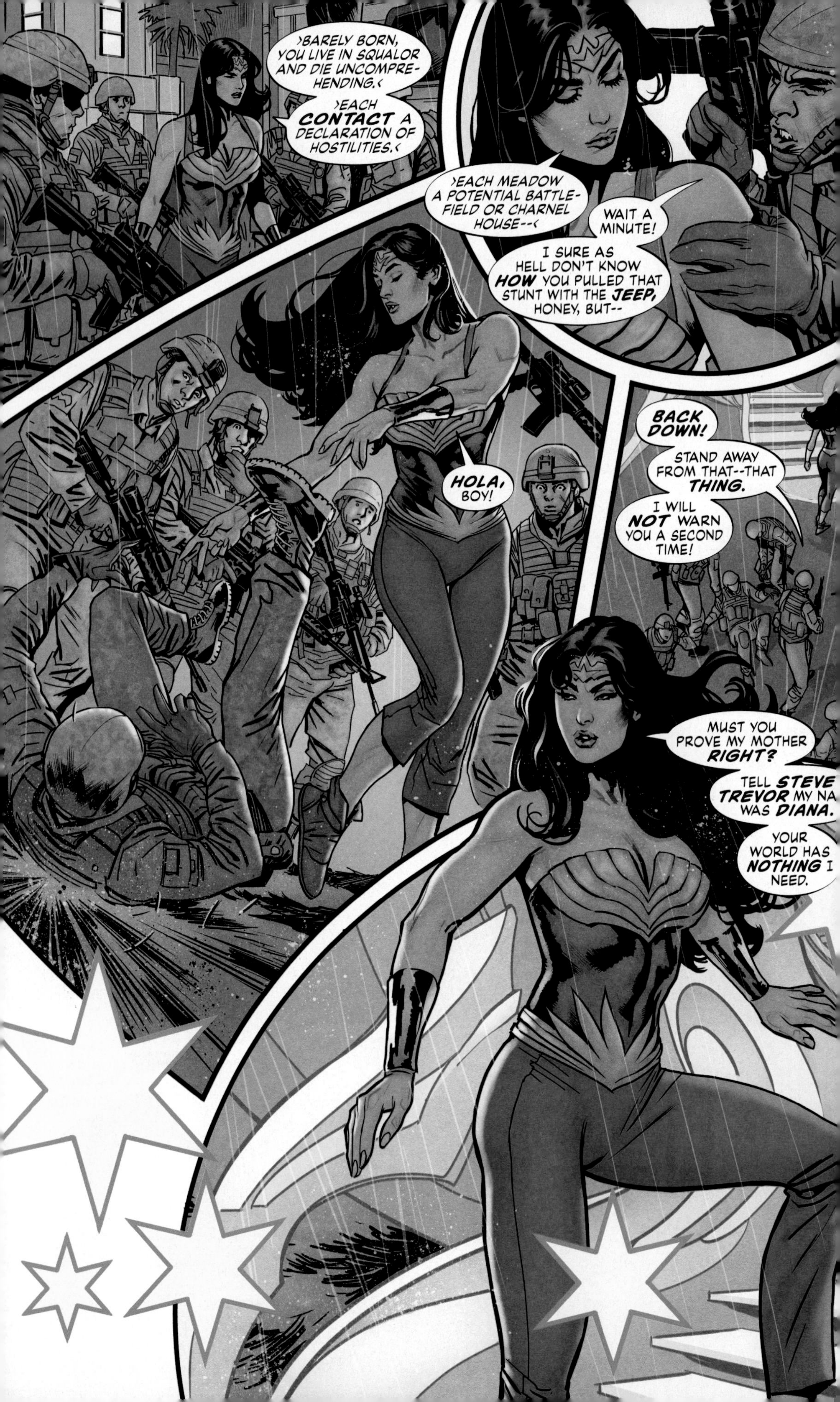
>BARELY BORN, YOU LIVE IN SQUALOR AND DIE UNCOMPREHENDING.<
>EACH CONTACT A DECLARATION OF HOSTILITIES.<
>EACH MEADOW A POTENTIAL BATTLEFIELD OR CHARNEL HOUSE--<
WAIT A MINUTE!
I SURE AS HELL DON'T KNOW HOW YOU PULLED THAT STUNT WITH THE JEEP, HONEY, BUT--
HOLA, BOY!
BACK DOWN!
STAND AWAY FROM THAT--THAT THING.
I WILL NOT WARN YOU A SECOND TIME!
MUST YOU PROVE MY MOTHER RIGHT?
TELL STEVE TREVOR MY NA WAS DIANA.
YOUR WORLD HAS NOTHING I NEED.

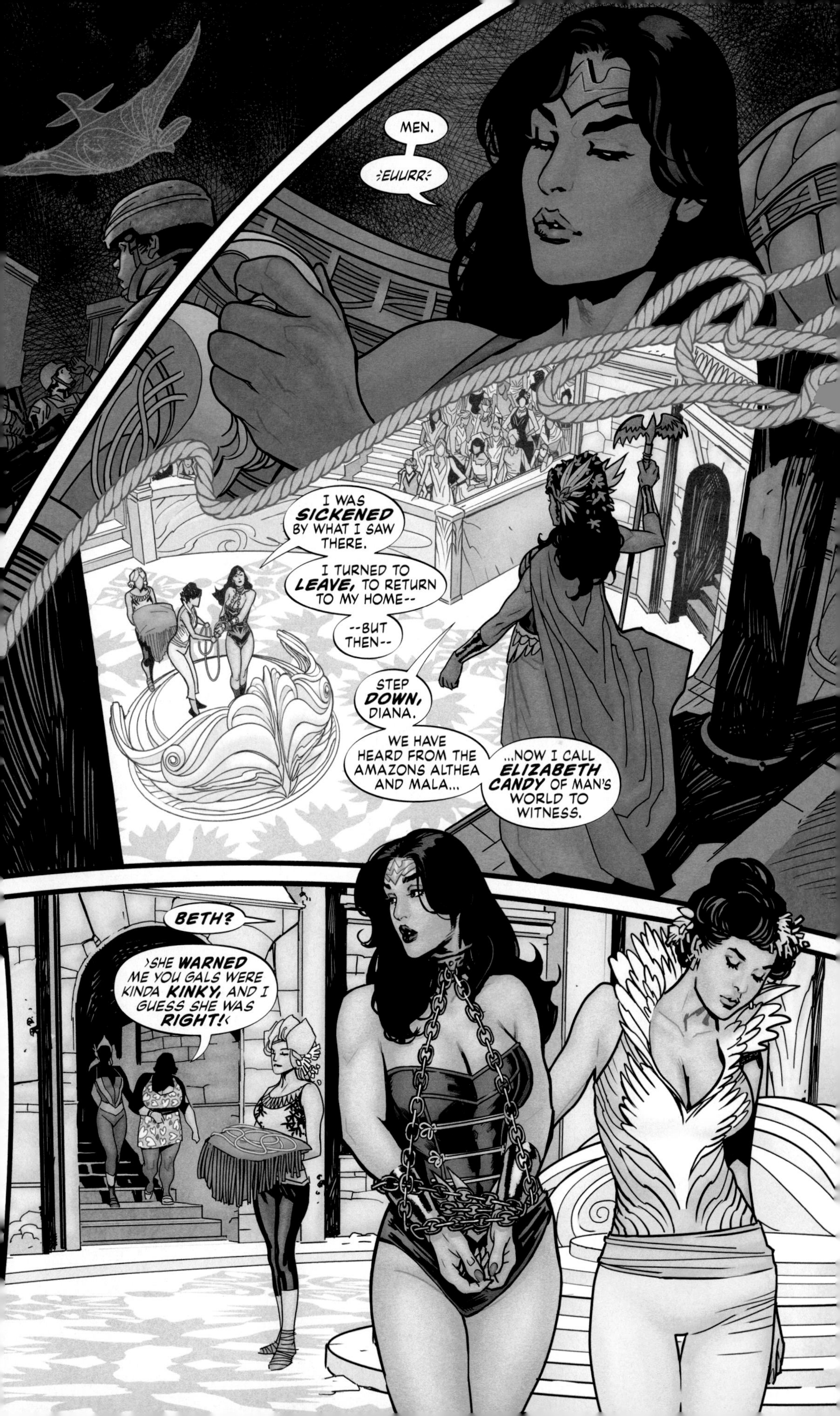
MEN.
≈EUURR≈
I WAS SICKENED BY WHAT I SAW THERE.
I TURNED TO LEAVE, TO RETURN TO MY HOME--
--BUT THEN--
STEP DOWN, DIANA.
WE HAVE HEARD FROM THE AMAZONS ALTHEA AND MALA...
...NOW I CALL ELIZABETH CANDY OF MAN'S WORLD TO WITNESS.
BETH?
›SHE WARNED ME YOU GALS WERE KINDA KINKY, AND I GUESS SHE WAS RIGHT!‹

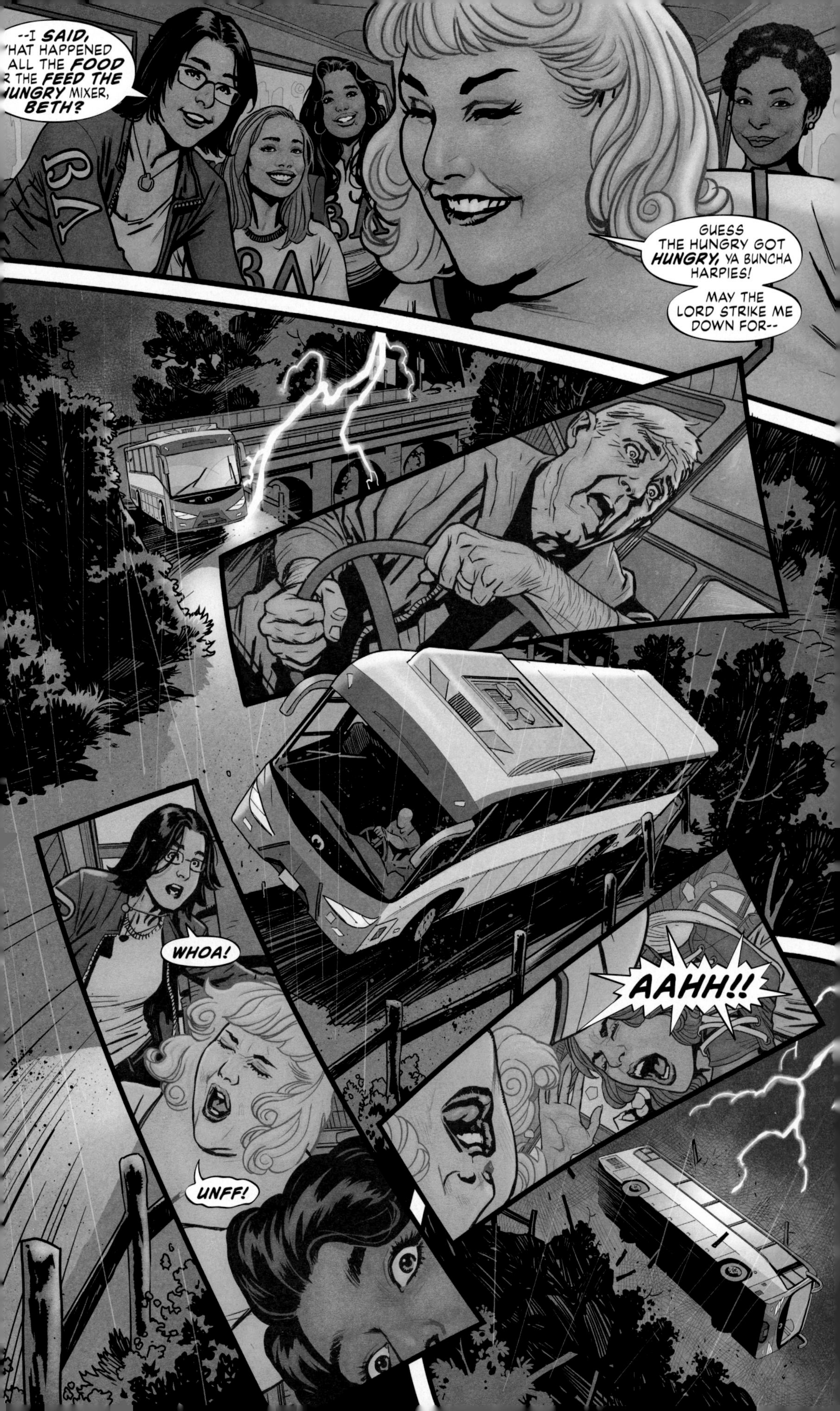
--I SAID, WHAT HAPPENED ALL THE FOOD FOR THE FEED THE HUNGRY MIXER, BETH?
GUESS THE HUNGRY GOT HUNGRY, YA BUNCHA HARPIES!
MAY THE LORD STRIKE ME DOWN FOR--
WHOA!
AAHH!!
UNFF!

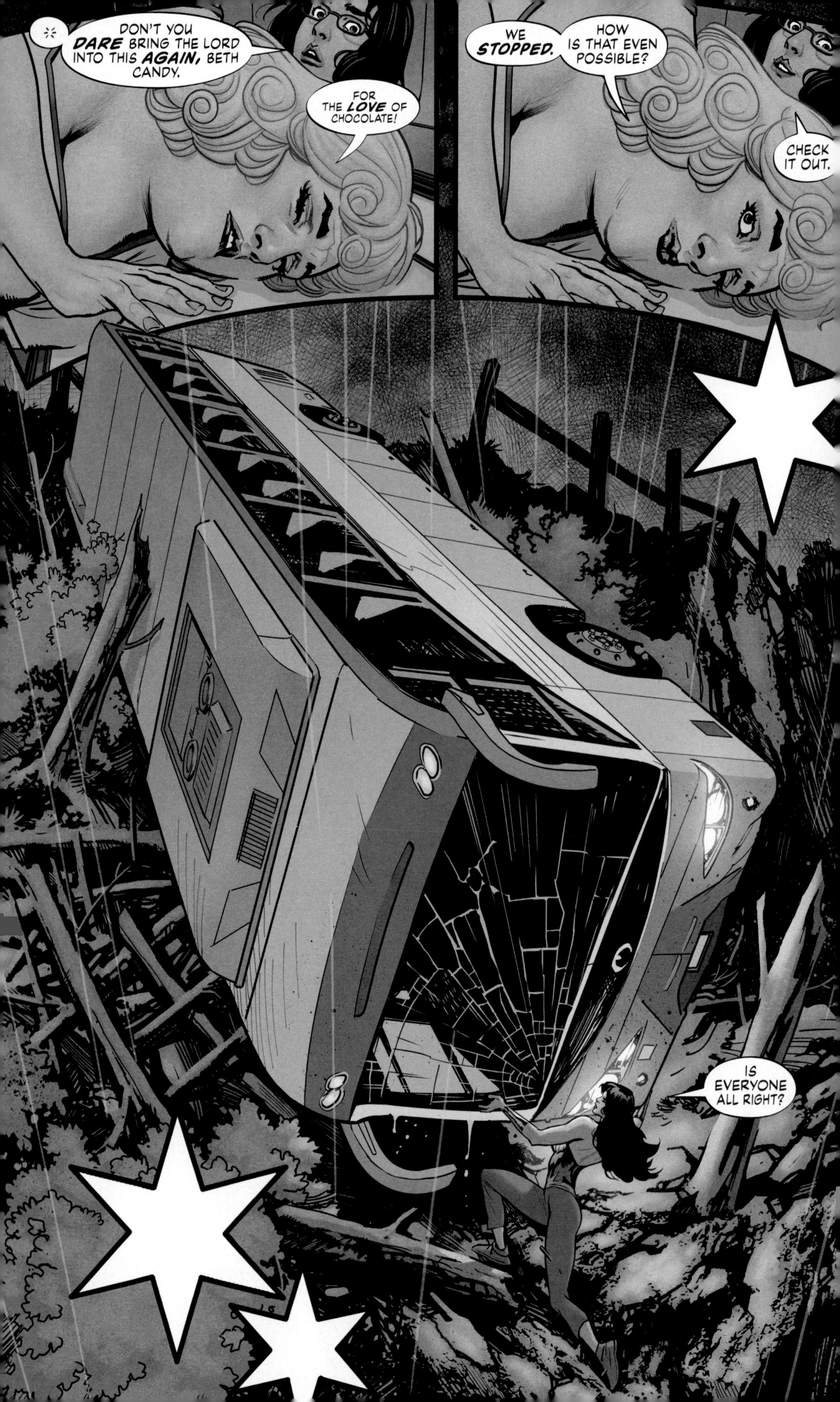
DON'T YOU DARE BRING THE LORD INTO THIS AGAIN, BETH CANDY.
FOR THE LOVE OF CHOCOLATE!
WE STOPPED.
HOW IS THAT EVEN POSSIBLE?
CHECK IT OUT.
IS EVERYONE ALL RIGHT?

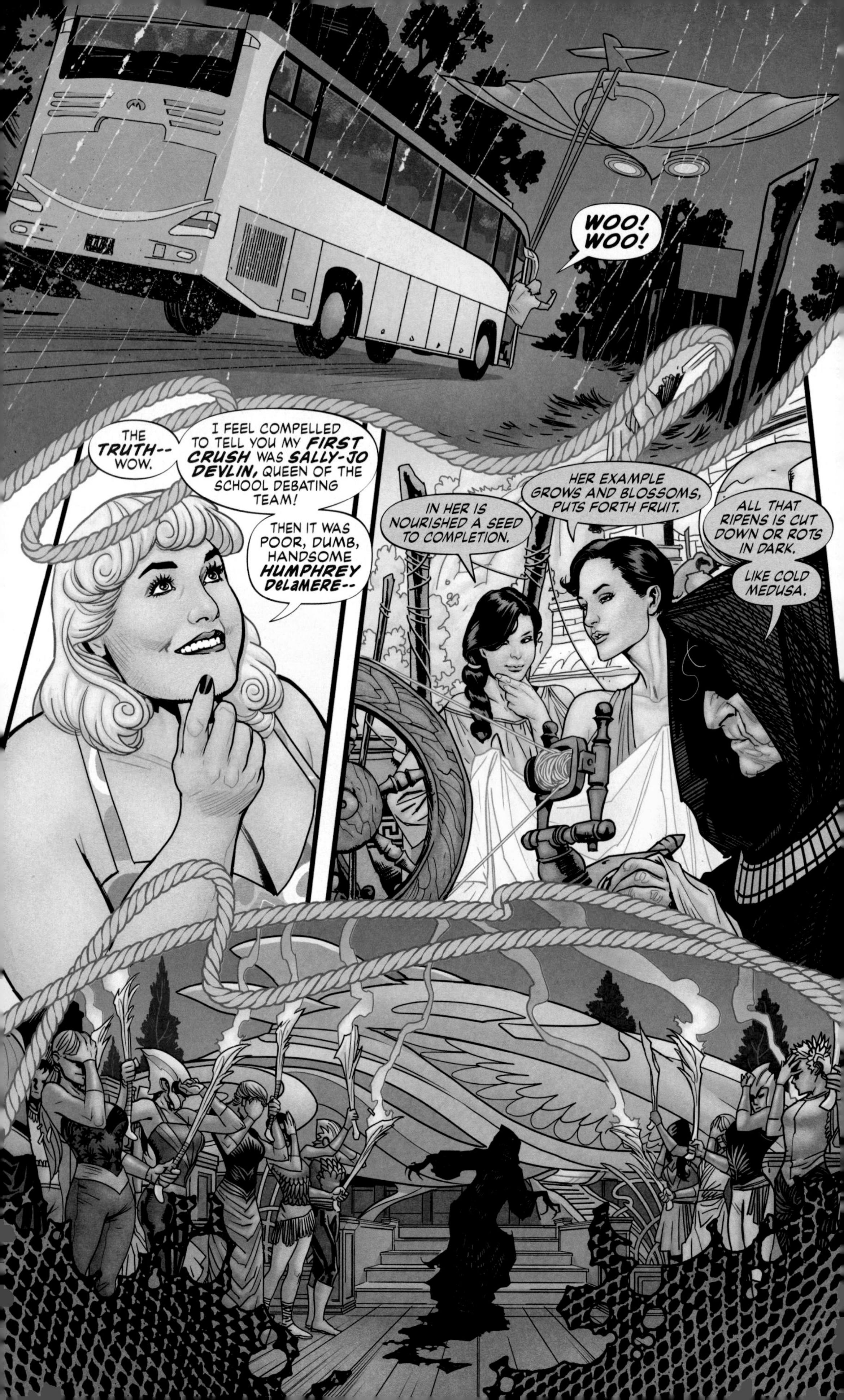
WOO! WOO!
THE TRUTH-- WOW.
I FEEL COMPELLED TO TELL YOU MY FIRST CRUSH WAS SALLY-JO DEVLIN, QUEEN OF THE SCHOOL DEBATING TEAM!
THEN IT WAS POOR, DUMB, HANDSOME HUMPHREY DeLAMERE--
IN HER IS NOURISHED A SEED TO COMPLETION.
HER EXAMPLE GROWS AND BLOSSOMS, PUTS FORTH FRUIT.
ALL THAT RIPENS IS CUT DOWN OR ROTS IN DARK.
LIKE COLD MEDUSA.

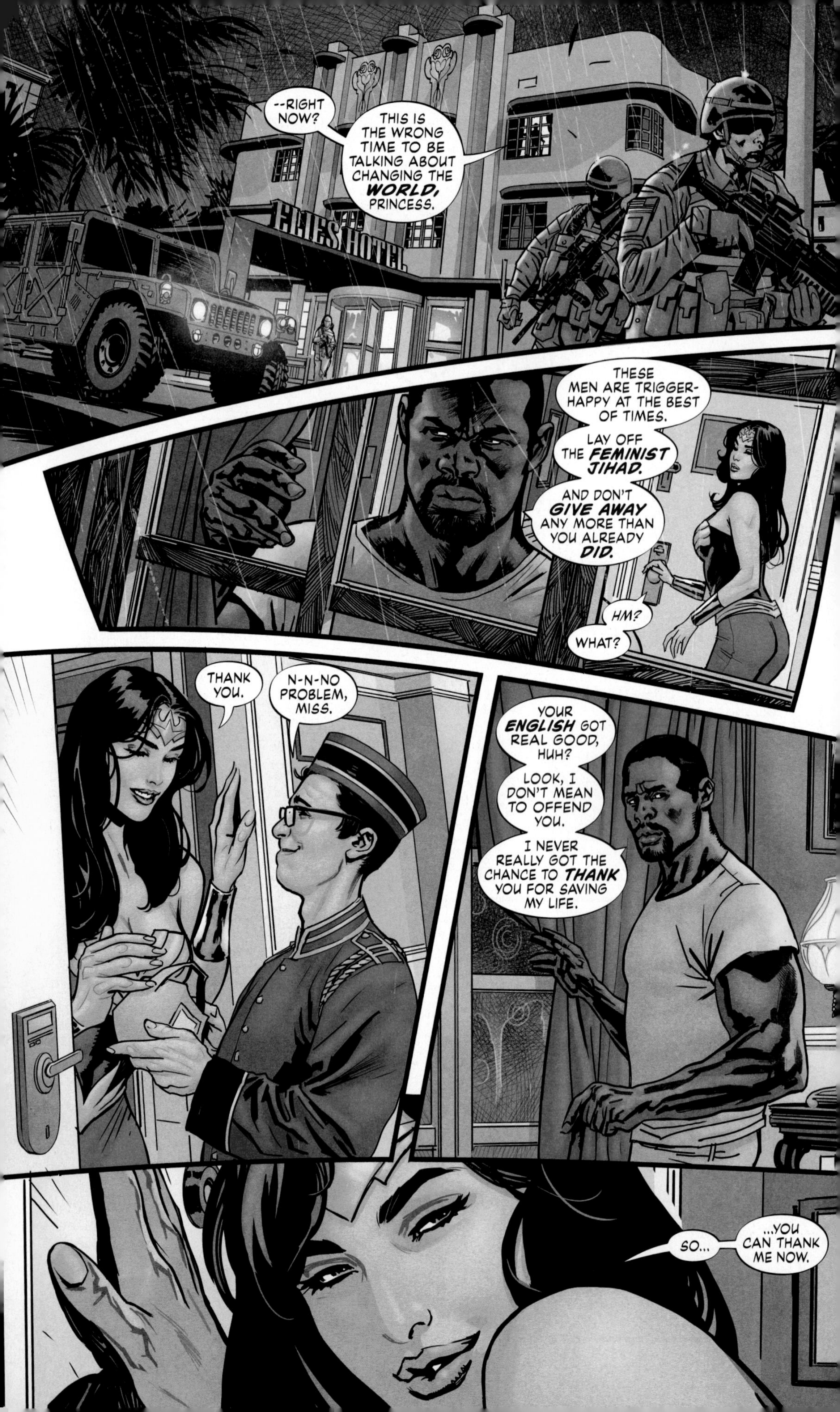
--RIGHT NOW?
THIS IS THE WRONG TIME TO BE TALKING ABOUT CHANGING THE **WORLD,** PRINCESS.
THESE MEN ARE TRIGGER-HAPPY AT THE BEST OF TIMES.
LAY OFF THE **FEMINIST JIHAD.**
AND DON'T **GIVE AWAY** ANY MORE THAN YOU ALREADY **DID.**
HM?
WHAT?
THANK YOU.
N-N-NO PROBLEM, MISS.
YOUR **ENGLISH** GOT REAL GOOD, HUH?
LOOK, I DON'T MEAN TO OFFEND YOU.
I NEVER REALLY GOT THE CHANCE TO **THANK** YOU FOR SAVING MY LIFE.
SO...
...YOU CAN THANK ME NOW.

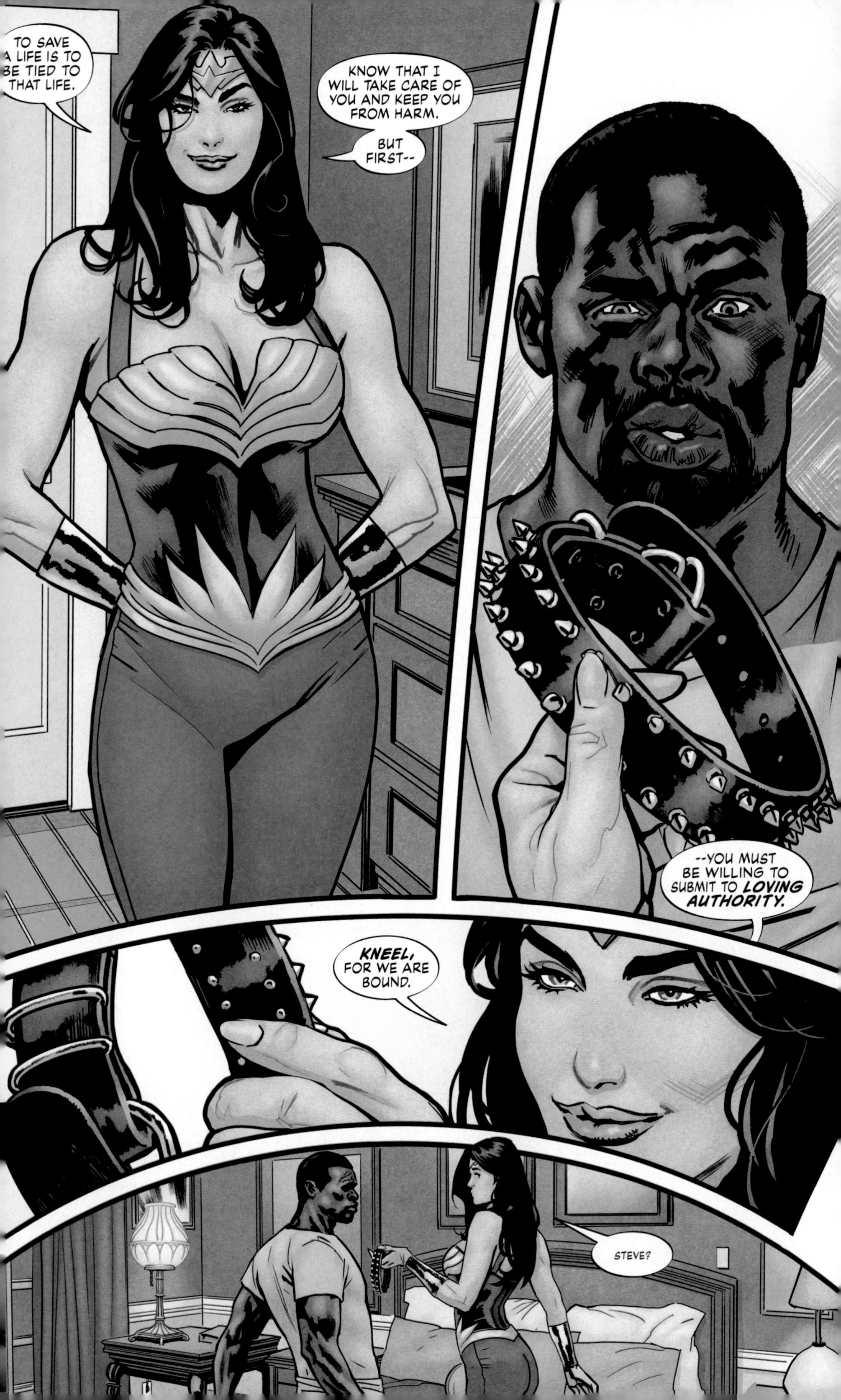

TO SAVE A LIFE IS TO BE TIED TO THAT LIFE.
KNOW THAT I WILL TAKE CARE OF YOU AND KEEP YOU FROM HARM.
BUT FIRST--
--YOU MUST BE WILLING TO SUBMIT TO LOVING AUTHORITY.
KNEEL, FOR WE ARE BOUND.
STEVE?

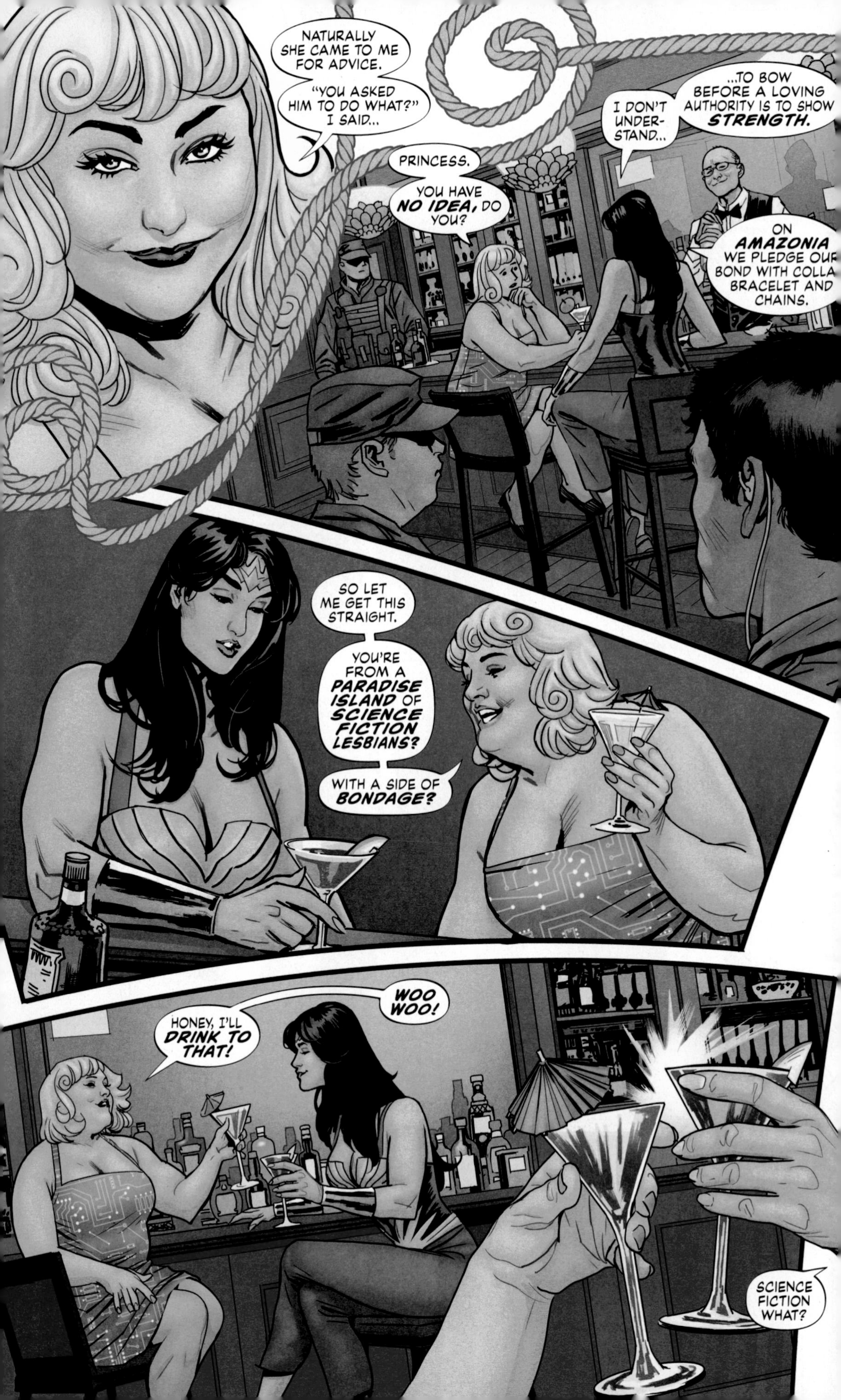

NATURALLY SHE CAME TO ME FOR ADVICE.
"YOU ASKED HIM TO DO WHAT?" I SAID...
PRINCESS.
YOU HAVE NO IDEA, DO YOU?
I DON'T UNDER-STAND...
...TO BOW BEFORE A LOVING AUTHORITY IS TO SHOW STRENGTH.
ON AMAZONIA WE PLEDGE OUR BOND WITH COLLA BRACELET AND CHAINS.
SO LET ME GET THIS STRAIGHT.
YOU'RE FROM A PARADISE ISLAND OF SCIENCE FICTION LESBIANS?
WITH A SIDE OF BONDAGE?
HONEY, I'LL DRINK TO THAT!
WOO WOO!
SCIENCE FICTION WHAT?

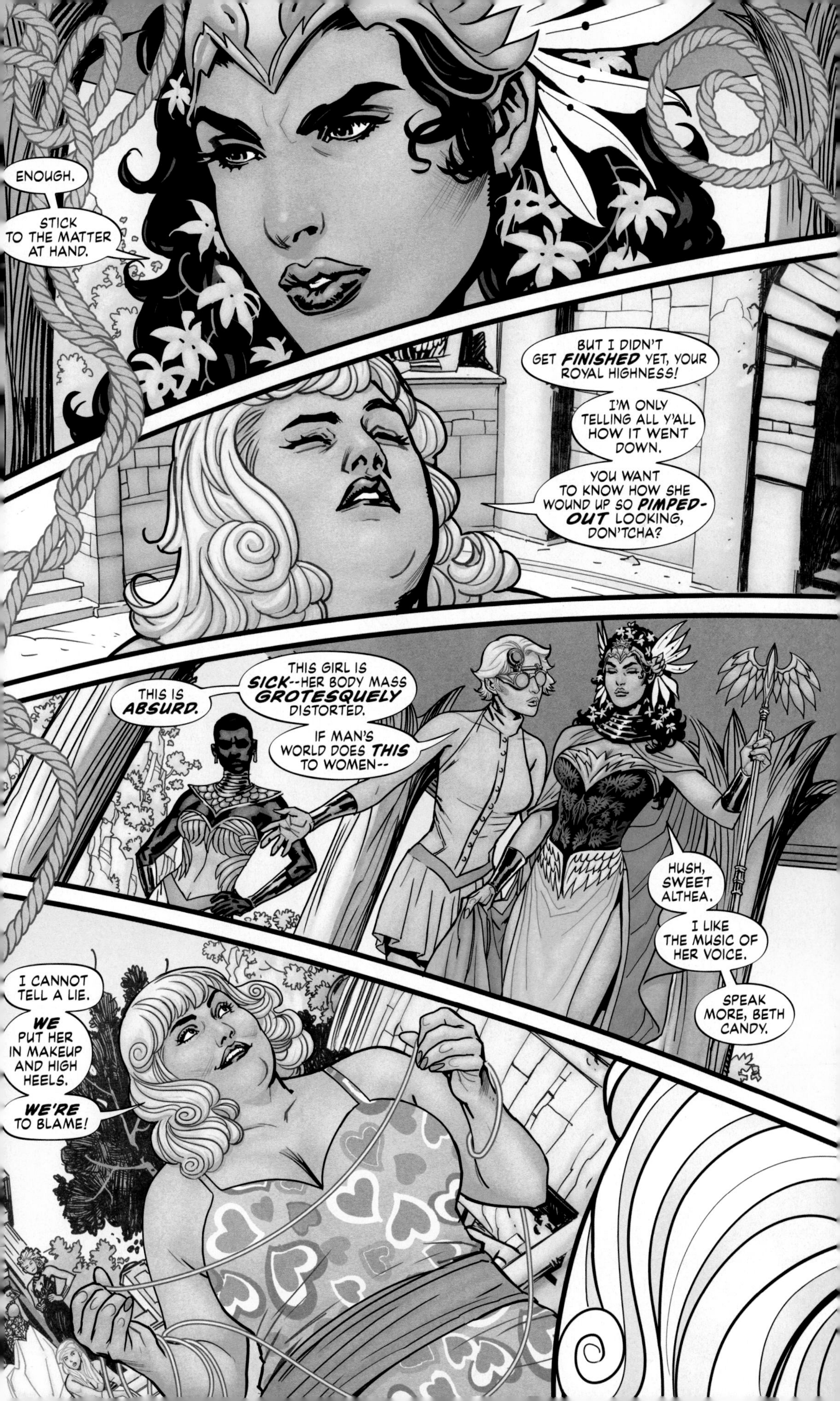
ENOUGH.
STICK TO THE MATTER AT HAND.
BUT I DIDN'T GET FINISHED YET, YOUR ROYAL HIGHNESS!
I'M ONLY TELLING ALL Y'ALL HOW IT WENT DOWN.
YOU WANT TO KNOW HOW SHE WOUND UP SO PIMPED-OUT LOOKING, DON'TCHA?
THIS IS ABSURD.
THIS GIRL IS SICK--HER BODY MASS GROTESQUELY DISTORTED.
IF MAN'S WORLD DOES THIS TO WOMEN--
HUSH, SWEET ALTHEA.
I LIKE THE MUSIC OF HER VOICE.
SPEAK MORE, BETH CANDY.
I CANNOT TELL A LIE.
WE PUT HER IN MAKEUP AND HIGH HEELS.
WE'RE TO BLAME!

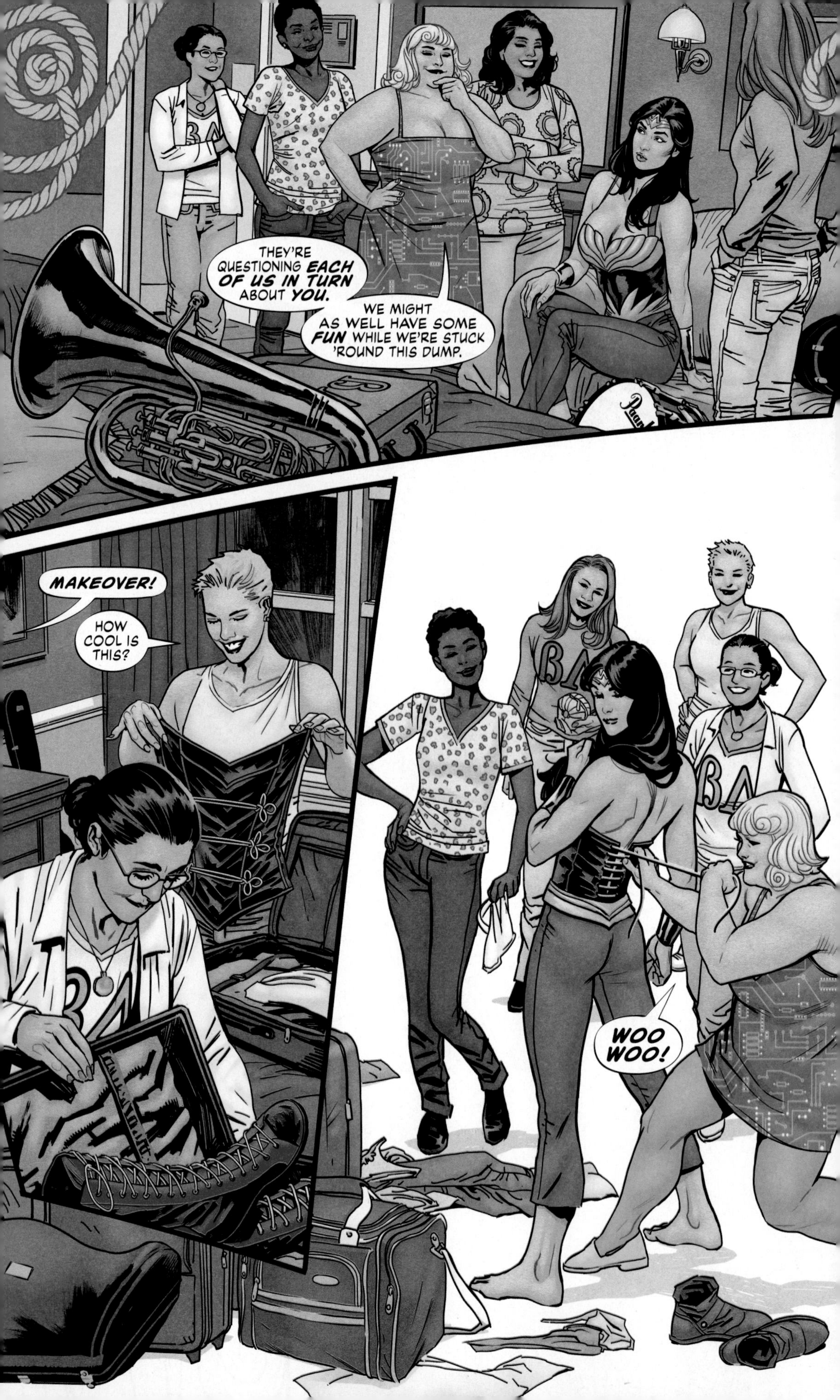
THEY'RE QUESTIONING EACH OF US IN TURN ABOUT YOU.
WE MIGHT AS WELL HAVE SOME FUN WHILE WE'RE STUCK 'ROUND THIS DUMP.
MAKEOVER!
HOW COOL IS THIS?
WOO WOO!

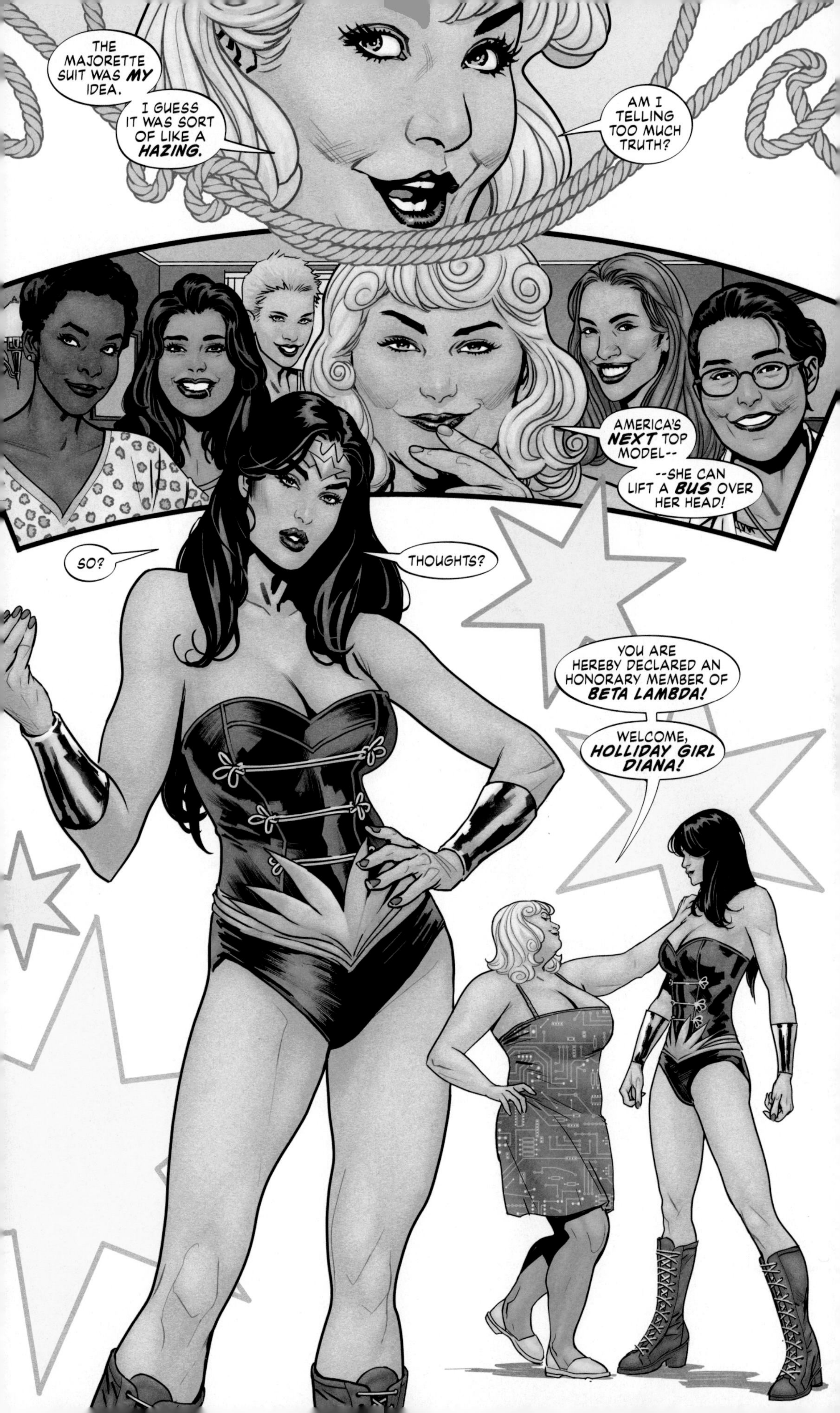
THE MAJORETTE SUIT WAS MY IDEA.
I GUESS IT WAS SORT OF LIKE A HAZING.
AM I TELLING TOO MUCH TRUTH?
AMERICA'S NEXT TOP MODEL--
--SHE CAN LIFT A BUS OVER HER HEAD!
SO?
THOUGHTS?
YOU ARE HEREBY DECLARED AN HONORARY MEMBER OF BETA LAMBDA!
WELCOME, HOLLIDAY GIRL DIANA!

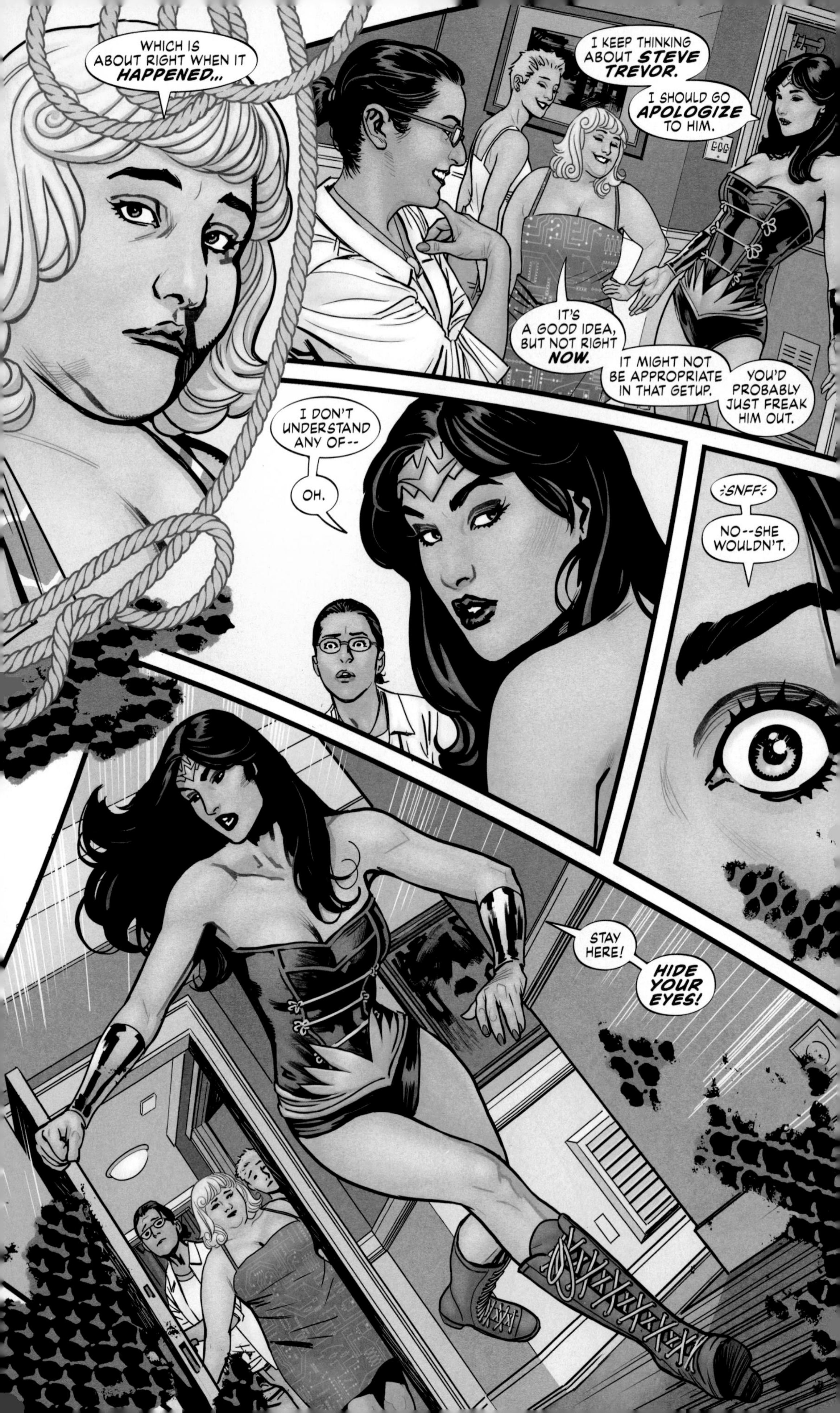
WHICH IS ABOUT RIGHT WHEN IT HAPPENED...
I KEEP THINKING ABOUT STEVE TREVOR.
I SHOULD GO APOLOGIZE TO HIM.
IT'S A GOOD IDEA, BUT NOT RIGHT NOW.
IT MIGHT NOT BE APPROPRIATE IN THAT GETUP.
YOU'D PROBABLY JUST FREAK HIM OUT.
I DON'T UNDERSTAND ANY OF--
OH.
SNFF
NO--SHE WOULDN'T.
STAY HERE!
HIDE YOUR EYES!

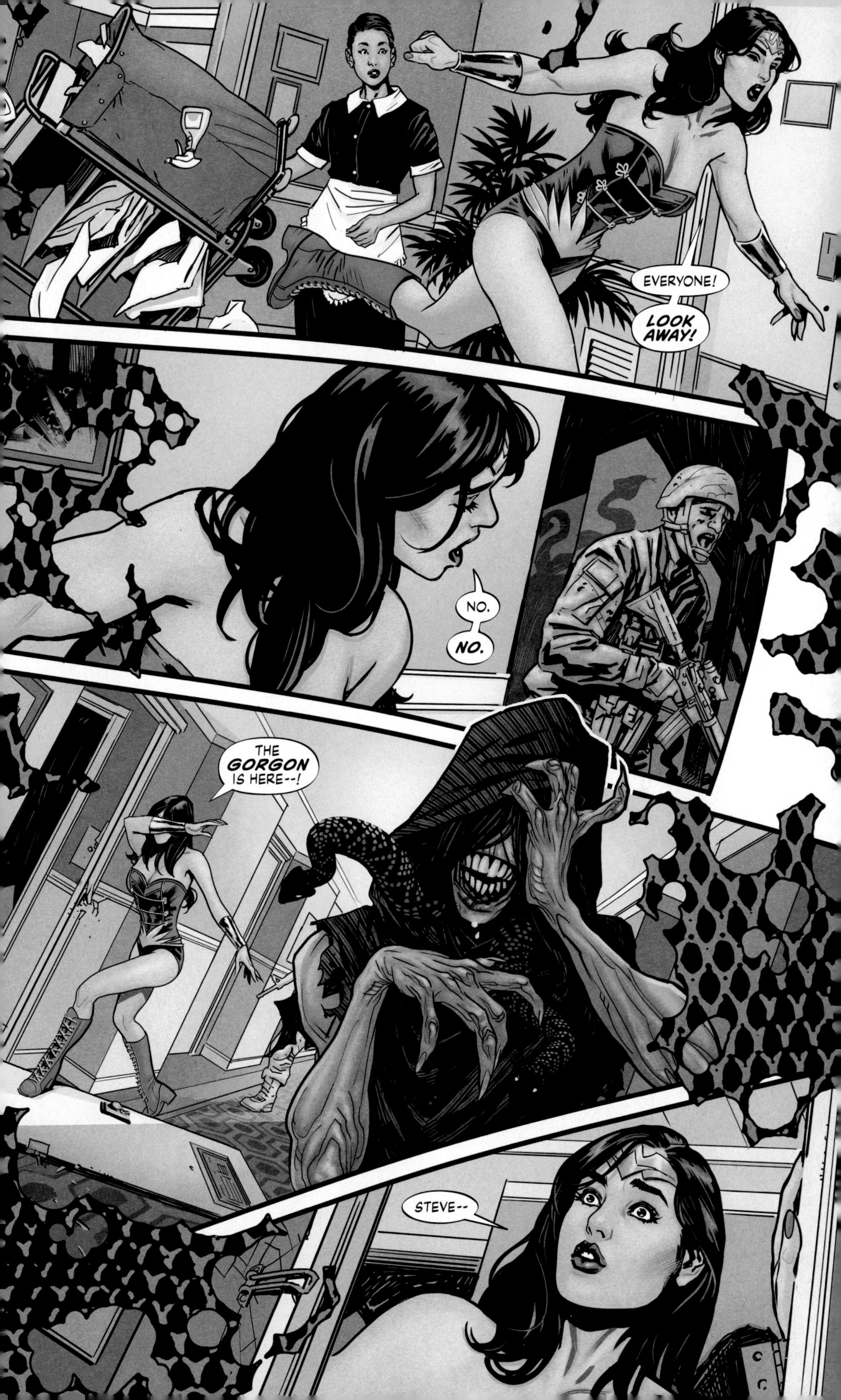

EVERYONE!
LOOK AWAY!
NO.
NO.
THE GORGON IS HERE--!
STEVE--

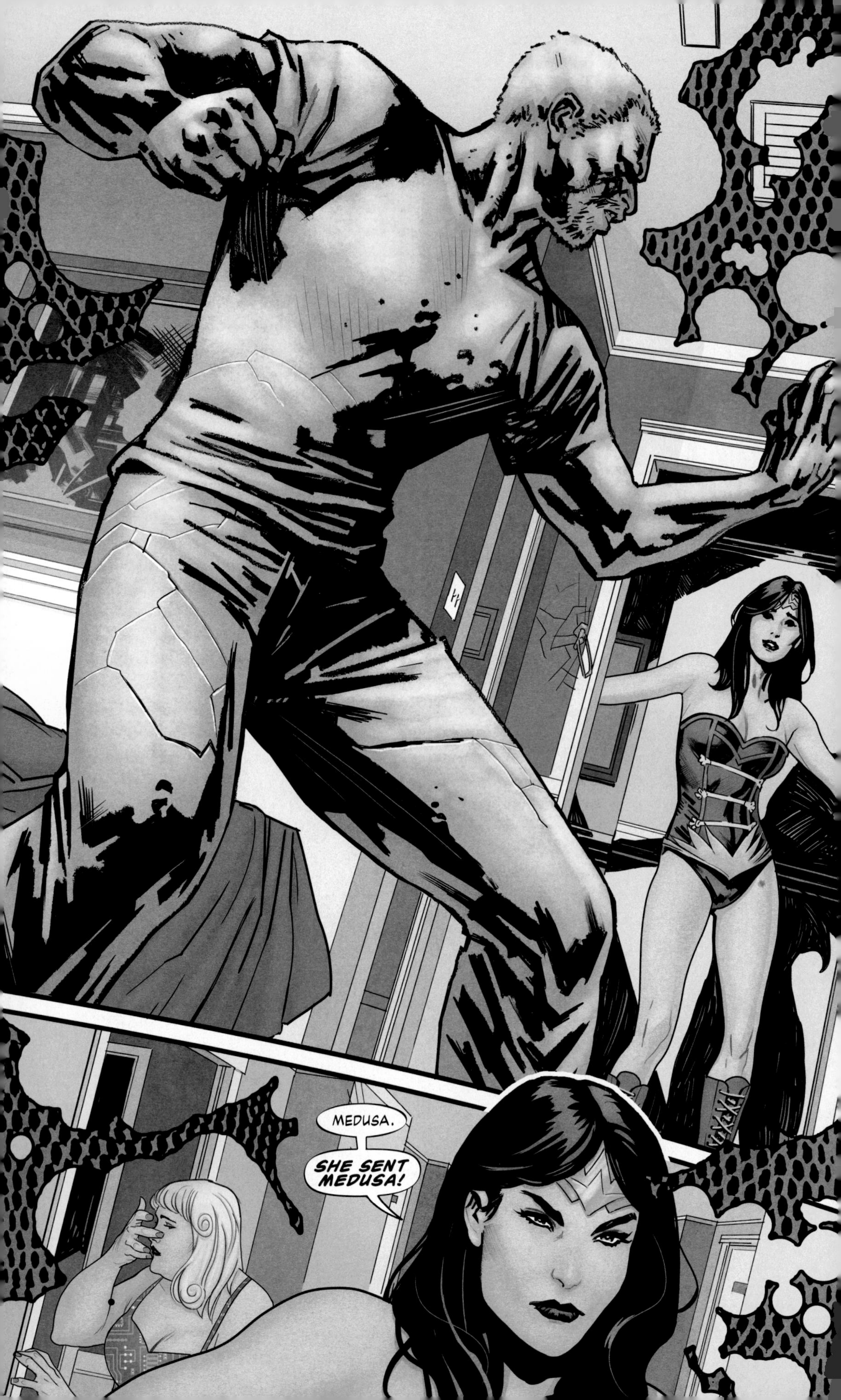
MEDUSA.
SHE SENT MEDUSA!

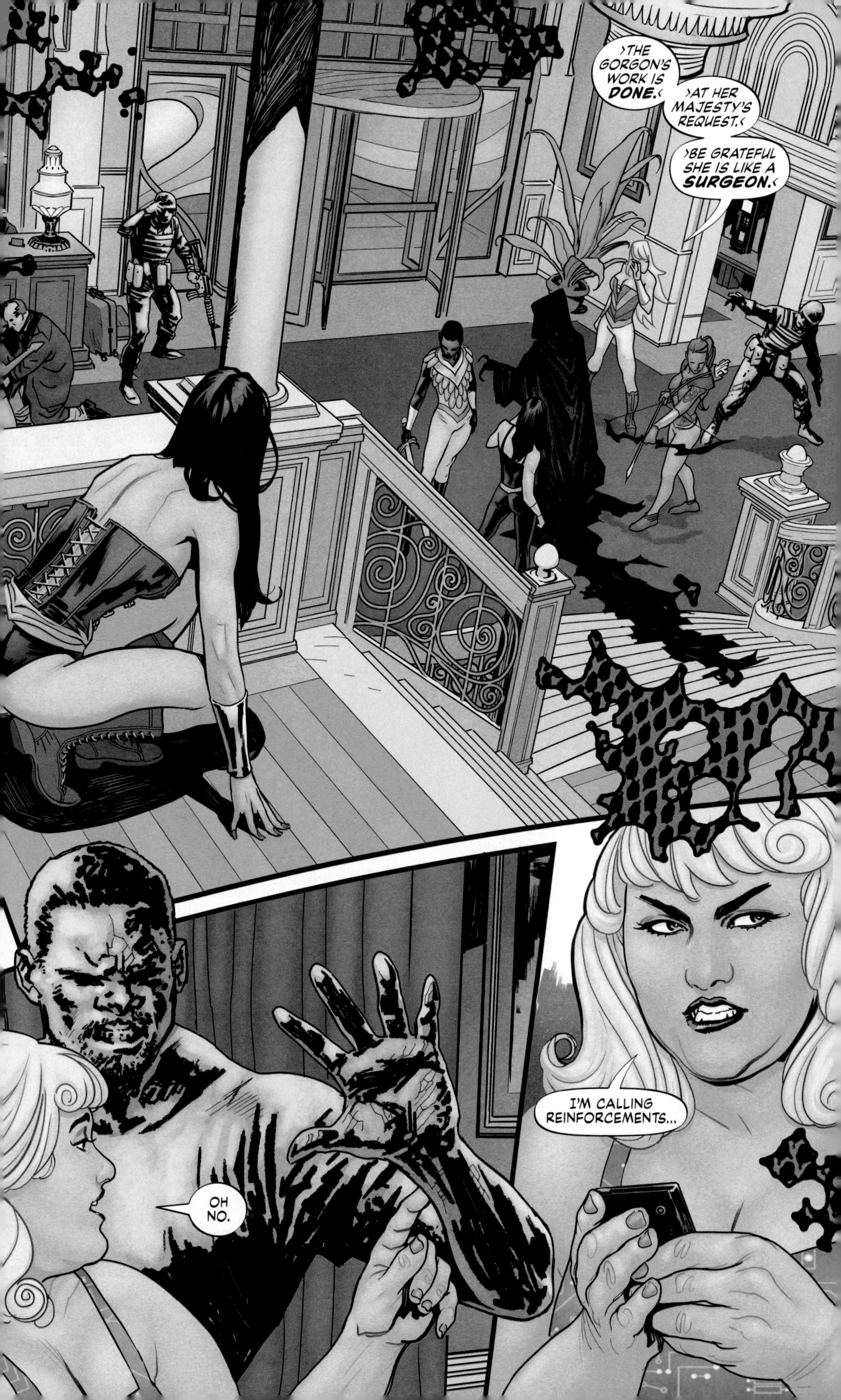

›THE GORGON'S WORK IS DONE.‹
›AT HER MAJESTY'S REQUEST.‹
›BE GRATEFUL SHE IS LIKE A SURGEON.‹
I'M CALLING REINFORCEMENTS...
OH NO.

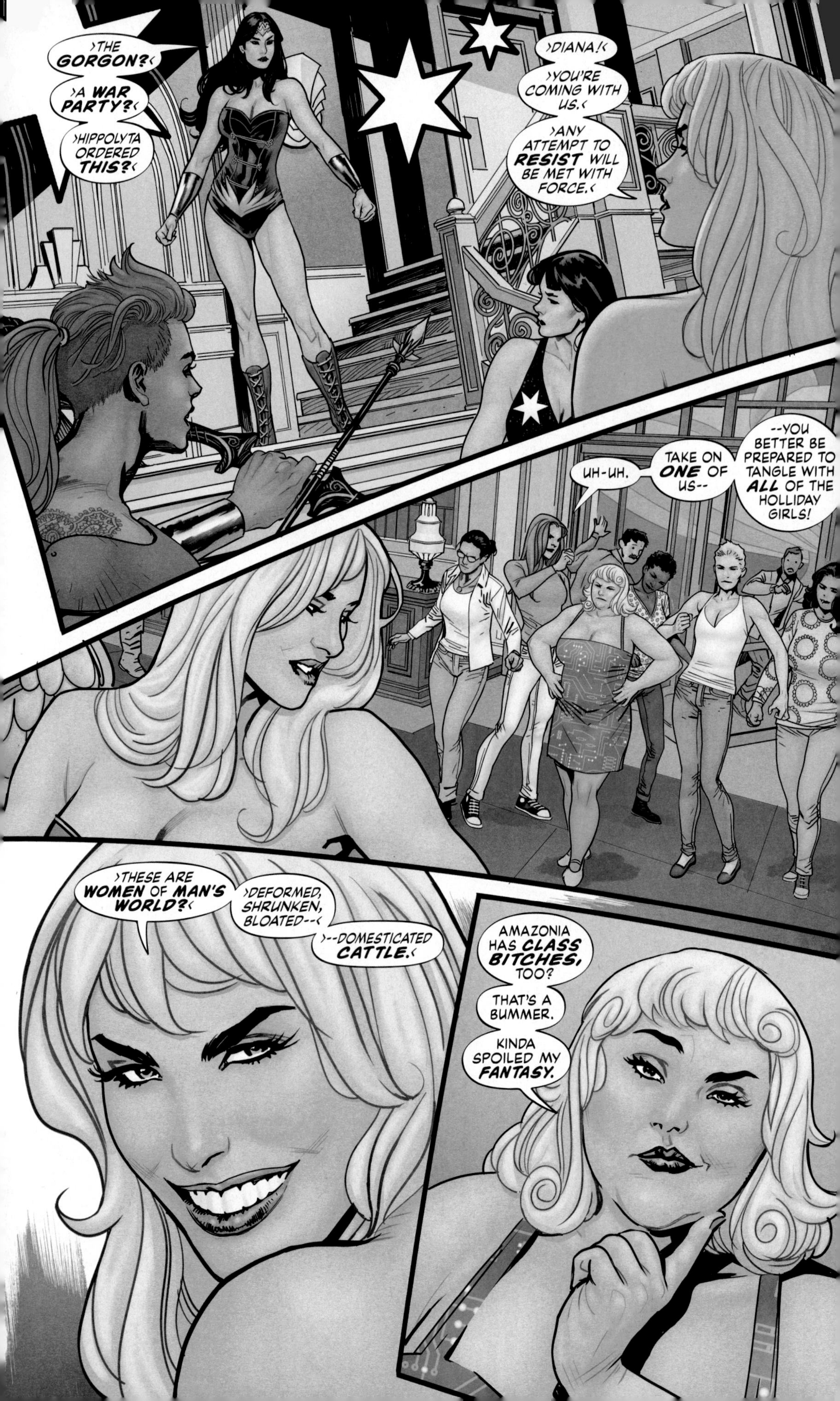

›THE GORGON?‹
›A WAR PARTY?‹
›HIPPOLYTA ORDERED THIS?‹
›DIANA!‹
›YOU'RE COMING WITH US.‹
›ANY ATTEMPT TO RESIST WILL BE MET WITH FORCE.‹
UH-UH.
TAKE ON ONE OF US--
--YOU BETTER BE PREPARED TO TANGLE WITH ALL OF THE HOLLIDAY GIRLS!
›THESE ARE WOMEN OF MAN'S WORLD?‹
›DEFORMED, SHRUNKEN, BLOATED--‹
›--DOMESTICATED CATTLE.‹
AMAZONIA HAS CLASS BITCHES, TOO?
THAT'S A BUMMER.
KINDA SPOILED MY FANTASY.

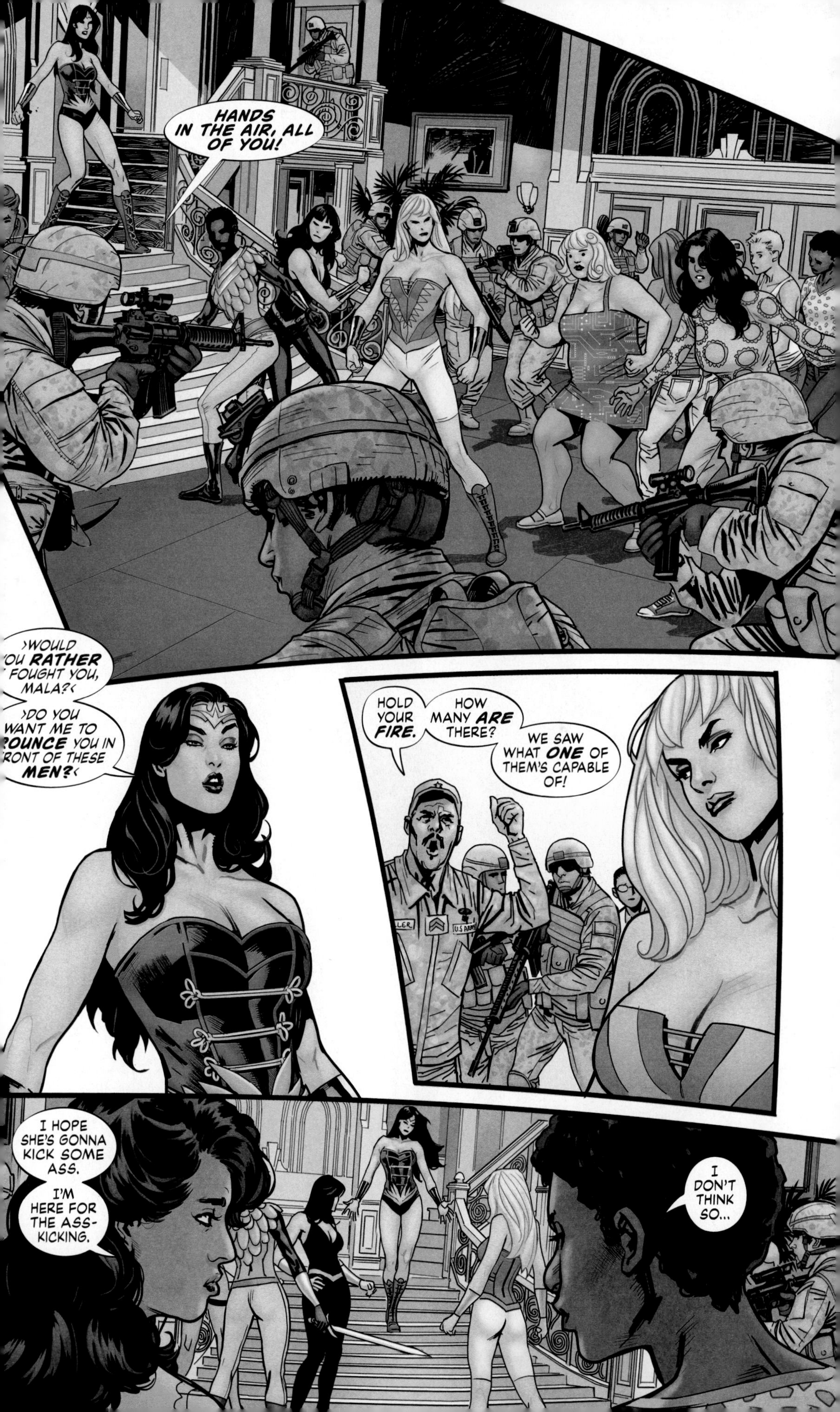
HANDS IN THE AIR, ALL OF YOU!
›WOULD YOU RATHER I FOUGHT YOU, MALA?‹
›DO YOU WANT ME TO TROUNCE YOU IN FRONT OF THESE MEN?‹
HOLD YOUR FIRE.
HOW MANY ARE THERE?
WE SAW WHAT ONE OF THEM'S CAPABLE OF!
I HOPE SHE'S GONNA KICK SOME ASS.
I'M HERE FOR THE ASS-KICKING.
I DON'T THINK SO...

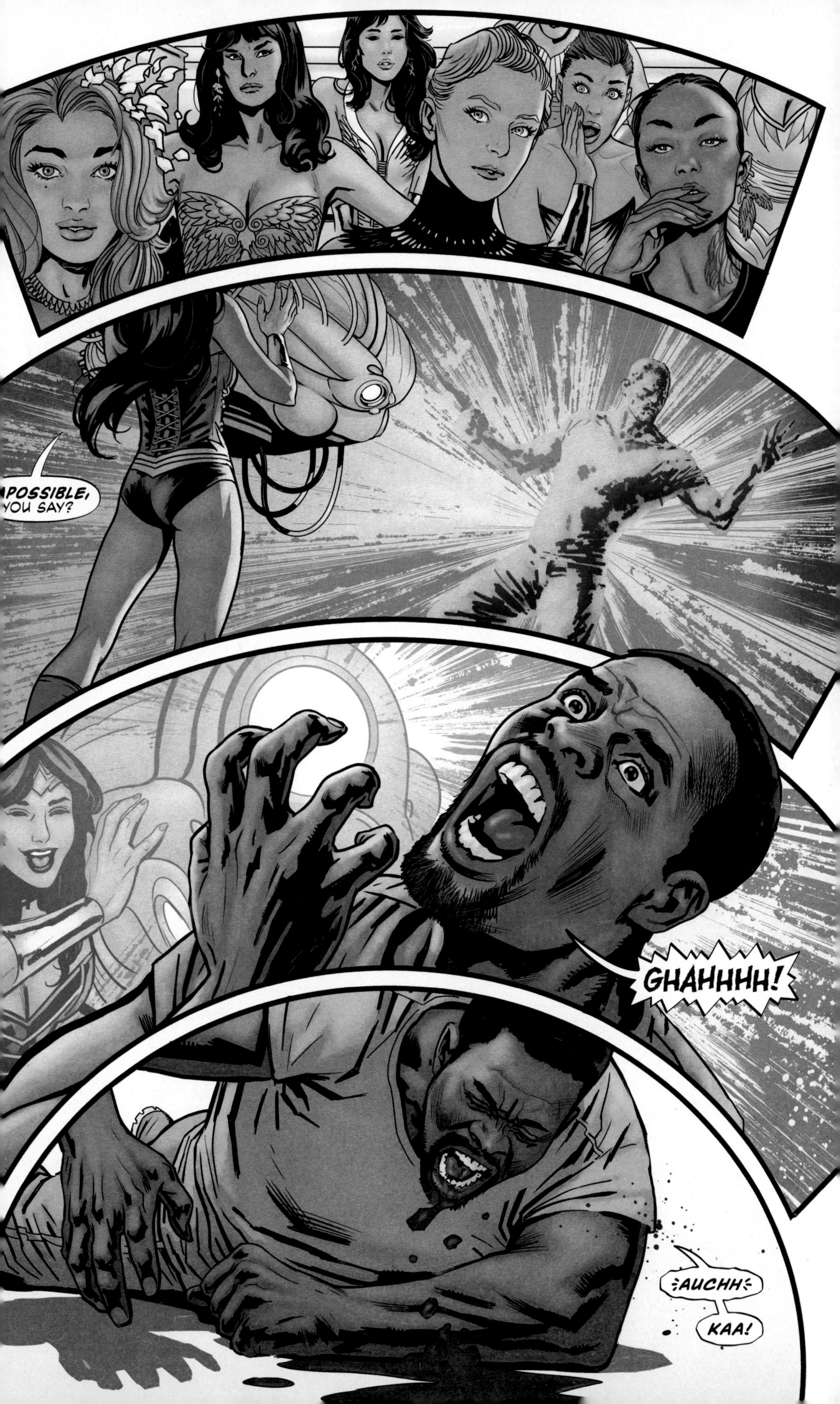
POSSIBLE, YOU SAY?
GHAHHHH!
AUCHH
KAA!

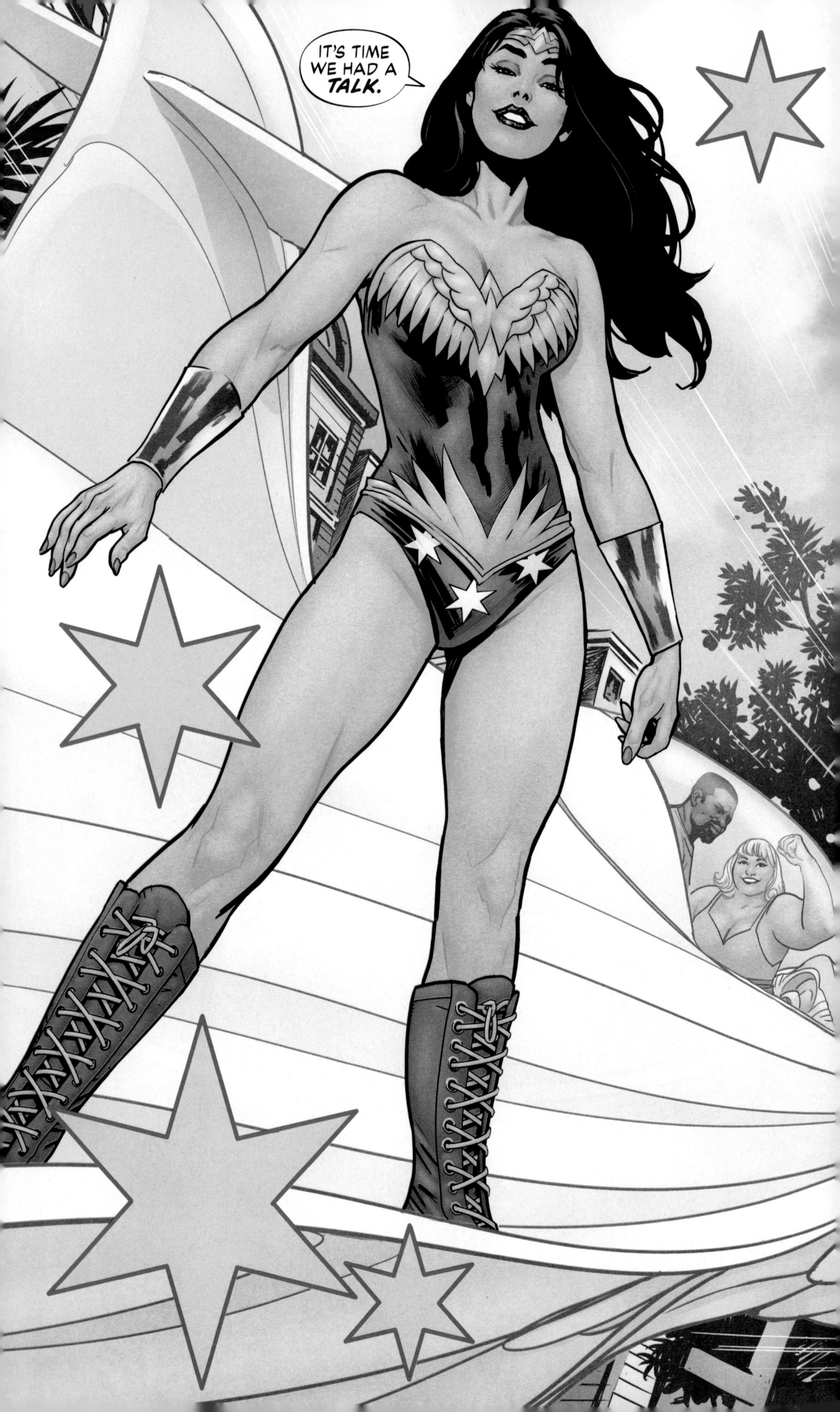
IT'S TIME WE HAD A TALK.

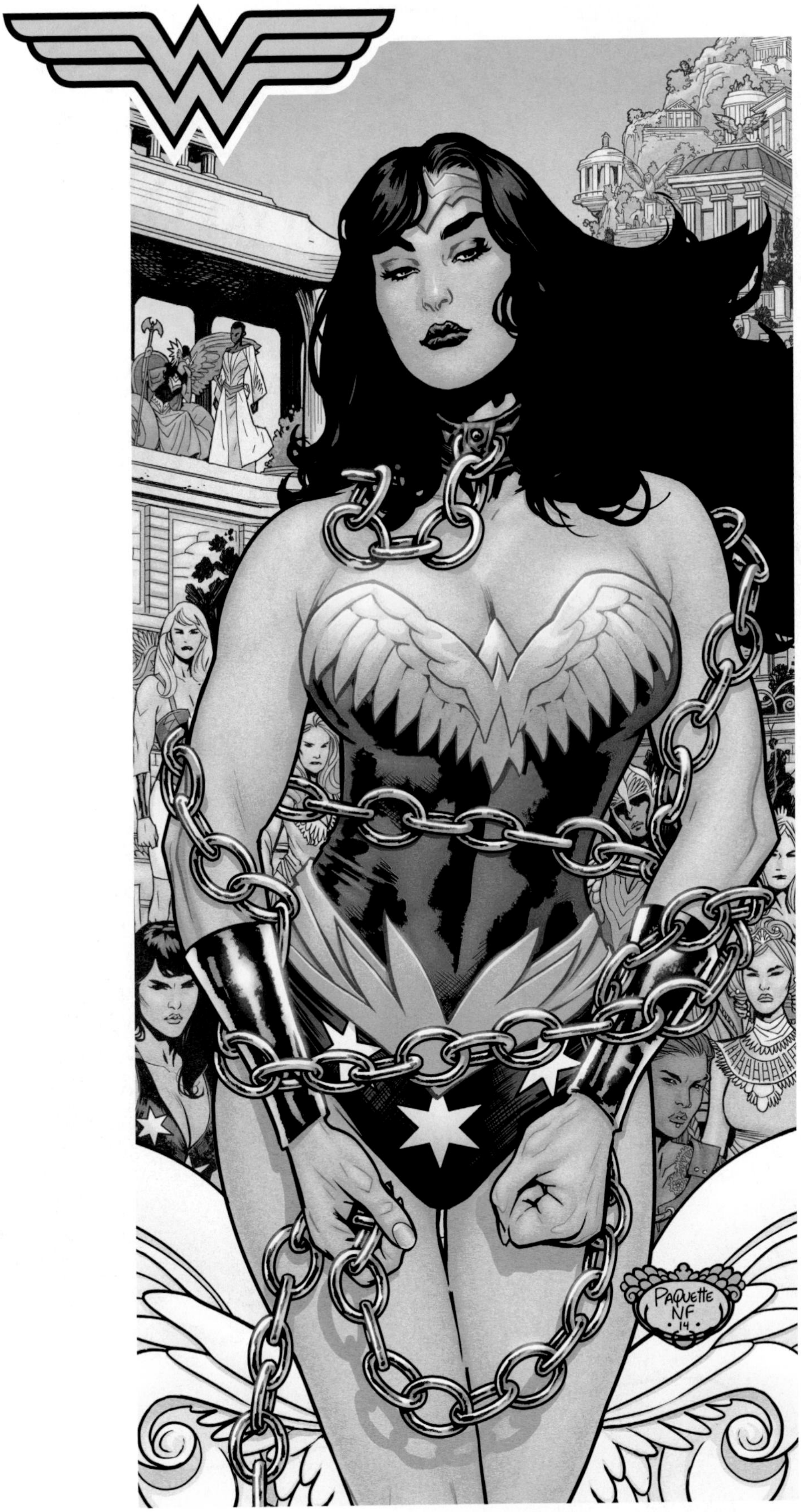
PAQUETTE
NF
'14

Earth One Sketchbook

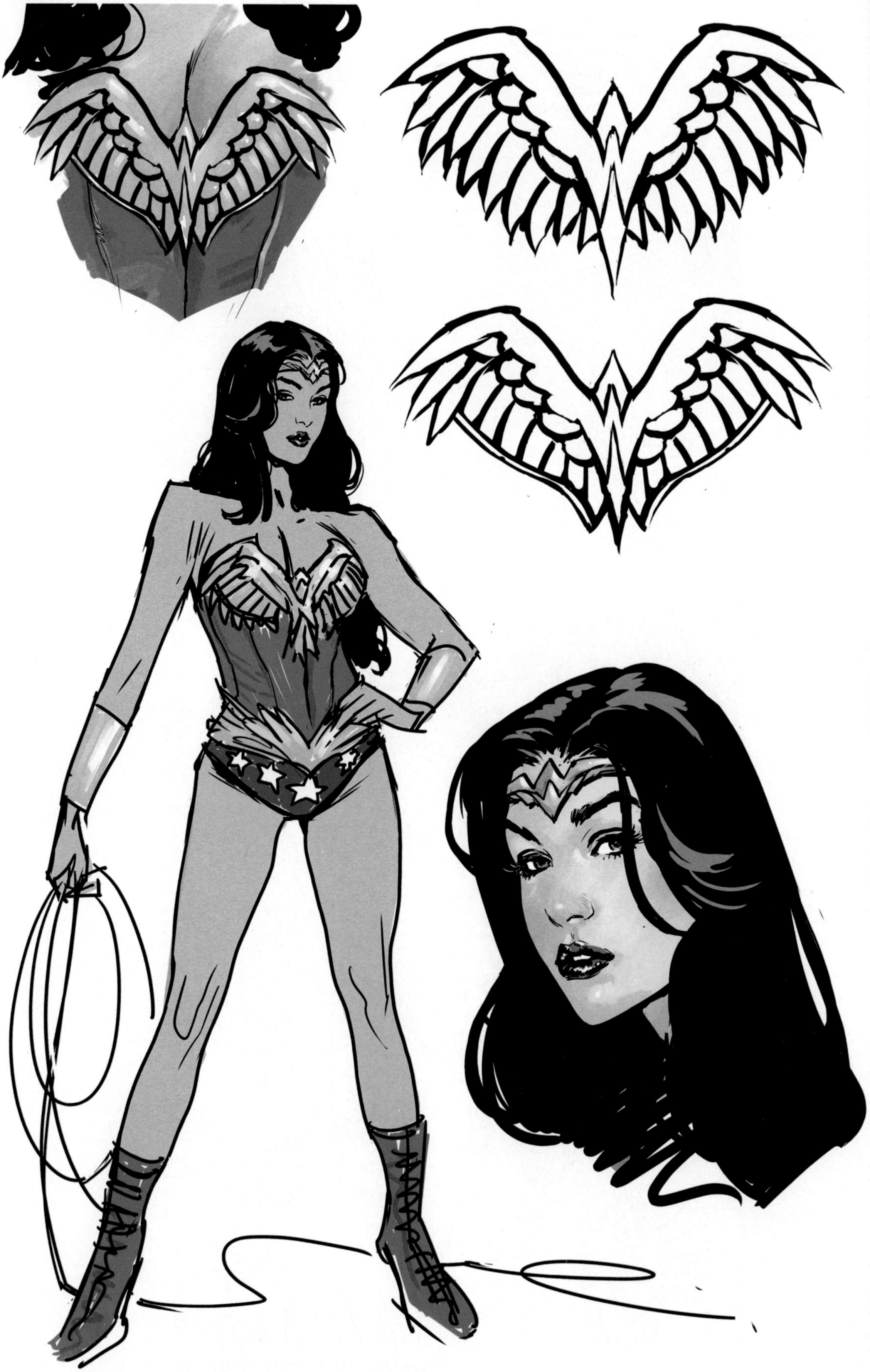

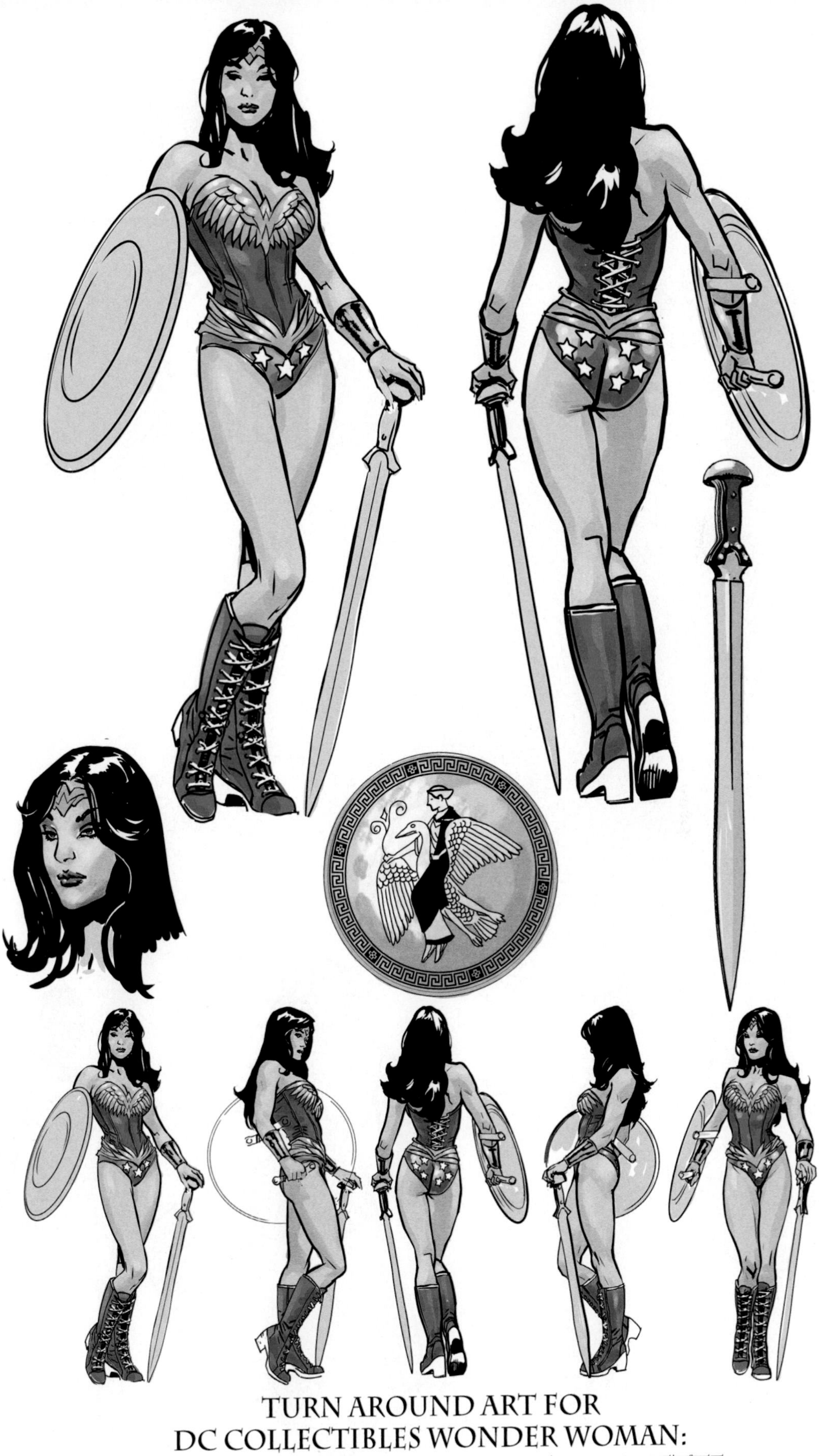

TURN AROUND ART FOR
DC COLLECTIBLES WONDER WOMAN:
ART OF WAR STATUE BY YANICK PAQUETTE

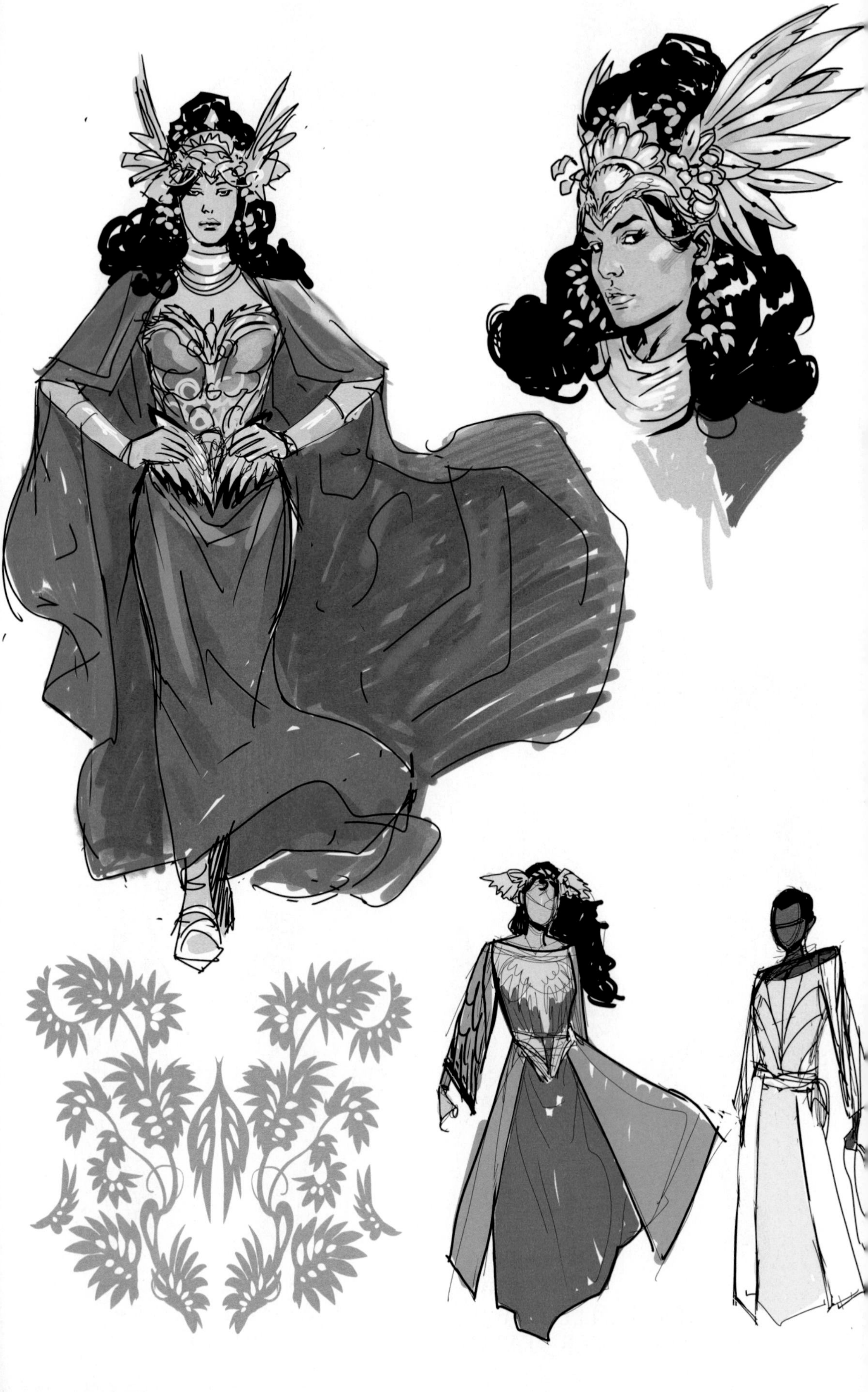

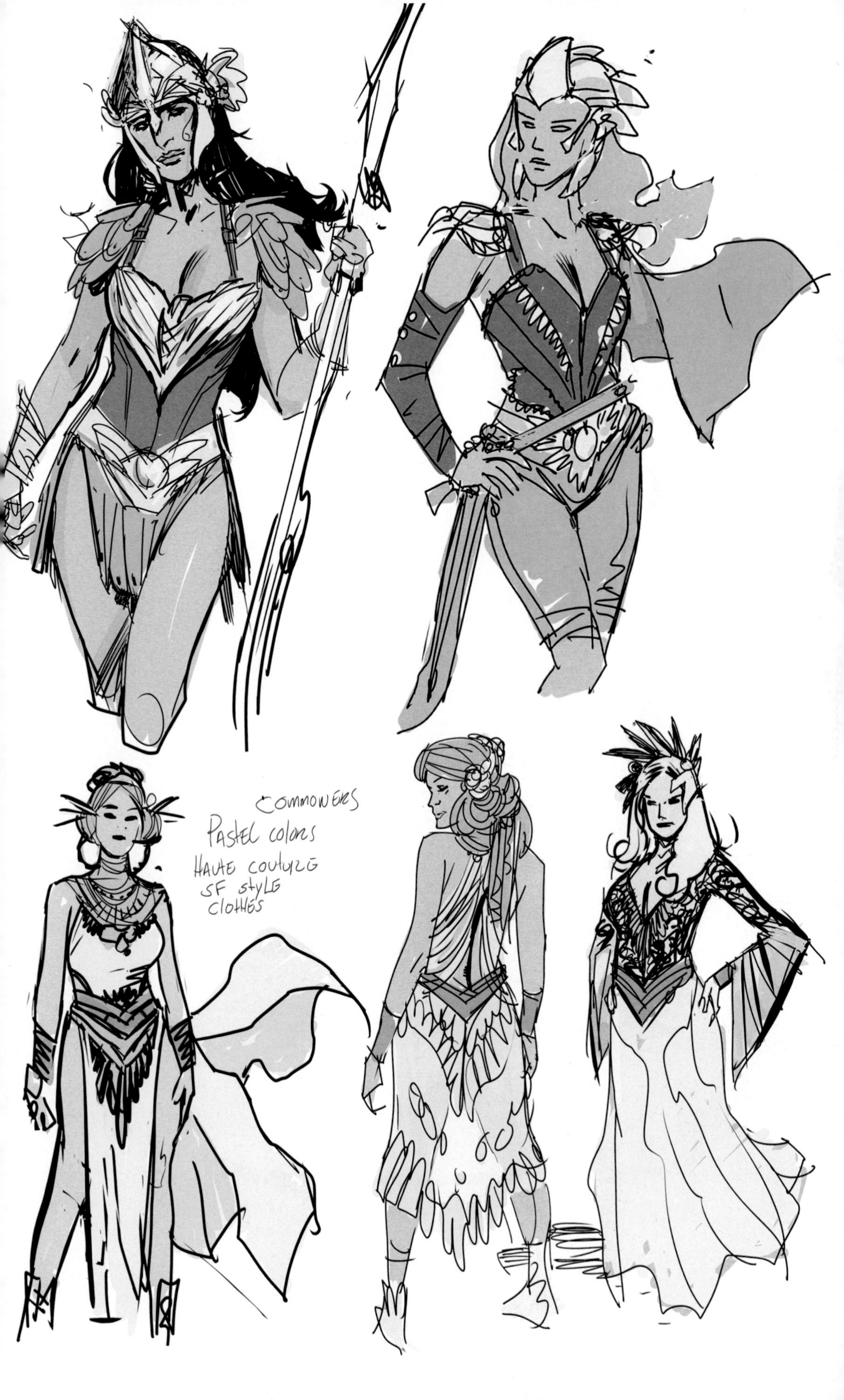
COMMONERS
Pastel colors
Haute couture
SF style
clothes

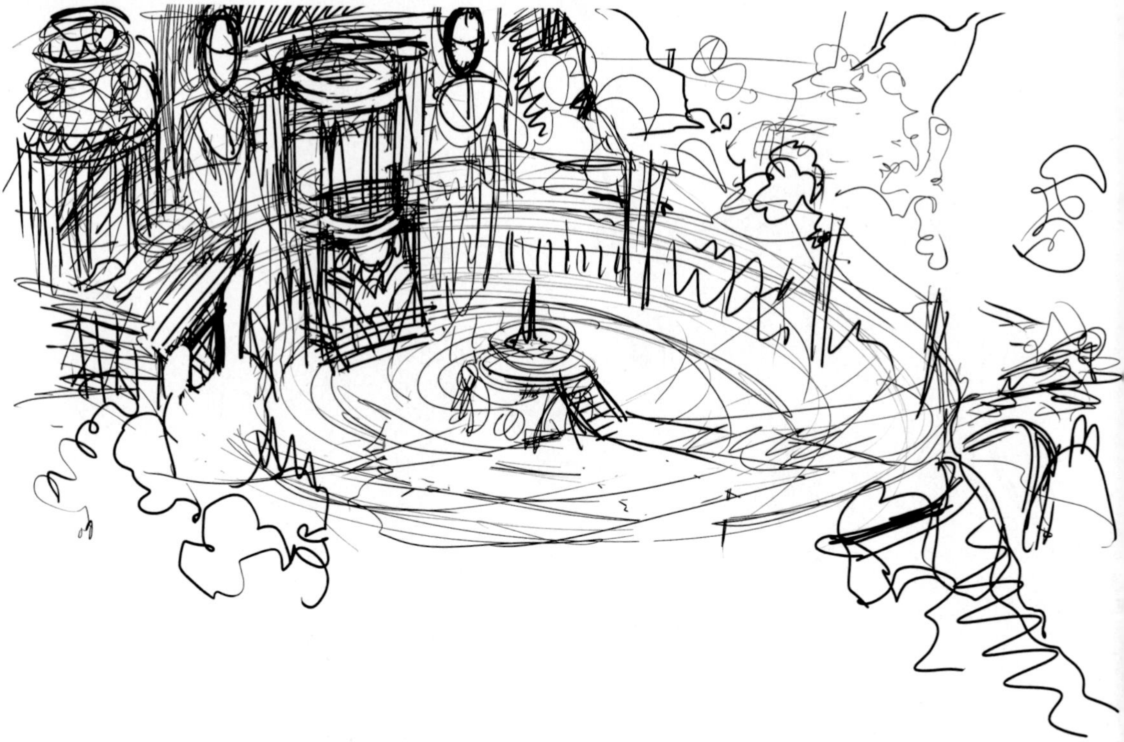

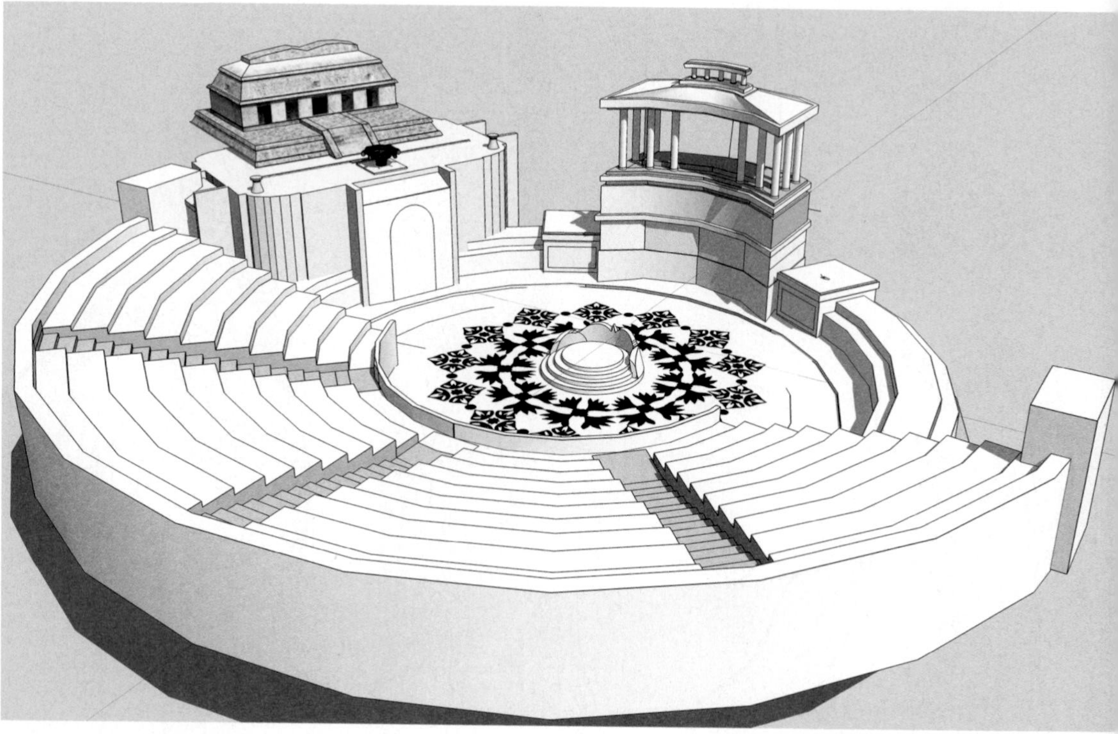

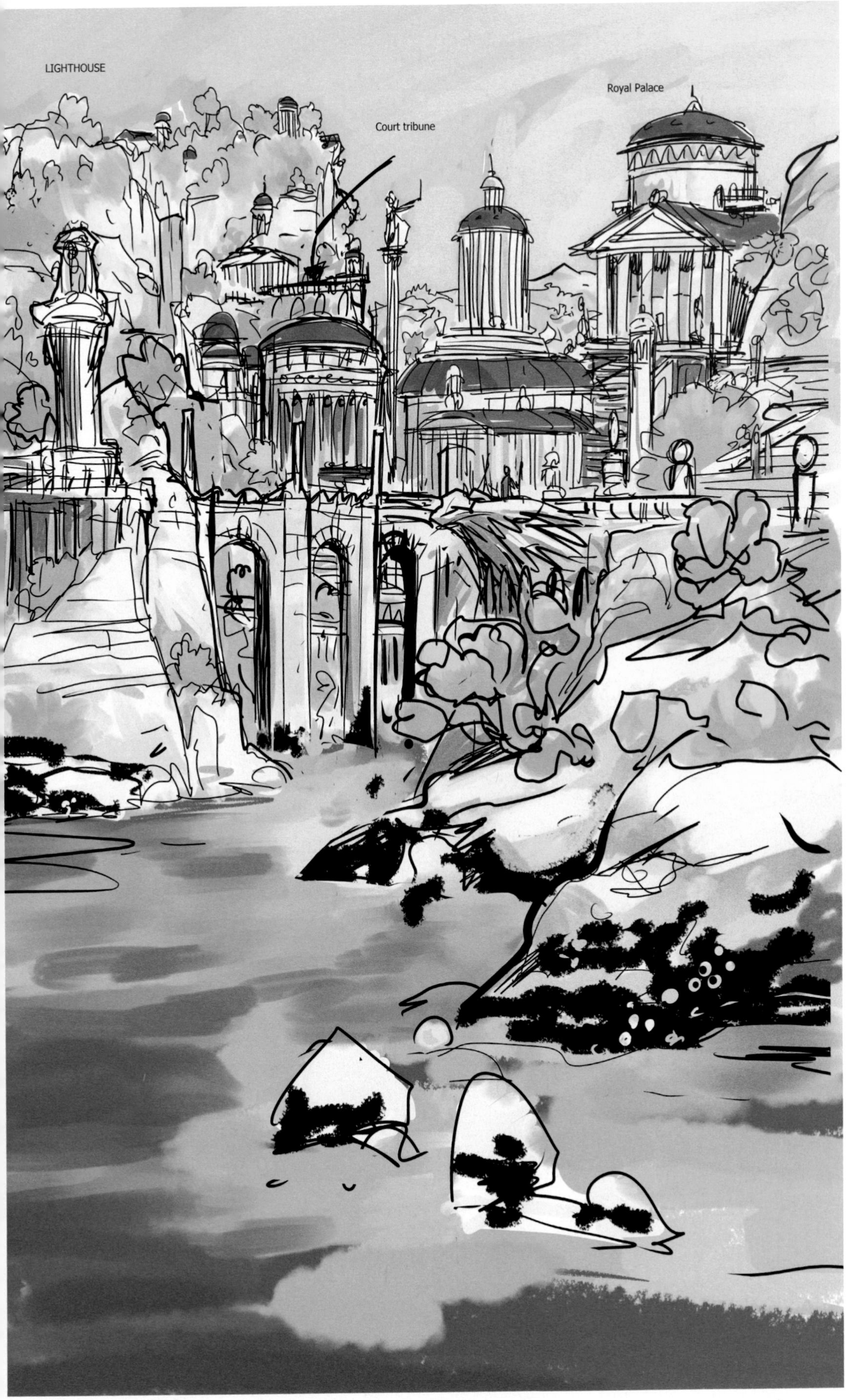
LIGHTHOUSE
Court tribune
Royal Palace

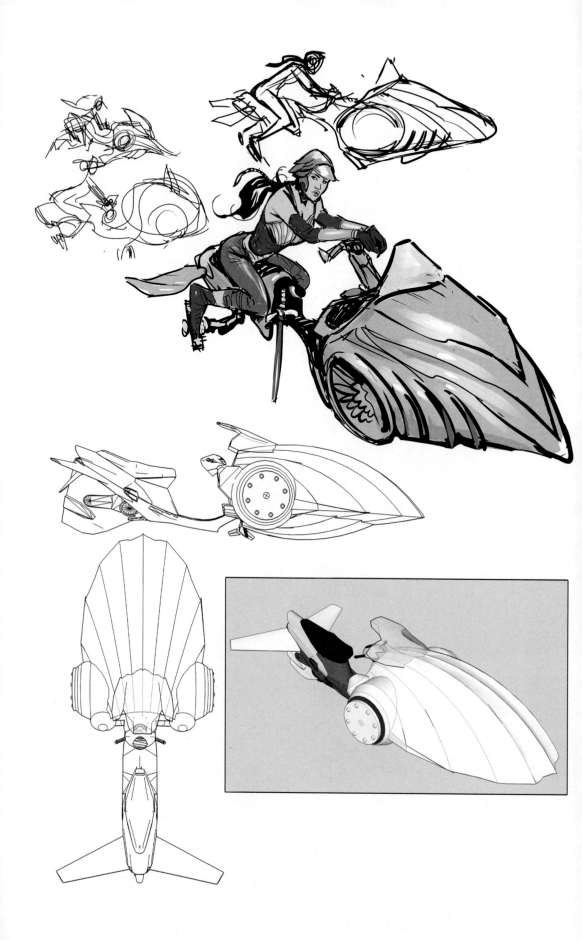

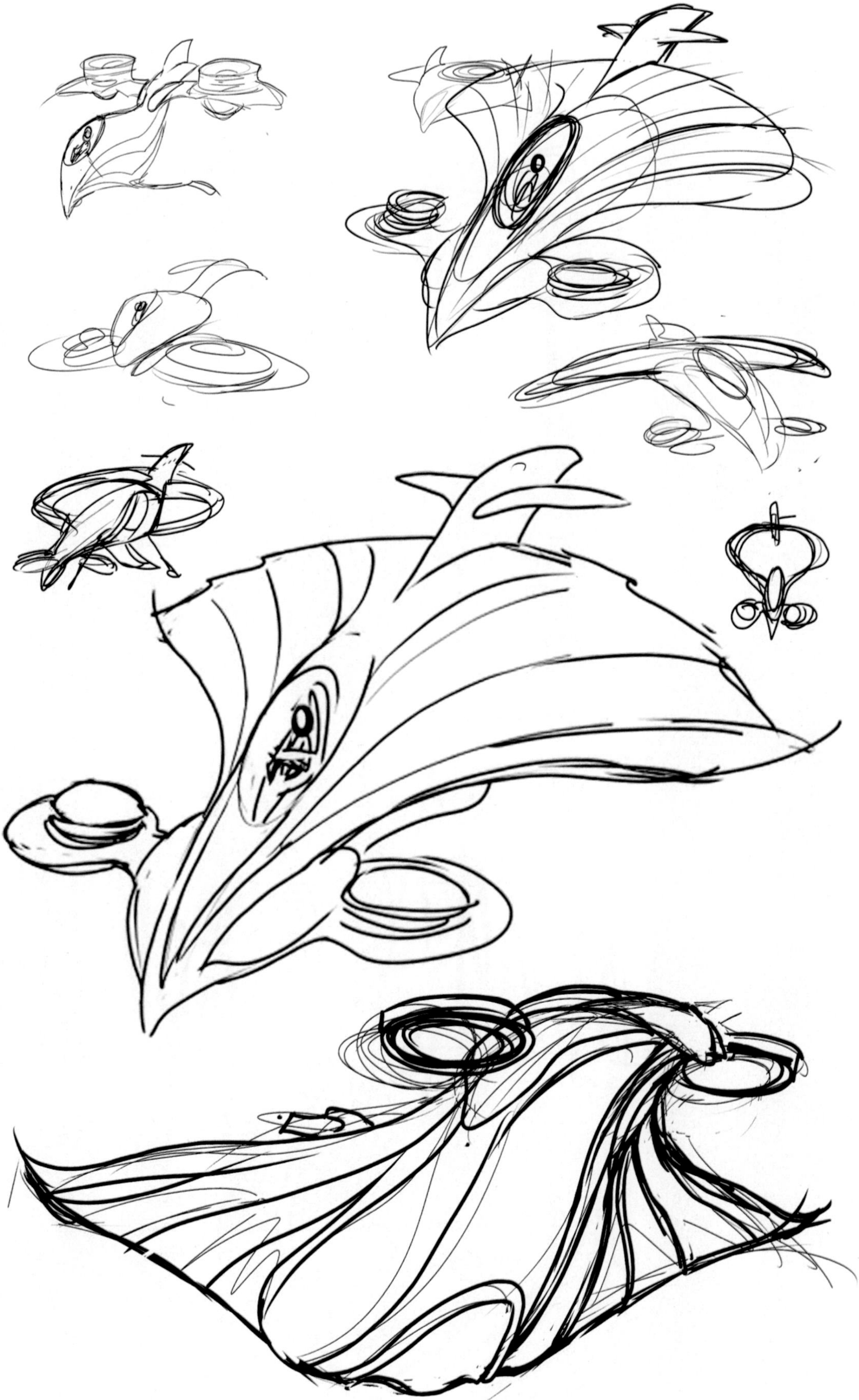

EARTH
ONE

*Grant
Morrison
Yanick Paquette*

DC COMICS™

EARTH
ONE

Grant Morrison

Yanick Paquette

DC COMICS™

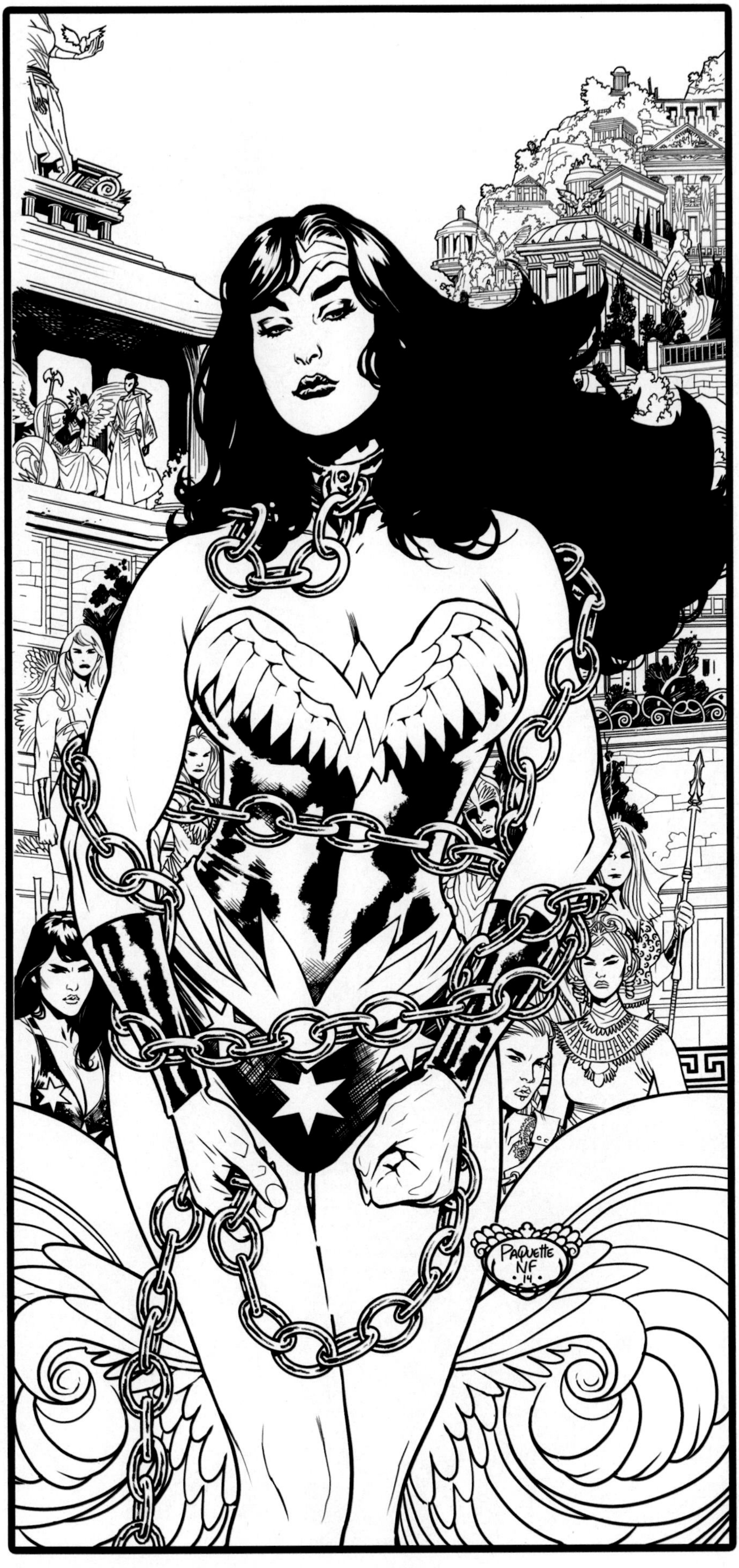
PAQUETTE
NF
'14

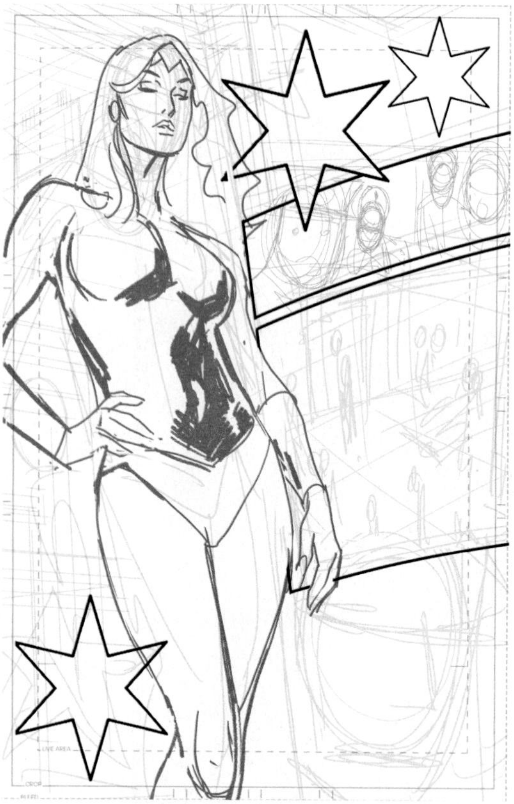

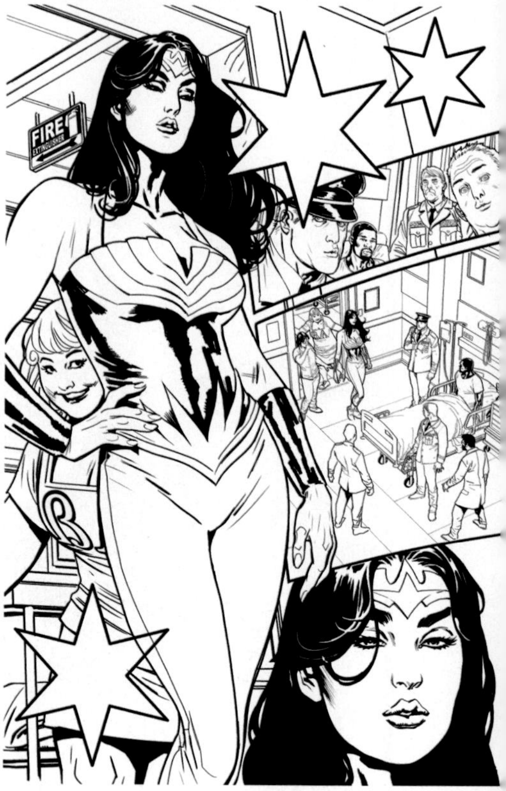
FIRE
EXTINGUISHER

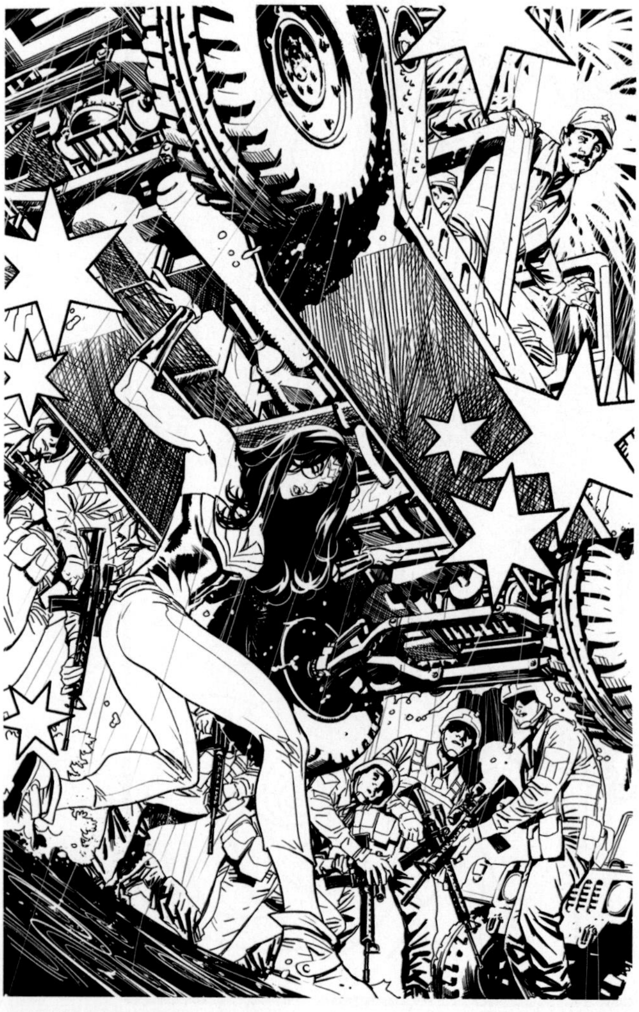

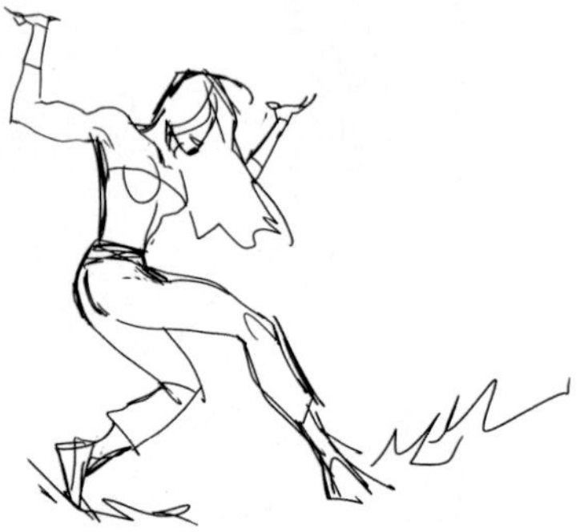

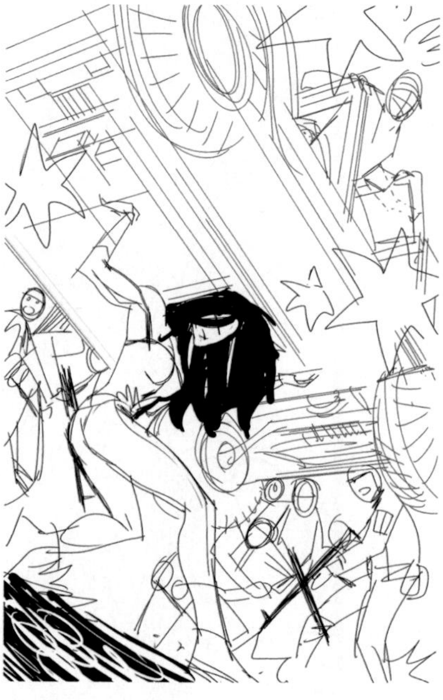

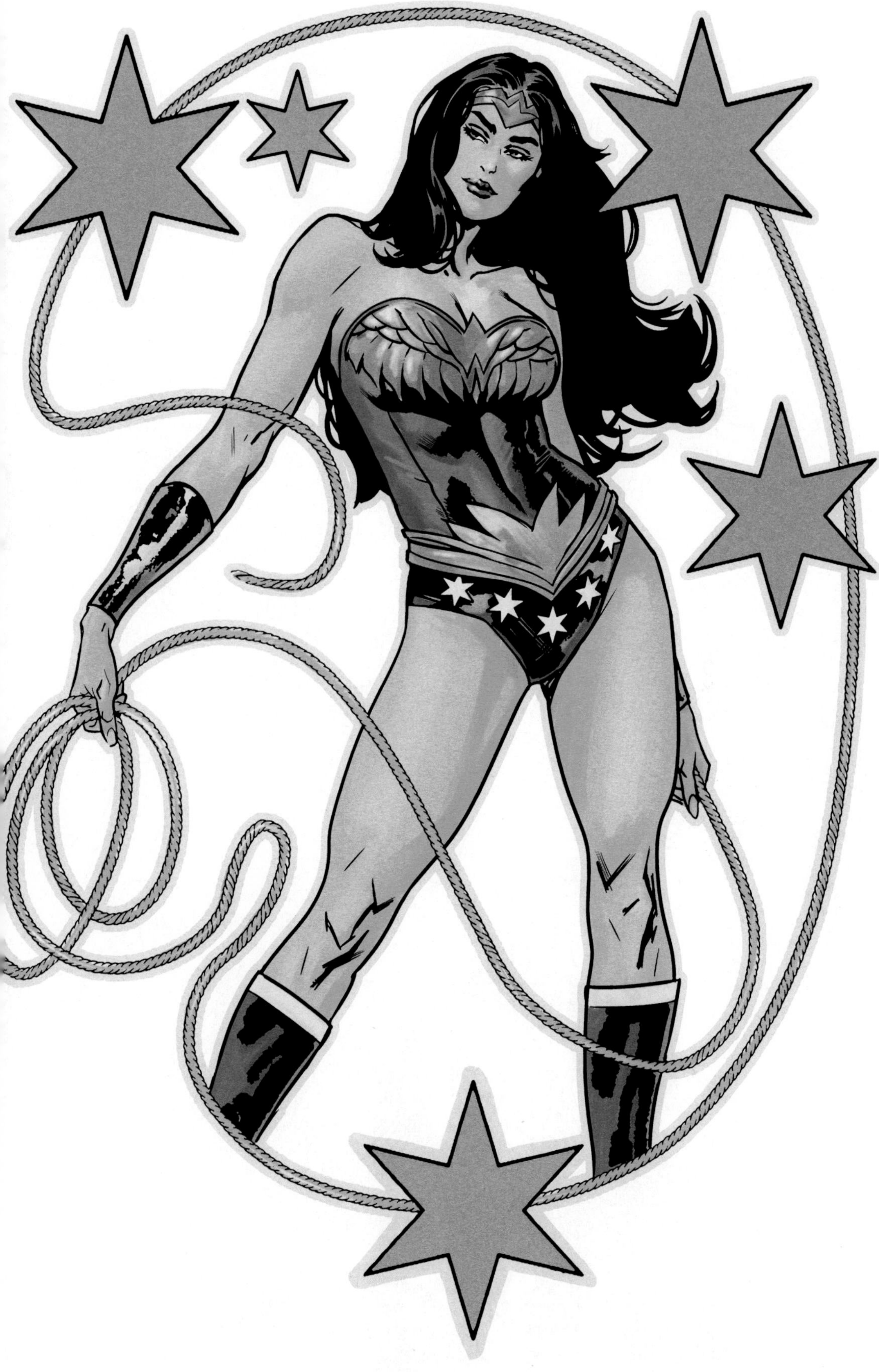

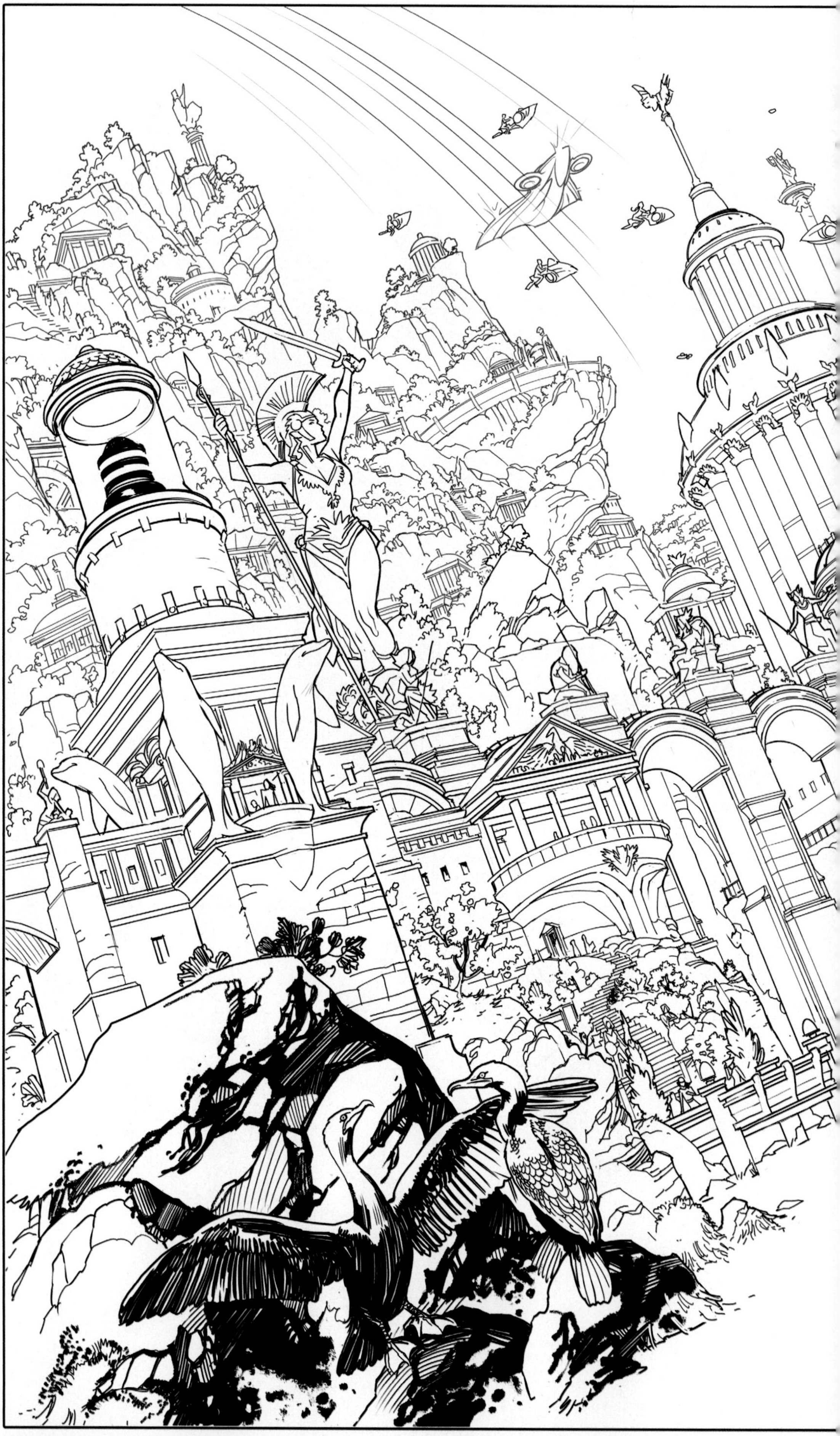

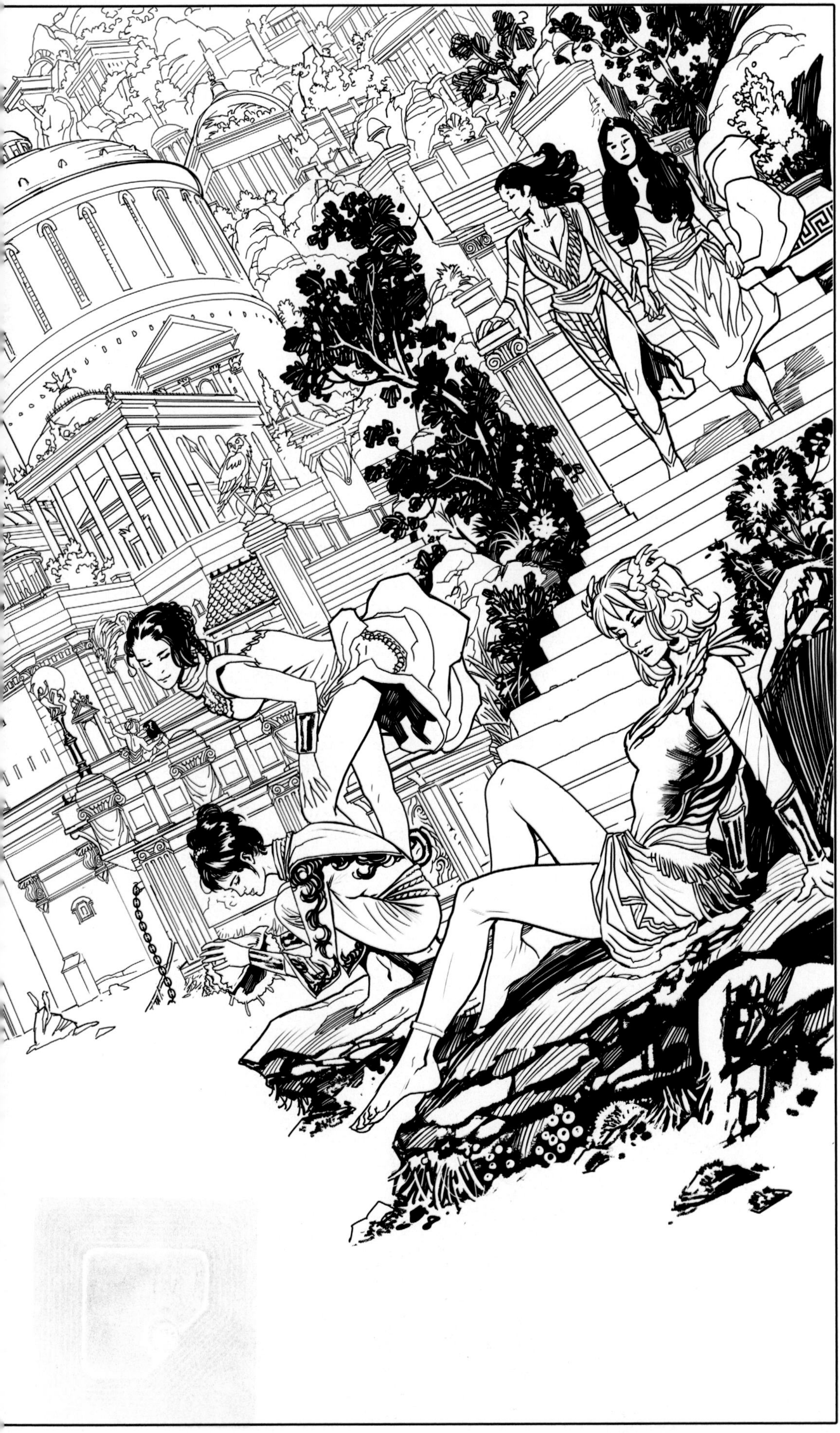

GRANT MORRISON Grant Morrison has been working with DC Comics for more than 20 years, beginning with his legendary runs on the revolutionary titles ANIMAL MAN and DOOM PATROL. Since then he has written numerous bestsellers — including JLA, BATMAN and *New X-Men* — as well as the critically acclaimed creator-owned series THE INVISIBLES, SEAGUY, THE FILTH, WE3 and JOE THE BARBARIAN. Morrison has also expanded the borders of the DC Universe in the award-winning pages of ALL-STAR SUPERMAN, FINAL CRISIS, BATMAN INCORPORATED, ACTION COMICS and the Grand DC Unification Theory that is THE MULTIVERSITY.

YANICK PAQUETTE is a Shuster Award-nominated Canadian artist who has been drawing comics since the late '90s. He illustrated many comics for both Marvel and DC, including various X-Men titles, two TERRA OBSCURA miniseries with Alan Moore and SEVEN SOLDIERS: THE BULLETEER and BATMAN INCORPORATED with Grant Morrison. An avid insect collector and naturalist from childhood, Paquette's tenure on Swamp Thing allowed him a rare occasion to conjugate his passion for biology and lush comics.